Claudio Garibaldi

The Psychology of the Enneagram Applied to Graphology

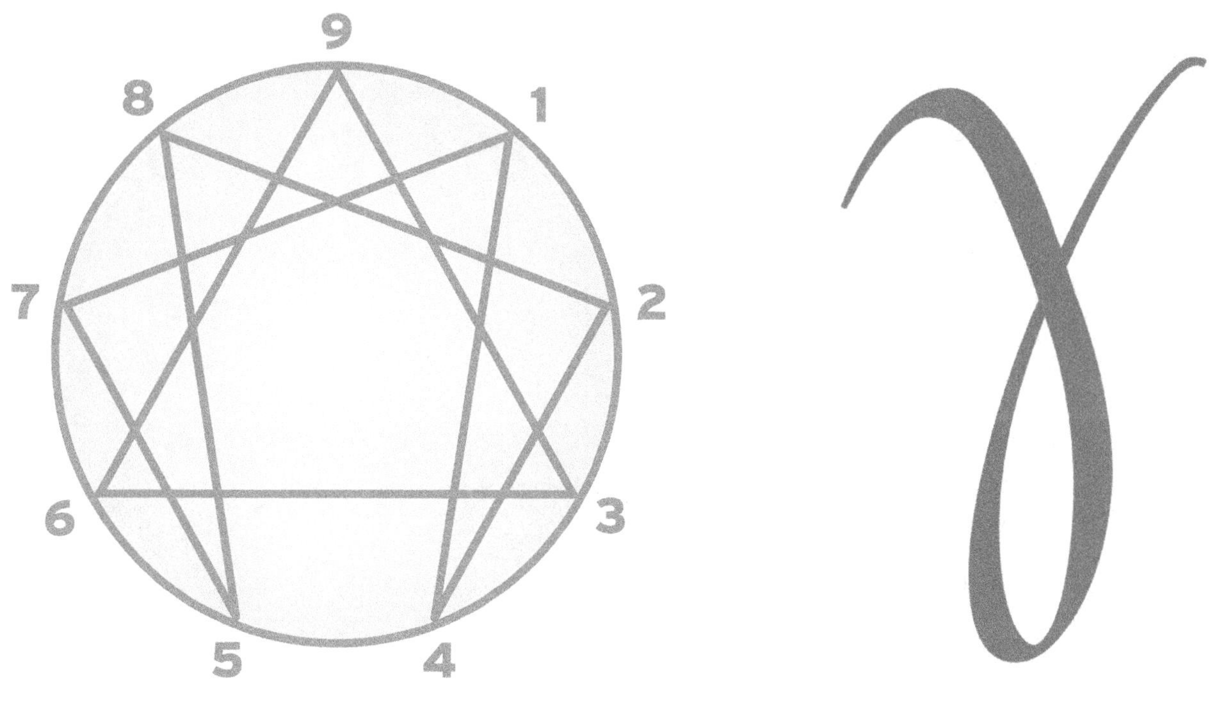

A Collection of Articles

Title | The Psychology of the Enneagram Applied to Graphology - A Collection of Articles
Author | Claudio Garibaldi

ISBN | 978-88-27816-72-1

Youcanprint Self-Publishing
Via Roma, 73 – 73039 Tricase (LE) – Italy
www.youcanprint.it
info@youcanprint.it
Facebook: facebook.com/youcanprint.it
Twitter: twitter.com/youcanprintit

Table of Contents

Foreword

The Enneagram is a dynamic personality system that allows for a deep understanding of ones' passions, emotions and behavior. Knowledge of the Enneagram has enabled me, as a handwriting analyst, to have a fuller awareness of the dimensions of writers' personality, allowing a better focus on core motivations that drive behavior.

In this compendium of articles published in *Enneagram Monthly*, Claudio Garibaldi's expertise guides us to discovering personality through the Enneagram coupled with handwritten expression. Throughout his long career, Claudio has researched how the Enneagram is reflected in handwriting and how it can be applied. His descriptions of the ways in which the graphologist can identify Enneagram types from handwriting are clear and nuanced, enabling the analyst to grasp the essence of the writer without losing sight of his or her individuality.

Claudio has given presentations about how the Enneagram can be integrated with graphology at conferences of *The American Society of Professional Graphologists* in New York twelve years ago and again recently in an online program. For many who attended these presentations, this was their first introduction to the Enneagram and represented a new way to explore graphology. Each time I hear Claudio speak or read his materials reveals another level of complexity for my personal understanding of what handwriting can reveal.

Claudio approaches handwriting analysis through the Italian Moretti system of graphology. This system is a new way to analyze handwriting for most Europeans and Americans. However, you do not have to know the Moretti graphology system to apply what Claudio teaches us about combining the Enneagram with handwriting analysis. His writings give important insights to all serious graphologists as well as those who are new to handwriting analysis.

I am pleased to recommend this compendium, not only to graphologists, but to anyone who is interested in understanding the underlying motivations in personality. Claudio Garibaldi's work broadens our perspective on how individuals think, feel and approach their world, and how it is expressed in the way we write.

Patricia Siegel

President, The American Society of Professional Graphologists

Graphology offers a picture of who we are to anyone capable of interpreting personality traits revealed by the involuntary chain reactions of impulses between brain and paper. Impulses that are generated by our nervous and muscular responses become a snapshot of our constitution, mental, emotional and physical state we are in at the moment of writing. I can't think of a more accurate, and spontaneous way of expressing the sum total of all levels of our being. Accurate interpretation of course is another matter that is half science and half art. Claudio Garibaldi demonstrated with mastery how personality assessment systems like the Enneagram can benefit from verification by using graphology. After all, psychological nudity is much more likely to be displayed innocently while writing than in a setting of being tested or by self-assessment.

Jack Labanauskas

Enneagram Monthly Publisher and Editor,
http://www.enneagram-monthly.com

Acknowledgements

I wish to express my special thanks to Patricia Siegel – President of *The American Association of Professional Graphologists*, who hosted one of my workshops in New York and always showed a deep interest for the Enneagram, and to Heidi H. Harralson – past President of *the American Handwriting Analysis Foundation* – who invited me to give some workshops in Arizona and in San José. I want to thank Jack Labanauskas – publisher and editor of *Enneagram Monthly* – who always demonstrated a real interest for graphology and a trust in my work. Lastly, a thought goes to Barbara Garro, Painter & Writer, and to Katherine Chernick Fauvre, an Enneagram author, who were the first persons welcoming my study when I decided to spend one year in the United States.

Introduction

This publication consists of a collection of articles published in *Enneagram Monthly* from 2005 to 2007. At that time, the study of the connection between the Enneagram and Graphology was a novelty, while today, perhaps thanks to these articles, it has become much more widespread.

Enneagram Monthly is an extensive journal dedicated to intelligent discourse about the enneagram, its current applications, and future potential. Since 1995, the *Enneagram Monthly* is the most internationally respected and referenced focal point of enneagram development.

The graphic expression of every human being is intimately connected to his neurophysiological structure, experience and history. The enneagram is benefiting from an international and transcultural dissemination because it describes human nature in a way that everyone can recognize him or herself, beyond belonging to a specific nationality. If it is agreed that the enneatype permeates the existential manifestations of each of us, we can say that it will have an influence on each individual movement of spontaneous handwriting. This is the empirical basis of the connection between graphic gesture and enneatype.

My goal for the last twenty-two years was to demonstrate this hypothesis is true. I have studied and researched about a thousand samples of handwritings belonging to subjects of different nationalities.

In addition to the theoretical elaboration, it was also necessary to verify directly the validity of what was formulated. This was done by organizing multiple workshops that I offered in several countries, such as the United States, Canada, Brazil, Hungary, Belgium and of course in Italy. It allowed me to experience the vast potential of the joint application of Enneagram and Graphology, a potential that unfolds in different sectors and in different ways. It is not just about theory. It is about self-knowledge and requires an individual's commitment to study and to work on themselves. Above all, in order to advise or teach the subject in a careful and effective way, one needs to know about him or herself.

At the beginning of my work I was mainly interested in transmitting knowledge to graphologists because, while they are very good at identifying individual traits by looking at handwriting samples, the science of graphology does not really teach us how to see the larger patterns formed by a cluster of traits. But it's really only when we can see this kind of larger pattern that it is possible to create a persona or profile based on handwriting data. As you can imagine, using the enneagram makes this much easier. So, a graphologist who knows the enneagram can work more efficiently and effectively.

The reverse is also true: someone who already knows the enneagram and learns the basic principles of graphology will be able to work more effectively with the enneagram. This is because graphology is very effective in revealing the nuances of a person's character. Two people of the same type may share the same core motivation, but the way this motivation manifests behaviorally can vary considerably. Graphology allows us to see subtle differences that are hard to discern. It's like using a microscope to look at type. And it does so using a methodology that has been developed and refined for centuries, especially in Europe.

Moreover, handwriting analysis is particularly effective for longitudinal studies. It allows us to monitor the personal evolution of individuals and to track changes in the effects of type at different stages in life.

My vision of how to apply enneagram and graphology has expanded to the needs of young university students, in terms of support for the development of their transversal skills, the business sector, coaching and much more.

In the near future, it is my intention to publish a book in which the link between enneagram and graphology will be presented in a more systematic way, with reference to temperaments, etc. In addition, I will outline possible areas of intervention.

This collection of articles aims to make available what was written and, above all, to stimulate curiosity by glimpsing the wealth, still largely unexplored, of the joint application of the analysis of movement in handwriting and the study of enneagram psychological types.

Claudio Garibaldi

Genoa, December 2017

HANDWRITING AND ENNEATYPE

CLAUDIO GARIBALDI

These articles aim to outline the possible connections between graphological theory and the Enneagram. We will take a journey of discovery and exploration, analyzing the expressive subtleties and psychological meaning of graphological signs, trying to understand how their language can help us detect their relevance to a certain enneatype or, on the contrary, guide us to exclude others.

We will use very general categories of graphological analysis, assuming that there cannot be a specific graphological sign for each enneatype, but rather a grouping of signs, exactly as each enneatype is a result of a grouping of traits.

Moreover, each graphological sign, with its own basic meaning, takes on a more specific meaning if considered in its graphic context.

These articles should not be regarded as a graphology correspondence course—in Italy a degree in graphology requires a three-year course at university level—but I will give some hints in order to stimulate curiosity and new thinking. We will analyze those hints thoroughly, but they should not be considered exhaustive..

For this introduction, a theoretical analysis seems appropriate. Next, I will present and analyze some samples of handwriting, and examine the individual graphological indicators in connection with the different enneatypes.

Goals of the Research

Before discussing more directly the various graphological signs, I will briefly describe what led me deeply and passionately to study the correlations between these two disciplines.

I think that for most people the initial encounter with and subsequent study of the Enneagram have ignited great transformations in their lives. To undertake the study of the Enneagram, seriously and with humility, brings forth changes in the way one relates to oneself, to others, and to life in general. Each of us who is interested in this symbol knows its beneficial power.

I bumped into the Enneagram by accident in a bookstore, leafing through the pages of a book in 1996. I had been studying and practicing graphology for a few years and considered it a discipline that was a source of self-knowledge and knowledge of humanity as well. The possibility of grasping the individual nuances of each and every writer I found fascinating then and it still continues to surprise me.

In the Enneagram I found the psycho-spiritual factor I had been looking for, perhaps subconsciously, for a long time. I remember very clearly that in my consulting job I had the feeling—and this should be regarded, perhaps, as my personal limitation—that while handwriting analysis could certainly elucidate a personality quite well, it could not suggest evolutionary paths, other than the benefits of self-knowledge within the frame of personality itself. In other words, to suggest only horizontal, though interesting, paths.

I felt unable to penetrate beyond the "mechanics of the compulsion," as we would say using Enneagram language; while I felt that I could find mechanical solutions to mechanical problems or at least describe them through the handwriting, I did not know how to help clients see this problem and also themselves from a broader perspective. I would have liked to give my clients a practical tool for some self-transcendence. In a way, I was feeling the need to develop an "existential graphology."

In his Preface to *Character and Neurosis*, Claudio Naranjo—undoubtedly one of the main authorities on the subject and also a collaborator with Raymond B. Cattel, a well-known inventor of psychological tests—gave a partial answer to what I was looking for. He stated that, "Together with constituting a clinical exploration of the same domain usually investigated by personality theorists embracing the mathematical and also a psychodynamic exploration of personality traits and their interconnections… the understanding that I present here may also be called a transpersonal or spiritual view of character and neurosis or, alternatively, an existential view—inasmuch as it equates spiritual "endarkenment" with loss of being."[1]

Surely, even without knowing the Enneagram, contemplating a particularly rigid handwriting, which we would assume to be of an enneatype One, we could easily advise a path of integration towards enneatype Seven— that is, towards greater flexibility, joy of living, freedom to express impulses, and so on. Nevertheless, I was feeling the lack of a broader vision that would take into account the transcendent element in a way that would be easy to see rather than abstract and vague. This is what the Enneagram defines as awareness of one's own

---

1 Naranjo C., *Character and Neurosis. An Integrative View* (Nevada City, Ca: Gateways Books, 1994, p. 22).

compulsive patterns, leading to a deeper contact with Being. The Enneagram unveils this trail with extraordinary simplicity and depth at the same time.

On the other hand, handwriting analysis, even though it always implies a certain degree of subjective intuition and lies on the borderline between science and art, has developed a whole set of strict criteria of measurement; precise standards of control, and interdisciplinary exchange with psychology. It was therefore necessary to take all these elements into account in order not to fall into simplistic inaccuracy.

In fact, "What Moretti (Girolamo Moretti, the founder of the Italian system of graphology,) has always been concerned about is understanding man in his unique and unrepeatable individuality. That's why he has unfailingly rejected all attempts to fit a person into schemes and classifications."[2]

As a highly esteemed professor of mine in Urbino wrote, "In recent decades a higher awareness has unfolded, an awareness of the unique and unrepeatable individuality of a person, regardless of specific factors such as learning, creativity, emotionalism, or motivation.

We can say that this is the main contribution psychology has given to mankind. Every concept of personality must include the descriptive and lasting aspects of individuality within a structure showing identifiable characteristics unique to each individual; at the same time giving the tools to compare different individuals. It is clear that this sort of reasoning has to possess enough plasticity, i.e. *flexibility within continuity*. Each individual must keep their integrity unaltered, neither constrained within too narrow schemes, nor nullified by rigid or overly straitened boundaries."[3]

Graphology has thus an idiographical approach and not a nomothetic one to personality, with the intention of capturing the specific individuality of each human being.

Approaching the study of Enneagram from my perspective as a graphologist, I had to ask myself, "is the Enneagram a mere typing of character?" and "Are all subjects belonging to the same enneatype, with the same wing, the same subtype, and a more-or-less identical level of integration or disintegration, almost alike?" The nuances are infinite and the question is not that simple, but within

---

2 Galeazzi-Palaferri-Giacometti, *La Grafologia*, Firenze, Sansoni Editore, 1986, p.47.

3 Giacometti F., "Lo studio della personalità e la grafologia", in: Galeazzi G. (a cura di), *La scienza grafologica oggi*, Roma, Città Nuova Editrice, 1977, p. 52.

Enneagram theory, we cannot assume that these answers are answered.

That's why at a certain point I decided to embark on an interdisciplinary path where the richness of the Enneagram could contribute to the theoretical development of graphology, and the particular methodology of graphology could widen and deepen the study of the specific expressions of the nine enneatypes.

After a time of intense reflection, I had an opportunity to meet Claudio Naranjo and talk about my intention to do research on the Enneagram and graphology. He was firmly convinced that graphology could be a very useful tool for individualization of enneatype, and, to demonstrate his conviction, he offered to gather nearly 400 samples of handwriting during his training programs (SAT) specifying for each sample both the enneatype and the subtype.

At that moment I felt that it was possible to start a proper research.

Theoretical Assumptions of the Interaction Between Enneagram and Graphic Signs

The main question is: if each enneatype refers to a deep structure of personality, can this personality structure in some way affect graphic signs?

Is it possible that the Ruling Passion and the Cognitive Fixation, which, according to the Enneagram, influence our whole existence, have no impact on that unique and personal expression of ourselves—our handwriting?

The goal of handwriting analysis is to describe and to define the peculiarities of each person. It is in fact impossible to find two people who have the same handwriting, just as it is impossible to find two identical people.

Essentially, writing is an expressive act that involves the whole organization of personality: innate inclinations, intellectual processes, quality of emotions, unconscious images. Handwriting is the product of a complex neurological, physiological, and psychological activity.

Is it possible that all these elements can contribute to recognizing our enneatype, wing, level of integration or disintegration, and the nuances of each enneatype? These are the questions to which we seek answers in our brief journey.

If the Enneagram is an archetypal map of the Ego, describing the conditioning and habits of personality, then the writing traits must be one of the behavioral expressions of the Ego itself.

Girolamo Moretti, based his theory on the concept of a "Predominant Passion."[4] He states that "Psychology must distinguish among all traits, the one that is the simplest and also most complex personal trait which singles out the unique nature of the individual."—i.e., the Predominant Passion—and he defines the individuality of a human being through the lights and shadows of this core of personality.[5] A student of Moretti, Giovanni Luisetto, states in his Introduction to his teacher's book *The Predominant Passion*, that: "*The origin and the aim of the Predominant Passion are the preservation and the defense of personality itself.*"[6] He also writes: "What I find especially original in Moretti's theory is the potential of characterizing in one glance the peculiarities of each human being, but comprised in universal psychological qualities."[7] The Predominant Passion represents the principle of unity, identification, and autonomy of a person. Therefore, the graphological concept of Predominant Passion appears quite rich and complex.

Claudio Naranjo, in *Character and Neurosis*, writes: "When we work with a specific individual we do find a specific facet of personality in the foreground amidst its universally shared structure,"[8] and "interpretations oriented according to a perception of the ruling passion and ruling fixation are *particularly* important to accept and heed."[9]

Moreover, as he states in relation to the "awakening" quoted in Gurdjieff's works, it is very important to take into account "that aspect of self-knowledge consisting in the discernment of one's chief feature, i.e., a pervasive characteristic of the personality that might be understood as a center of it."[10]

We can therefore infer that, on an epistemological level, it is possible to find many points of intersection between these two disciplines: the Enneagram refers to the Ruling Passion, while graphology refers to the Predominant Passion. The two concepts are not exactly alike, but they complement each other, creating the groundwork for fruitful research, and for practical applications in the path of self-knowledge.

---

4 Moretti G., *La Passione Predominante*, Studio Grafologico "Fra Girolamo" – San Francesco – Ancona - Italy, 1962
5 Moretti G., op. cit. p. 8
6 Moretti G., op. cit. p. 23
7 Moretti G., op. cit. p. 7
8 Naranjo C., op. cit. p. xxxii
9 Naranjo C., op. cit. p. xxxii
10 Naranjo C., op. cit. p. 12

The brain has discrete, complex and highly developed sensory and motor regions. They are responsible for the production of handwriting, which is a complex psychomotor skill. The main properties of handwriting are cultural, perceptual, technical, linguistic, motor and biomechanical.
In his theory of signs, Moretti reveals an awareness of those very profound neurophysiological processes. These processes lie at the heart of the relationship between that "internal language" which derives from the brain's processing of stimuli and/or reflex responses, and its external (and therefore recordable and interpretable) counterpart. This "exterior language" of spontaneously produced handwriting or "Movement of Spontaneous Handwriting" (MSH), forms the specific object of graphological study.
Moretti also relates the scriptor's psychomotor activity to the graphic "sign", a phenomenon which is at the same time crystallised and vibrant, and which by its very nature serves as a mirror of the writer's psychological and physiological constitution.
Our personalities are the end product of the interaction of many different traits or qualities, which serve to provide us with our individuality. In the same way, handwriting is the most personal and individualised form of self-expression. It manifests itself as gestures (in motion) and physical patterns which we call graphical (or, better yet, graphological) signs.
The main task of graphology is to identify in handwriting that which distinguishes one individual from the other. In other words, Moretti was searching for what exactly it is that makes two people different from one other.
The sign is a "dynamic psychological synthesis", which is strictly connected with all the other signs that are present in a handwriting. It is like a constellation who's core is the Dominant sign.
Since a human being is a psychosomatic unity, each sign is a registration of the psychological and physiological structure of the writer. **Each graphological sign reflects the whole personality**, which includes the cognitive, emotional, volitional, operational and the somatic level.
For example, the sign which is defined *LIGHT*, (i.e. a script with light pressure throughout) indicates:

- At the **COGNITIVE LEVEL**: a subtle, acute mind, fine discrimination; the individual is able to see shades of meaning.
- At the **EMOTIONAL LEVEL**: keen sensitivity, introversion; the individual responds to the subtlest shades of feeling but does not manifest this.
- At the **VOLITIONAL LEVEL**: poor physical stamina, strong mental endurance; the individual easily tires at the physical level, but the mind is constantly active.
- At the **OPERATIONAL LEVEL**: the individual feels more at ease with theoretical matters than with practical ones.
- At the **SOMATIC LEVEL**: frail constitution, elongated muscles, reduced muscle mass, fair complexion, delicate skin, thin hair, soft voice, gentle gait, polite behavior.

Considering the sign *"LIGHT"* separately, these are its main characteristics. But what really matters, is how it relates with the combinations of other signs in that specific handwriting. Only by taking into account multiple signs and combinations will we be able to have insights into the nature of the writer.

The notes in the side-bar have been pulled out by:

- Cristofanelli P. & Torbidoni L. *The Graphological System of Girolamo Moretti, and his Typology of the Four temperaments*, available from The Academy of Graphology, London
- De Petrillo V. – Millevolte A. *The Application of the G. Moretti Graphological System* – Brain Edizioni 2000, Roma
- Found B., *A scientific approach to the analysis of the handwriting behavior: Validating individual identification and the assessment of character*, lecture made at the International Graphological Colloquium held in Canada on May 2004

The charts show a synthesis of the connection points between the Enneagram and Moretti's graphological system.

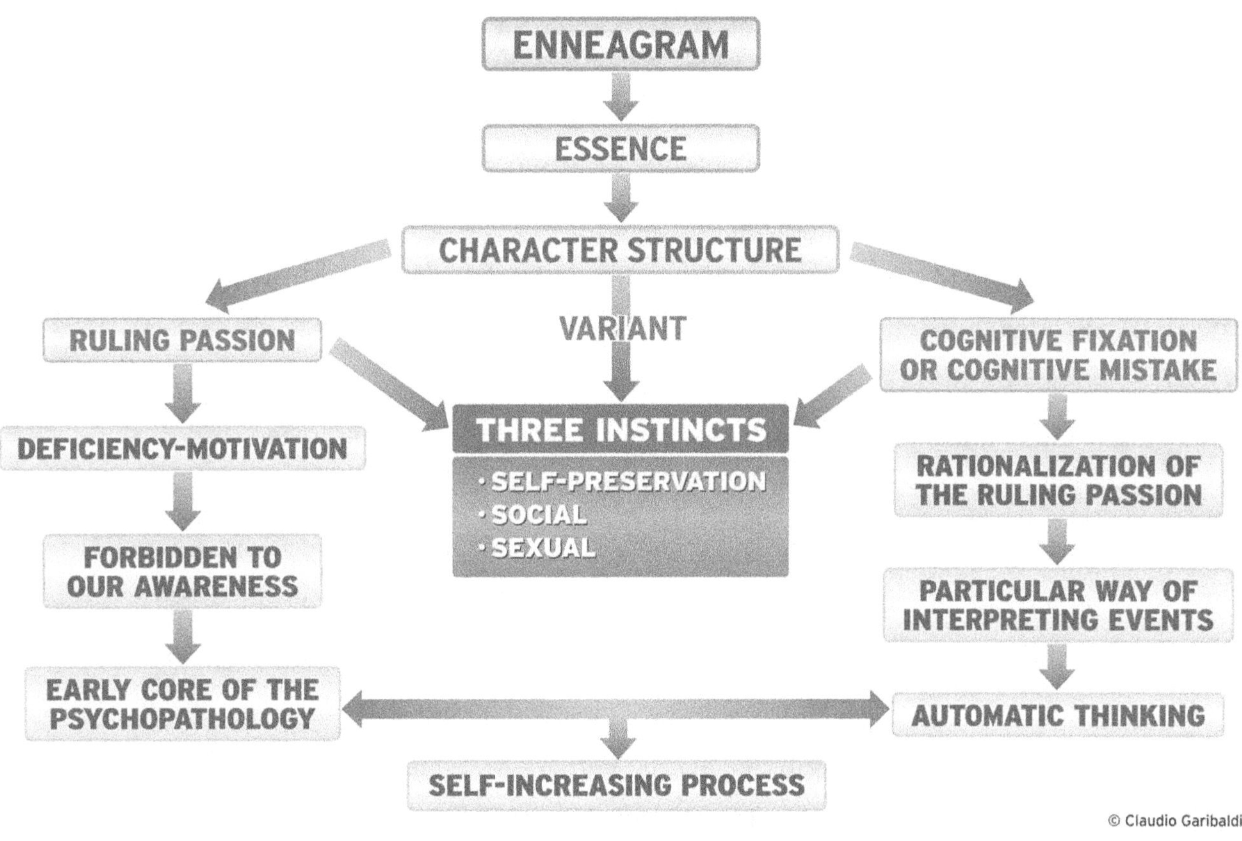

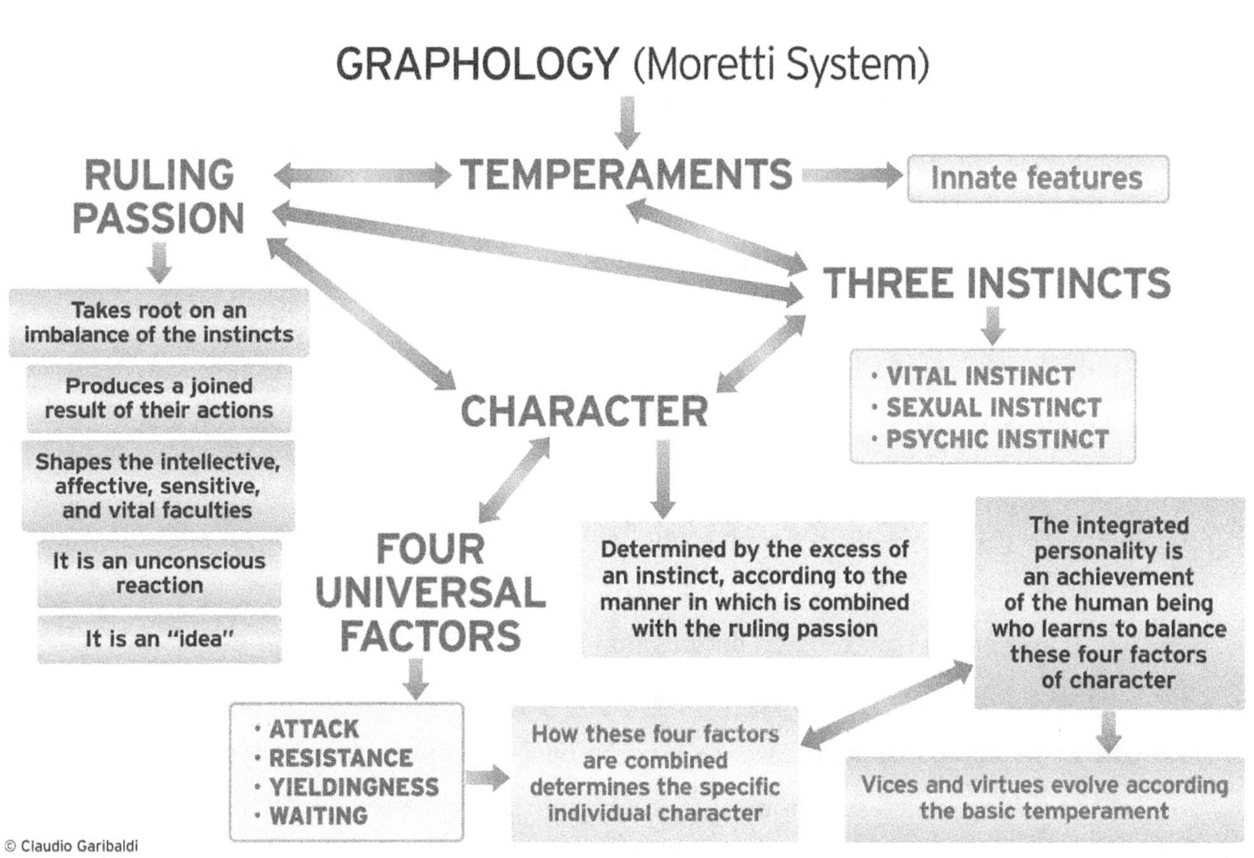

How can Graphology and Enneagram Interact?

Graphology and the Enneagram are often quoted in various contexts—for example during the personnel selection process within companies. Both disciplines are used, but in a separate and distinct way. There is not a specific procedure that includes from the start a standardized synthesis of meaning and operational information, incorporating the psychological categories outlined by the Enneagram and graphology.

I'm also not aware of the existence of a standardized and truly systematic procedure using graphological indexes in order to individualize the enneatypes, although a lot of pioneering work with a different emphasis, and a different method, which does not include the graphological concept of Predominant Passion, can be found in Usha Mullan's books. Moreover, two different but interesting approaches to the subject have been made by the colleague and friend Carol A. Meyer, who refers to the study of Vimala Rodgers in the area of Applied Graphology, and specifically to the teachings of Don Riso and Russ Hudson in the area of the Enneagram, (but in my opinion graphologists should consider all relevant authors on the subject), and by Barbera McMenemin with her *Bi-Zonal* Paradigm. Finally I heard that in Helen Palmer's workshop in France, last year, a little space has been given to graphology applied to Enneagram, but I don't know the name of the graphologist(s) who were there, nor the contents of their work.

The concept of Passion ("Ruling" or "Predominant") is intrinsically connected to one of the three basic instincts inherent to human beings. In graphology we have the psychic, the sexual, and the vital instincts, while the Enneagram refers to the sexual, social, and self-preservation instincts.

However, in graphological theory the sexual instinct includes both the sexual and the social instincts (they are both relational), whereas the Enneagram considers them two separate energies. The self-preservation instinct on the other hand, is common to both (graphology calls it "vital instinct," but the concept is substantially the same). The Enneagram does not use the concept of psychic instinct, which is a very important one in graphological theory.

This is not to be taken as a limiting and incompatible diversity, but rather as part of Moretti's graphological theory, aimed at capturing the uniqueness of every human being. It is based on the empirical assumption that each person's handwriting is different from any other, even though there are also general categories of analysis of the writing movement. The psychic instinct is the drive, ontologically inherent to every human being, to realize one's own uniqueness.

The Enneagram also refers to an individual specificity. The division into nine types is only a starting point for an analysis of personality whose uniqueness unfolds after the evaluation of the impact of the wings, the direction of integration or disintegration, the instinctual subtypes, and the developmental level of the individual. The dynamic integration of those elements defines the individual characteristics. *Therefore, handwriting analysis offers a specific and useful advantage, allowing one to better focus and deepen the structural tendencies of each enneatype.*

In a similar and dynamic way, the Enneagram describes in a precise, broad, and deep manner the pathways to self-knowledge and development of our own resources. The Enneagram can assist the handwriting analysis process by providing a map pertinent to the individuals evolution, and fleshing out the analysis with tangible and practical proposals that can be offered to the client. *We could consider handwriting analysis as the "microscope" or the "magnifying glass" on the individual personality, whereas the Enneagram could serve as the window on the vaster spiritual side of each writing.*

Handwriting analysis allows us to monitor in a concrete way the personal evolution over time and to verify actual changes and accomplishments in life. Such an evaluation will consider the balance and the awareness the writer has gained in managing his or her existential uniqueness. Since our handwriting is not static it is in a constant process of change that is fueled by our instinctual drives, the quality of emotions and affectivity, mental patterns, and relational dynamics. In fact, according to Moretti, the human being is constantly in a relationship, both with an internal and an external "self".

Both graphology and the Enneagram consider the cognitive element along with the familial and external environmental factors as decisive in refining and maturing our disposition.

According to Enneagram theory, for each Passion we develop a correspondent cognitive "fixation," a specific way of interpreting reality. The Passion takes shape during the childhood, as a result of the interaction between inborn predispositions and our home environment. It then settles into a cognitive interpretation – or fixed view – about ourselves, others, and situations. Thus, the cognitive process has undergone an unconscious distortion.

Moretti's graphological method gives great importance to the Predominant Passion, and he wrote a book exclusively on that subject. It is not possible, in this short article, to summarize all the nuances of this concept. Basically, the Predominant Passion is an *Idea*—not a feeling or a sensation. This is another way to state the conceptual connection between passion and Fixation made by the Enneagram. Moretti often points out that the Predominant Passion is a goddess, a despotic queen of a totalitarian regime, and that, she completely influences intellectual, sensitive, and vital faculties with the goal of enforcing its direction, inspiration, and aspiration. It is very difficult for a person to recognize her tricks.

A further contribution graphology could bring consists of the different evaluation of the enneatypes according to gender. Most Enneagram authors implicitly state that Passions and Fixations have exactly the same structure and dynamic in the feminine and masculine universe. In graphological theory, most signs have not been assigned a differential meaning according to gender, even though we know that some signs are more typical of women and others of men. Nonetheless, in the branch of graphology generally used with family and couple relationships, much weight is given to gender identity which is considered to be a specific and very influential component of personality. In my research I would like to keep an open door about this dimension, taking into account gender differences especially when evaluating persons of the same enneatype.

Why it Makes Sense to Look for a Connection Between the Enneagram and Graphology

Both disciplines aim at acquiring deep and detailed knowledge of the individual and see the person as a psycho-physical structure interacting with in a social environment. Both disciplines see personality not as restrictive and set in stone, but as an organic process expressive of who we are.

Graphology doesn't make direct references to Essence, but refers to the personality as an "organization" of a various vital components of personality which are structured around an innate temperament. Temperament, according the graphological theory, is an inborn imprint that directs the evolution of character. This implies that there exists an "organizing element," in other words, a person has real latitude for change, beyond the innate conditioning and his or her specific evolutionary story. This organizing element affecting each human being has the power to give new meaning to each of the individual existential paths, to channel energies in new ways, and to modify mental patterns. The organizing element participates completely in the dynamics of personality, but has the potential to transcend itself through the awareness of one's own identifications and compulsions.

Graphology does not claim to have penetrated and defined this "organizing principle" which operates in every human being beyond the personality. Indeed Moretti, referring to the Predominant Passion, says that the regulating mechanism of Passion itself is made by virtue. Virtue as a concept in graphological theory contains the idea of habit. So, Moretti defines virtue as the *habit of attention.*

Giovanni Luisetto, writes in his introduction to Father Moretti's book *Graphology of the Seven Deadly Sins*, 1937, that, as a result of the struggle against the Predominant Passion: "What was considered a restriction becomes broader action; what was an obstacle becomes an object requiring attention; what was lust can become mysticism; what was anger is transformed to mildness, what was sloth becomes courage to take action."[11] These surprising and remarkable words written seventy years ago by a scholar not familiar with the Enneagram, carry deep resonances with what the Enneagram calls "transformation of the compulsions," "freedom from and awareness of our own automatisms," and "non-identification with the personality."

The Enneagram as well as graphology, go into depth in knowledge of personality. This paves a preferential lane for reading signals that could guide us in the transformation of our identifications, that are the cause of our suffering. The personality, according to the sacred symbol of the Enneagram, is the gate through which we can contact our *Essence,* which is our true core. This is the real scientific and humanistic contribution that the Enneagram can bring to graphological theory—to indicate the path for self-transcendence. Graphology on the other hand can help going into greater depth exposing specific nuances of the writer.

In conclusion, at an epistemological level, the Enneagram and graphology both refer in similar but different ways to the same structural and dynamic components of personality. The Predominant Passion (according to the graphological theory)—or the Dominant Passion (according the Enneagram)—

---

11 Luisetto G., "Introduction", in: Moretti M. G., *Graphology of the Seven Deadly Sins*, Seconda Edizione, Ancona, Istituto Grafologico – S. Francesco delle Scale, 1974.

are considered pivotal to personality and arise from the interaction of the innate substratum, instincts, and relational dynamics of childhood. The points of intersection contain the foundation for theoretical research and for practical applications for both disciplines.

In the next article, we will start to go into individual enneatypes, using samples of handwriting, and trying to single out the main graphological features for each type.

HANDWRITING AND ENNEATYPE ONE

As mentioned previously, there is no specific graphic indicator for each enneatype, but rather a cluster of signs. Moreover, it is necessary to bear in mind that each sign, even though it has its own basic significance, takes its full meaning from the graphological context in which it is included.

We will highlight the main signs or combinations of signs that are most typically found in each enneatype. A single sign may indicate a certain enneatype (and even the person's level of development) if accompanied by certain other signs or, equally telling, if certain signs are conspicuously absent.

Certain signs can be regarded, according to their underlying psychological dynamics, as more likely bearing on a certain enneatype, and incompatible with another. For instance, it is psychologically reasonable to assume that a predominantly angular handwriting is more likely or essential to the dynamic of the passion and fixation of a type One, rather than a type Nine. This does not mean that certain Nines, especially more developed Nines, could not have some form of angularity in their handwriting.

Looking deeper at *Angular* handwriting, it is graphologically simple enough to be understood even by the layperson. It is reasonable to think that for an average Nine, going away from a "lazy roundness," from a "generalization in the perception of stimuli," from the "narcotization of the affirmation of one's own needs" (*Curved*) towards a more "active assertiveness," a more efficient "discrimination of differences" and "courage to openly express one's own identity" (*Angular*), represents an evolutionary step. Likewise, for an average One with a different kind of compulsion than the Nine, who for instance tends to be excessively rigid about adhesion to rules (*angularity* in conjunction with other characteristics), it would surely be healthy to learn to let go of some tension, both physical and psychological, expressed also by a marked graphical angularity. This would enable a type One to come closer to an expressive fluidity (which requires gestures that are softer, more fluid, with more launch, and *curvilinear*), peculiar to the direction of integration towards Seven.

We should understand that the meaning of graphological signs is always relative and their importance lies in the combinations of different signs. Above all, it is necessary to evaluate handwriting from a broad perspective, without assuming that there is a typical single sign for each enneatype. Such an assumption would diminish the rich complexity of the Enneagram, which demands, in the process of attaining self-knowledge, that one take careful account of many variables such as basic type, wing, subtype, direction of integration/disintegration, level of development, and quality of Essence.

Evaluating and looking at the relationship between the two disciplines in this way makes it easy to determine how graphology can assume a tutoring function in guiding a person to accurately type him- or herself, while at the same time graphologists can broaden, with the help of Enneagram, the vision of personality.

Let's have a closer look at the main signs and at some samples of type One.

According to Claudio Naranjo, some of the basic characteristics of the type One personality consist of *rigidity*, *control* and the dominance of the superego. Those qualities find their origin especially in the repression of anger which in turn reinforces the qualities.

Both the connection with emotions and their expression seem to be quite inhibited, resulting in a general feeling of tension.

Moreover, type Ones are generally considered responsible and conscientious. They place a great deal of importance on self-discipline and loyalty. Quite formal and fair, Ones exhibit little spontaneity, maintaining too much control over their own behavior. More inclined to duty than to pleasure, they bring a hint of formality into their personal relationships.

The One's thinking is logical, methodical, and excessively bound by rules, resulting in a loss of creativity and intuition. They have a strong interest in principles, moral rules, and ideals.

Ones like order and are quite meticulous. Another dominant trait is *perfectionism* combined with a critical attitude towards others and themselves.

On the whole, type Ones' handwriting displays a sense of coercion of impulses. Consequently, their "Movement of Spontaneous handwriting" (MSH) cannot be very fluent or agile, simply because control pervades the expressiveness of the gesture. These angular rather than curvilinear gestures point at the compulsion of this Enneagram type, but it is the entire cluster of graphological signs that, when taken together, define this type. Those signs, when together, tend to reinforce each other's aforementioned characteristics of hypercontrol, rigidity, and inhibition of the spontaneous manifestation of emotions.

They are mainly:

- *A angles*
- *B angles*
- *Steady*
- *Stable baseline*
- *Straight extensions*
- *Upright*
- *Careful*
- *Clear*
- *Strokes of sobriety*
- *Strokes of subjectivism*

A angles: This is the sign indicating angles, either pointed or blunt, mostly at the bottom of *ovals*, but in fact at the bottom of most letters.

In general a high degree of angularity is a result of minor or major control of MSH (gesture).

The tension expressed by the angle occurs both when the person's handwriting symbolically gets into reality (descending stroke of the oval going towards the baseline, which represents the demarcation between the conscious and the unconscious, the point of contact among instincts and the actual expression in the environment), and also when symbolically meeting the Other (right-oriented, horizontal, or slanting stroke at the bottom of the oval, which follows the previous descending stroke, in order to give shape to the letter itself). This second part of the graphic movement of drawing the oval shows the level of adaptability, and of expansion—if mostly curvilinear—or the level of defensiveness and of retraction—if mostly angular—when confronted with the impact of life's realities (see chart).

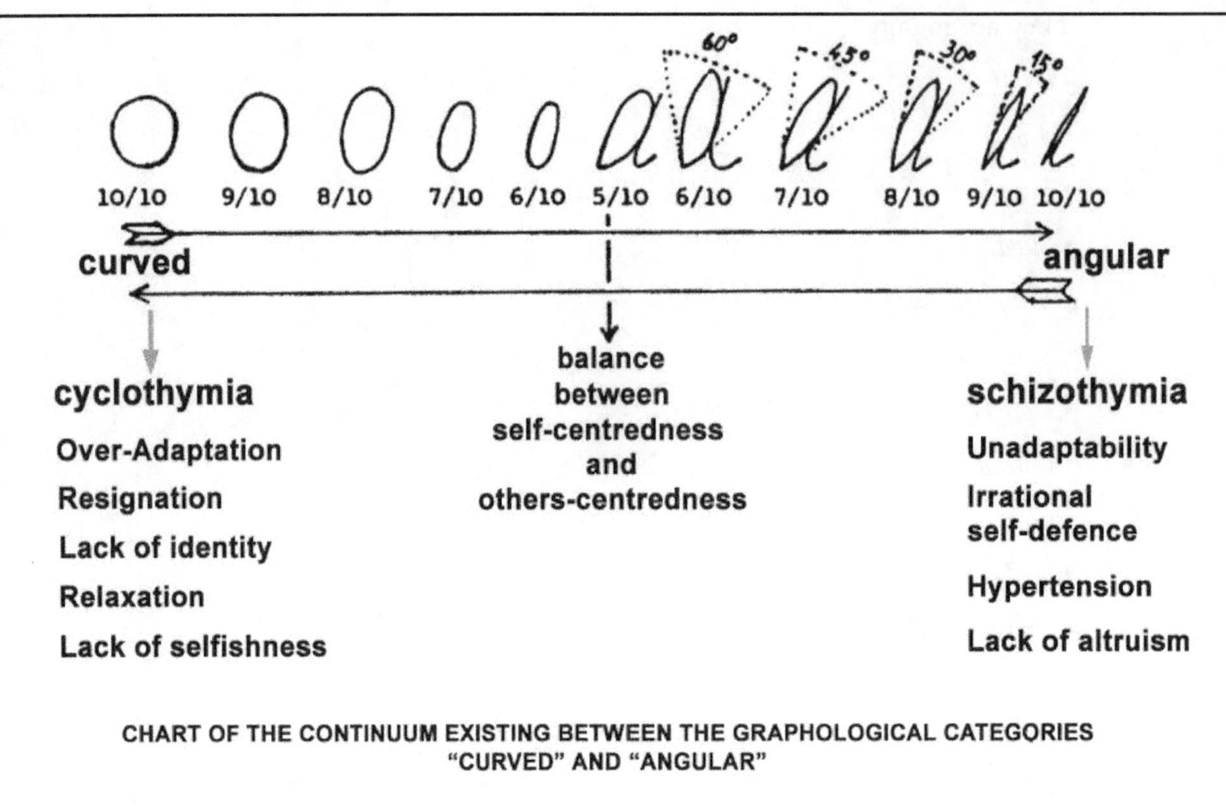

CHART OF THE CONTINUUM EXISTING BETWEEN THE GRAPHOLOGICAL CATEGORIES "CURVED" AND "ANGULAR"

The basic meaning of this sign is resentment—that is, the control the Ego automatically exerts when clashing against the inevitable impact that occurs with any encounter with an Other. The excessive defense of our own Ego causes a sense of anger. This "resentment of the Ego" means that "the Ego is listening and giving lots of importance to the stimuli coming from the outside, or from inside (impulses), considering them as a provocation to which the ego must react and exert control over." Thus, the ego feels angry.

Type One is also called Ego-Resentment. Claudio Naranjo states that the anger or resentment of the One has to be considered "as a more inward and basic antagonism in the face of reality than an explosive irritation"[12]

The compulsions of each enneatype are a form of identification with the ego, and we have to think of *angularity* in handwriting as an indicator of an inner stance in opposition to people and reality. This opposition, according to the sharpness of the angle, will range from an appropriate assertion of ego requirements to the irrational and strong defense of one's own needs (*i.e.*, to want always to be right at all costs).

---

12 Naranjo C., *Character and Neurosis. An Integrative View* (Nevada City, Ca: Gateways Books, 1994, p. 28).

By contrast, curvilinear writing indicates a spontaneous and instinctive adaptation to situations that can range from a capacity to understand and identify oneself with the other, to, when extreme, a sort of amorphousness and incapacity to define the boundaries of one's own identity.

It can't be emphasized enough that the only way to gain deep insight into the nature of a person's handwriting is by taking into account the overall interaction among all the signs. Each handwriting has its own unique set of consonances and dissonances.

In the handwriting of many Ones, we can see how angularity is the first compulsion indicating "opposition," if not explicitly - thanks to the mechanism of the reacive formation - at least inwardly.

The psychological traits represented by this angularity are various and always need to be seen in context with other signs. Some of the positive ones are: determination, fighting spirit, awareness and defense of one's own rights, reactive liveliness - always within reasonable boundaries.

But if we have *A angles* to a high degree and in a context of general rigidity, they indicate a poor capacity for adaptability, tension (even excessive tension) arising from the defensive systems of the personality, prejudice, resentful and aggressively reactive inwardness, jealousy, a need to appear distinguished, sudden irritability, anger, a spirit of contrariness, and a tendency towards dissatisfaction and persecution mania.

In contrast, the type Nine - who denies legitimate needs, tends towards resignation, and relinquishes his assertiveness - will surely have handwriting that is more curvilinear. Generally speaking, the Nine is the enneatype that is more likely than the other types to have handwriting with a high degree of the sign *Curved*. We could say that should a Nine's handwriting become more angular, he or she has probably begun a path toward individuation and assertion.

There is a close connection between *A* and *B angles*. The latter is represented by two or more angles - usually one at the base and another at the top of the letters *o*, *a*, and their derivatives (*d*, *g*, *c*, *p*, *q*, and *h*). The more pointed the angles, the higher the degree of angularity; the more blunted they are, the lower the degree of angularity.

The *B angle* is one of the fundamental signs of will. It indicates tenacity; but when present in high degree it indicates stubbornness. The mindset of tenacious persons is to prevent other people from invading their space. They defend the rights of the ego, holding on to the principle of never giving up. It's as if there were a persistent disposition to resist. While a certain degree of tenacity is needed for self-preservation, as it protects one's legitimate needs, only secondarily does that tenacity require others to respect those needs.

Stubbornness is a completely different matter. In that case, defensiveness and resistance are caused by an instinctive prejudice that assumes one's own point of view is the only right one. There is no willingness to understand other people's way of being. Stubborn people are not balanced in their judgment and they are prone to disintegration, because they use an excess of energy to defend to the bitter end their opinion that they are right.

Steady: We find this sign when the handwriting is firm and has moderate angularity and a high degree of the three elements that according to the Moretti's graphological theory are indicators of resoluteness: *B angles* (steadiness due to tenacity), *Straight Extensions* (steadiness due to inflexibility), and a *Stable Baseline* (steadiness and upright character).

Steadiness indicates, in its positive sense, determination, tenacity, restraint, self-control, and self-confidence.

On the negative side, steadiness can show inflexibility, poor adaptability, a sense of being special and aloof from others, arrogance, pretentiousness, and a sense of superiority.

Stable baseline: We can observe this sign in handwriting that proceeds horizontally in a straight line, without rising above or falling below the baseline.

This sign indicates the ability to keep one's own behavior and thoughts linear and coherent. It implies conscientiousness, restraint, self-control, self-confidence, and a refusal to compromise.

A highly *Stable Baseline* points to a reliable person who is not easily overwhelmed by enthusiasm and carefully weighs the available resources needed to attain a goal.

Once they make a commitment, they will do their best to keep promises, and can make great sacrifices. Once they have determined to do something, they will not be swayed by others' negative opinions, and will stay the course.

On the negative side, this sign can also indicate moralism, formality, and a lack of emotional richness, plasticity, imagination, and emotional adaptability.

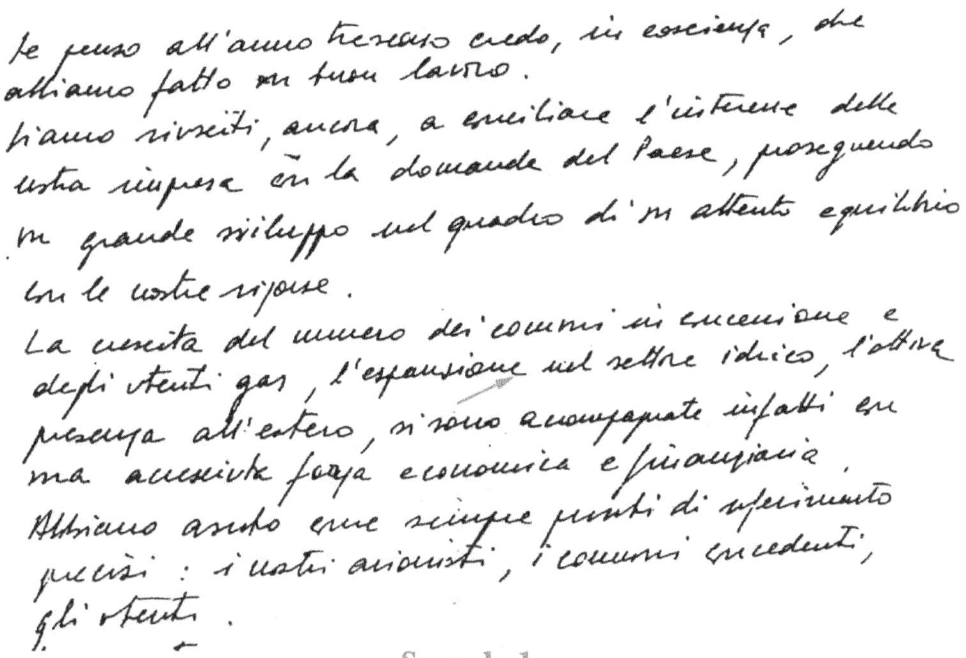
Se penso all'anno trascorso credo, in coscienza, che
abbiamo fatto un buon lavoro.
Siamo riusciti, ancora, a conciliare l'interesse delle
nostre imprese con la domanda del Paese, proseguendo
un grande sviluppo nel quadro di un attento equilibrio
con le nostre risorse.
La crescita del numero dei comuni in concessione e
degli utenti gas, l'espansione nel settore idrico, l'attiva
presenza all'estero, si sono accompagnate infatti con
una accresciuta forza economica e finanziaria.
Abbiamo avuto come sempre punti di riferimento
precisi: i nostri azionisti, i comuni concedenti,
gli utenti.

Sample 1

Sample 1 Male – Enneatype One. Chairman of a big company. The HW is *Steady*, *Angular*, with *Straight Extensions*, *Stable Baseline* (the baseline is *rising*), but its movement is stable), rather *Careful*, with *Sober* final movements, but also with some hints of *Strokes of Subjectivity* (see the final "e" of the word "espansione" in line 8). The *Slant* is *rightward*, with a bent to the sign *Parallel* (see the description in the next part of this article). A general impulsiveness and irritability is also noticeable, it is however somewhat diluted by the external expression (see the width of the *Margins*, especially the left one).

Upright: This is script in which the vertical axes are mainly perpendicular to the baseline. It indicates self-control that persists in all manifestations, including the expression of affection and speech, and in gestures.

People with upright handwriting are generally psychologically stable and hold on to habitual attitudes. They tend to be linear and consistent in their convictions; if they take on commitments, they will do their best to honor them. They are self-controlled and not given to frivolity. They prefer deeds to words, and are aware of their own sense of self-sufficiency—which sometimes can turn into conceit. But by nature they are little inclined to manipulate others.

Upright script also indicates mastery over internal and external pressures.

A person whose handwriting has a high degree of uprightness could be prone to harshness of character, inflexibility, vanity, pride, and making moralistic judgments. When *Upright* is in a context of agitated or worked-up, it suggests oscillation between yielding to passion and holding it at bay. Such handwriting generally indicates habitual muscle tension.

Straight extensions: The letter extensions are straight, with no bending. This indicates inflexibility of character, not to be confused with firmness, whose indicator is the *Stable Baseline*, nor with self-control, whose indicator is the *Upright* sign.

A person whose writing has a high degree of straight extensions is rigid and unable to adapt, even if it is to their advantage. They neither bend nor give in, and hold their personal point of view as flawless. Even in the face of extenuating circumstances, they stick to their inflexible judgments.

If in a position of authority, they may apply the law literally, with no room for interpretation.

They judge themselves by the same criteria, keeping their word and promises and treasuring the image of blameless righteousness that such behavior confers.

These traits become negative only if the extensions are overly tense and rigid; otherwise, on average (*i.e.*, when only some extensions are upright while others are not), or if they are neutralized by other signs such as *Curved* or *Space between Letters*, the straight extensions assume a positive meaning - uprightness, honesty, faithfulness, and reliability.

Careful: The sign *Careful* when present to a high degree points at a lack of spontaneity. Such people are polite, well mannered, and impeccable in attitude and behavior.

At the same time, they tend to follow rules and are attached to formality and order. They comply with plans and methods, are inflexible and narrow-minded, and expect others to follow the same frame of reference.

They become inwardly annoyed when matters don't seem to work according to expectations or if things are not done with the same scrupulous accuracy that rules them. This attitude is not conducive to a spirit of adaptability. As a result, they are always tense and dissatisfied with the performance of others, especially with how others do things.

Clear: When individual letters are clear-cut and easy to read, without the contextual help of letters nearby. This sign is associated with people who like to state their thoughts precisely, behave in a distinguished manner, and are fond of order, both on psychic and moral levels. They are annoyed by and reject approximation and superficiality. Uncomfortable with instinct and the complexity of feelings, they nevertheless try to express them accurately (*i.e.*, inner feeling and thinking are congruent with external manifestation).

Strokes of sobriety: When the strokes, especially the ones at the end of the word, are cut short or barely visible.

The basic meaning is an attitude that moderates all manifestations of the personality, holding back impulsiveness in speech and responses to stimuli. But the restrained final stroke can change to what in graphology is defined as:

Stroke of subjectivism: The final stroke of the word that runs parallel to the baseline and is carried out in a restrained, accurate and basically rigid way. This sign occupies a place in the field meant for *Space between Words*, which symbolically stands for the time and space given to the critical thinking that occurs between a word and the following one. Filling that space with a rigid stroke is as much to say, "There is nothing to be added to the last word written."

Psychologically, this kind of stroke implies a pretension to superiority and infallibility, to standing as a model for others, a need to feel distinguished and to consider one's own thinking unquestionable.

At this point it should be obvious how the sign *A angles*, *B angles*, *Stable Baseline*, *Uprightness*, and *Straight Extensions* have an inner coherence of meaning and also how they are in tune with the basic characteristics of type One.

1

There are days when everyone I meet appear as symbols, and individually or together they form a prophetic or occult writing that describes my life in shadows. The words I exchange with familiar or unfamiliar faces are phrases for which I have no dictionary, though I have an idea of what they mean. They speak, they express, but its not of themselves that they speak, nor to themselves that they express; theyre words and are not clearly indicative, but they allow glimpses. In my twilight vision, however, I only vaguely distinguish what these sudden glass panes on the surface of things let show

Sample 2

There are days when everyone I meet appear as symbols, and individually or together they form a prophetic or occult writing that describes my life in shadows. The word I exchange with familiar or unfamiliar faces are phrases for which I have no dictionary, though I have of what they mean. They speak, they express, but it's not of themselves that they speak, nor to themselves that they express; they're words are not clearly indicative, but they allow glimpses.

Sample 3

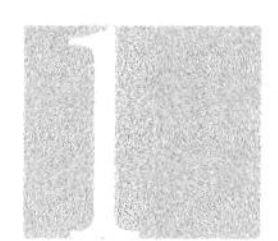

Samples 2-3 Females – Enneatype One. The main signs are: *angular ovals*, *Straight Extensions*, *Stable Baseline*, *Clear*, *Space between Words*, *regular left margin*, *Careful*. In this context *Careful* means that in the handwriting the "form" predominates over "movement". The writings appear to pay attention to and control that impulses be expressed in an adequate manner. Consequently, the will is pretty strong, and there is mental clarity. As a whole the MHS is contained. Moral rules are important to both writers, and so is fairness. The sample # 2, appears less composed than sample # 3, and I believe this is due to a greater influence of the Two wing.

At the same time this cluster of signs is not very compatible with:

• Type **Two**, is "anti-rigid" more than any other types. How else could the Two tune in so fluidly to other people's needs? How could the Two seduce, manipulate, express warmth and at the same time maintain the control and carry on all that criticism to which the type One is so passionately dedicated?

• Type **Three** has a similar need and attitude towards realization and action as the One. Both have perseverance when engaged in practical tasks. Therefore, graphologically speaking, some of the aforementioned signs apply also to the Three, in particular those showing determination, for example *A angles*, *B angles*, and *stable baseline*.

Ones, however, are highly conditioned by an inner sense of criticism and a rigid adherence to rules that makes them less flexible than Threes. Ones, in order to realize their goals, neither project the most appropriate image, nor feel inclined to compromise. In contrast, Threes are more flexible, perhaps more opportunistic, and mold the rules to fit the desired goal.

Thus, the Three's handwriting will be less restrained, the slant more changeable, the signs of austerity almost absent; the extensions could be straight, but also concave to the right.

The Three's handwriting will contain more demonstrative additional signs, such as starting and final strokes that are large and curved, as if showing the capacity to smile even if internally they don't feel like smiling. Ones can also smile even when they feel resentment, but perhaps their facial muscles appear strained and stiff. Threes are much better at putting on a mask to hide their true feelings.

Threes reserve their criticism for things related to achieving maximum efficiency, for example, in teamwork; but if the situation requires it, they can easily hold back criticism. Threes are better able to maintain a broader view of a situation without getting stuck in details.

For average Ones, however, criticism is almost compulsive. They have a hard time letting things go and getting over them. Ones can get stuck in formal details and following rules that may be totally irrelevant to the Three.

That's why, on the whole, the handwriting of type One, although similar in some graphical indicators, appears more rigid and restrained when compared to that of type Three.

• Type **Four**: It is not by accident that the direction of integration for type Four is towards One. Generally, Fours lack stability because of an unsteady inner image of themselves caused by mood-swings and inefficiency during spells of uneasiness. In contrast, Ones by nature are not overwhelmed by their emotional needs and can carry out their duties in a more consistent way. Graphologically speaking, the Four's handwriting lacks firmness and structure while the One's handwriting could be sometimes considered as hyper-structured. We know that Fours need to develop more emotional self-discipline, while maintaining their creativity. So, developing some graphological (and psychological) characteristics of the type One such as *straight extensions, stable baseline,* and *B angles* would indicate an increase in emotional stability and would be very positive for the Four**.**

• Types **Five** and One have similar psychological traits. Both are intellectually oriented, love coherence and freedom of thought, are perfectionist, and behave in a rather withdrawn and restrained manner.

Ones, however, seem more intense (their handwriting uses more pressure than the Five's), giving little space to spontaneous expression of their own desires. This intensity is at the same time countered by strong self-control, as if there were an ongoing inner struggle.

The Five, on the other hand, will distance from their emotions right from the start in order to observe them.

In the Five's handwriting we might find many of the abovementioned graphological signs, but in general the letters will be smaller, the pressure lighter or "dryer," with larger spaces between letters and words. The Five's handwriting looks less formal, because their defensiveness and control is accomplished by distancing themselves mentally from situations, rather than emphasizing the irreproachability of their own behavior, as a type One would do.

• Type **Six**: Ambivalence, indecision, doubt, and fear are characteristics that contrast with the coherence and firmness of type One**.** In the handwriting, self-doubts, fears, and ambivalence cannot be expressed through some of the typical graphological signs of the One, such as *uprightness, straight extensions,* and *stable baseline*. However, the handwriting of a counterphobic Six will contain some similar reactive signs, but is much more fluctuating than that of the One.

The counterphobic Six will for example display a less homogeneous pressure throughout (a sign indicating ambivalence). Moreover, the One belongs to the gut center, while the Six to the head center. The Six struggles with inner conflict between intellectual evaluation of people/situations, and spontaneous expression of internal drives (head and gut); and that translates into a more erratic pressure compared to the One who is more stable and grounded in the gut.

• Type **Seven** is characterized by a multi-sided and unsystematic thinking process. Sevens tend not to inhibit impulses, are not into tradition, and have a flexible interpretation of rules. They are inclined to partake in the pleasures of the life, which they do not place after duty. If Sevens show the graphological signs we are talking about (the cluster of signs peculiar to the One) in their handwriting, they are most likely not being themselves, but could benefit from some of these traits. Similarly, self-controlled Ones should develop some traits of the Seven and learn to let go of a little tension and self-control.

• Type **Eight** is gifted with the same strength and instinctual determination as the One, but is more flexible when it comes to interpreting rules, so that they will fit the Eight's agenda of preserving a sense of power and control over the environment. We rarely find the handwriting of a type Eight with the sign *careful* (very common in the One). Eights are not subject to inhibition of impulses or the expression of anger as are Ones; therefore the Eight's handwriting will be livelier and often messier.

• Type **Nine** seems less active, less "tonic," less determined or gritty and less committed to following stable lines of behavior and thinking that concern ideals, rules and duties. They are more inclined to comply with situations rather than oppose them. When Nines don't want something, passive resistance is their way to communicate it. The average handwriting of type Nine will seem spineless and less angular when compared to the handwriting of type One.

L'enneagramma è un modello geometrico
che affonda le sue radici in molte di
quelle tradizioni, soprattutto orientali, che
hanno coltivato più la conoscenza della mente
che quella del mondo – È utilizzato come
strumento scientifico, per dare ordine e concretezza
alle conoscenze psicologiche su se stessi e su
gli altri: un filo d'Arianna nel labirinto

Sample 4

Sample 4 Female – Enneatype One: HW with the signs *Careful, Upright, Stable Baseline, Straight Extensions, Clear,* hints of *Strokes of Subjectivity* and *Strokes of Affectedness* (those last ones consist in the initial traits of the letter, implying a sense of aesthetic preciousness). In this context, an indication of the need to show her softness and amiability – which is not quite validated due to the general propensity towards control and the lack of spontaneity in the hand writing. The behavior is somewhat formal.

Ci sono giorni nei quali ogni persona che incontro e, ancor più, le persone abituali della mia convivenza obbligata e quotidiana, assumono aspetti di simboli e, isolati o fra loro connessi, formano un alfabeto profetico od occulto che descrive in ombra la mia vita.
Da quando il caldo è cessato e la prima leggerezza della pioggia è cresciuta fino a farsi sentire, nell'aria è rimasta una quiete che l'aria del caldo non aveva, una nuova pace a cui l'acqua dava una sua brezza.
Fernando Pessoa – "Il libro dell'inquietitudine"

Sample 5

Samples 5-6 HW of two females enneatype ONE: in common are the graphical signs of *Careful, Upright, Clear, Stable baseline, Straight Extensions, Sober Final Strokes*. One of the dominant traits is the need to control the spontaneous self-expression.

Ci sono giorni nei quali ogni persona che incontro e, ancor più, le persone abituali della mia convivenza obbligata e quotidiana, assumono aspetti di simboli e, isolati o fra loro connessi, formano un alfabeto profetico od occulto che descrive in ombra la mia vita.
Da quando il caldo è cessato e la prima leggerezza della pioggia è cresciuta fino a farsi sentire, nell'aria è rimasta una quiete che l'aria del caldo non aveva, una nuova pace a cui l'acqua dava una sua brezza.

Sample 6

El maestro le dijo: todos los budas y todos
los seres consientes no son mas que la mente
única aparte de la cual no existe nada.
Esta mente que no tiene comienzo es no
nacida y es indestructible, no es verde ni
amarilla ya que no tiene forma ni apariencia.
Solo la mente única es el Buda, y no
hay distinción entre el Buda y los seres
sintientes, pero los seres conscientes están

Sample 7

Sample 7 Male – Enneatype ONE: HW with the sign *Steady* (includes *Straight Extensions*, *Stable Baseline*, a strong *Pressure* with a good degree of tension and decision, *A Angles* and *B Angles*).

I forgot I have a
workshop on Friday
until 4:30pm
I will be free all
day Saturday until
5pm and all day
Sunday. Let me
know when you are
free to buy your
sweater. See you

Sample 8

Samples 8-9 Females – Enneatype ONE with a Two Wing. The *Ovals* are pretty *angular*, present are the signs *Straight Extensions*, and *Careful*. The *baseline* is *rising*, but consistent in its course. These handwritings emanate a deep need of order and harmony. At the same time, there is a fight present between control of the movement (and then of the behavior), and an expressive élan of impulses. The sign *Rightward slant* has been taught at school to the writers, but, in this context, it also expresses the wish of letting go towards spontaneity.
The influence of the Two wing is pretty marked in both samples. For example, in sample # 9, note how the word "*movement*" is restless compared to the previous word. There is a need to let go of control and of going toward others. In the sample # 8, the influence of the Two wing manifests trough *enlarged ovals*, and *reduced angularity* (see the difference among the oval marked by the arrows: some of them are very narrow and overflowing of ink, while others one a are very open and curved).

Allport, Gordon &
— Vernon
Studies in Expressive
Movement
(has a chapter re
graphology)

Sample 9

1

In the first part one of this article, I proposed that the graphological basis of enneatype One consists of the following signs:

- *A Angles*
- *B Angles*
- *Steady*
- *Stable baseline*
- *Straight Extensions*
- *Upright*
- *Careful*
- *Clear*
- *Strokes of sobriety*
- *Strokes of subjectivism*

This group of signs is almost always present in type One's handwriting. We could say that they express the core psychological traits of type One. But in order to recognize the various ways in which a ruling passion and cognitive fixation manifest, we need to take additional signs into consideration.

The individuality of each handwriting emerges when these and other meaningful graphological indexes are put together.

Before discussing additional signs, here are some handwriting samples of types One, both,with the Two and Nine wings.

In general, the One w/Nine maintains the graphological basis mentioned above, but is more *curvilinear* and rather *static*. The handwriting (HW) of the One w/Two is also more *curvilinear* than the basic type One, but more lively and dynamic compared to the HW of One w/Nine.

Here we come across a first tricky question, but one that graphology can help to investigate: How much do the wings influence the basic type, and how does this influence relate to the subtypes?

Handwriting analysis can allow us to go deeply into quantifying and qualifying psychological structures. We should be able to distinguish both the subtype and also the wing and how strong or weak their influence is, but this level of analysis requires more research and is a goal for the future.

It would also appear that One w/Nine matches the characteristics of Self-Preservation subtypes closer than the One w/Two, who is more compatible with the tendencies of the Sexual subtype; this supposition must be verified as well.

Ci sono giorni nei quali ogni persona
che incontro e, ancor più, le persone
abituali della mia convivenza obbligata e quotidiana, assumono aspetti di
simboli e, isolati o fra loro connessi,
formano un alfabeto profetico ed occulto
che descrive in ombre la mia vita.

Sample 10

Sample 10 Female – Enneatype ONE w/9: the HW shows characteristics of some rigidity (*Careful, Upright, Straight extensions, Stable baseline, Narrow space between Letters*), which together with the sign *Clear* make up the graphological base of the type One. The strong influence of the Nine wing emerges from the extra curvilinear aspect and the slow gesture of the Hw (the average One's HW is more *Angular*) and from the slightly drooping final strokes, also defined as *Strokes of Phlegmatism.*
In this case the writer has typed herself as a One; but analyzing the HW gives food for doubt, because the tension of the stroke is not tonic enough for a One. We could classify the scriptor as on the cusp between One and Nine. Nevertheless, the attempt of a rigid control that emanates from the HW supports her choice of type One.

Ci sono giorni ~~in cui~~ nei quali
ogni persona che incontro e, ancor
più, le persone abituali della mia
convivenza obbligata e quotidiana,
assumono aspetti di simboli e, isolati

Sample 11

Sample 11 Female – Enneatype One w/9: we can say the same as stated about the previous sample (#10), however, the tension of the Movement of Spontaneous Handwriting (MHS) is quite tonic. The HW shows the characteristics of a good degree of *Steadiness*, but the curvilinear context discloses the influence of the Nine wing. (In this case we know that it is a Self-Preservation One. In my experience it is quite likely that Self-Preservation Ones have a Nine wing, while Sexual Ones are more likely to have a Two wing. But this assumption is yet to be verified).

Ci sono giorni nei quali ogni persona che incontro
e, ancor più, le persone abituali della mia con
vivenza obbligata e quotidiana, assumono aspetti
di simboli e, isolati o fra loro connessi, formano
un alfabeto profetico od occulto che descrive in
ombre la mia vita.
Da quando il caldo è cessato e la prima
leggerezza della pioggia è cresciuta fino a
farsi sentire, nell'aria è rimasta una

Sample 12

Sample 12 Female – Enneatype One w/2: the difference from a One w/9 is quite evident. We have greater agility, easiness, and fluidity here. Nevertheless, in the background there is control, and a kind of perfectionism inherent to type One: *Stable Baseline, Upright, Clear, Careful*, presence of *Straight extensions*, *Narrow space between letters* (if she were a type Two, the HW would be softer. But also in this case, we are on the cusp between two types).

There are days when everyone I meet appears
as symbols, and individually or together
they form a prophetic or occult
writing that describes my life in
shadows. The word I exchange
with familiar or unfamiliar faces

Sample 13

Sample 13 Female – Enneatype One w2: the HW in substance is careful and formal, but there is as if an urge to throw herself toward others (the HW starts *Upright*, and, progressively, becomes *Rightward*. After a while it comes back to *Upright*). The *letter extensions* sometimes are *straight* and *rigid*, and sometimes *Concave to right*. The course of the baseline is fluctuating.

L'enneagramma è un modello geometrico
che affonda le sue radici in molte
di quelle tradizioni, soprattutto orientali,
che hanno coltivato più la conoscenza
della mente che quello del mondo.
È utilizzato come strumento scientifico
per dare ordine e concretezza alle cose.

Sample 14

Sample 14 Female – Enneatype Two w/1. Here again we are on the cusp between two types. The writer, after an Enneagram workshop, typed herself as a Two, but her HW contains both a good dose of curvilinear, which conveys characteristics of availability and empathy; as well as a tendency toward self-control and rigidity (signs: *Straight extensions - Upright - Careful*). The rhythm of the graphic gesture is rather not homogeneous indicating that emotionality exerts a strong influence on the thinking process. In general, type One is better at maintaining clarity of mind because of self-control.

Then, we could say that this HW belongs to a type Two but with a very strong One wing. Finally, in this HW the passion of pride is more evident than the passion of anger (anger implies inner reactivity and HW will show a fight between "reaction", and "control". In this HW anger cannot be considered as a primary reaction, but is triggered when the writer feels that her pride is attacked. It is a subtlety, but is important to consider).

Perciò, ho pensato di scriverti anch'io, con la sper
questo mio <campione> possa essere analizzato e
indicare le caratteristiche fondamentali della m
soprattutto in relazione alla professione che svolg
parere, l'insegnamento la mia strada, oppure se
possa meglio realizzarmi seguendo altre vie, indi

Sample 15

Sample 15 Script showing the sign *Austere* (sample taken from Palaferri N., *L'indagine grafologica e il metodo morettiano*, Padova, Ed. Messaggero, 1999).

tedesca un'articolo riguardante il Suo la
e la Sua capacità in campo grafologico. Il co
spondente raccontava degli anedotti e dei fat

Sample 16

Sample 16 Script showing the sign Austere. The strictness and the inflexibility of the MHS is evident (sample taken from Palaferri N., op. cit.).

Let us consider the signs that, although coherent with the graphological basis of type One, express different manifestations of the personality.

Austere: A sign that I found quite often in One's HW.

We find this sign in the HW that is rigid and strict in the stroke (strong pressure, and *Straight Extensions*), and manifests stiffness and control (*Upright*, restrained final traits).

Handwritings containing this sign indicate a person gifted with remarkable moral courage and reliability who bravely faces challenges and problems, is very determined and not influenced by pressures of circumstances. Even if wrong in a position, they nevertheless remain coherent and consistent because of the integrity of intentions. In spite of exuding a sense of sternness in a group setting, their opinions are respected for their impartial judgement.

They expect agreements to be honored and do not tolerate shortcomings, adhering to rules with no patience for favoritism or weaknesses.

They have a lot of self-control over habits, do not indulge in excesses and have the moral courage to endure hardships although there is an inclination to feel guilty or self-doubt for their own performance.

The strong influence of the super-ego inhibits spontaneous feelings and actions causing a tendency towards hypertension and control.

- Originalmente tu non riconosci che la conoscenza
innata e la sua coscienza sono il tuo Buddha
interno, pertanto corri in altri posti a cercare Buddha
Pertanto tu che parlasse a te del
tuo conoscimento innato e della tua coscienza.
Come una medicina per curare questa infer=
mita di questa ricerca agitata, quando tu
cerchi fuori questa infermità della tua cura
se ti fissi (prendi in forma
fissa) a questa (coscienza) conoscenza innata. questa è
l'infermità del Zen che è caratteristica di un
seguitore fanatico- È come l'acqua che si fa
gelo= Tutto il gelo è acqua ma non può
essere utilizzato per calmare la sete _

Sample 17

Sample 17 Male – Enneatype One: HW with the sign Austere (the reproduction of this sample does not show sufficiently the strong pressure, hence the intensity of the original sample).

Sample 18

Sample 18 Female – Enneatype One: script showing the sign *Austere*.

Solemn: this sign indicates standoffishness, an almost hierarchic and pompous aspect resulting from a tidy and careful MHS, with straight letter axes and a quite large vertical dimension of the letters.

Psychologically this sign represents a sense of personal dignity and of honor, but also an extra layer of ostentatious dignity, resulting in a lack of spontaneity and naturalness—elevating simple communications to proclamations as in an authoritative delivery of a judgement.

Sample 19

Sample 19 Script showing the sign *Solemn* (sample taken from Palaferri N., op. cit.).

Another cluster of signs peculiar to enneatype One point more specifically to a strong sense of duty coupled with a tendency towards formality and excessive rigor. These signs are characterized by a need to distinguish oneself, the prevalence of the thinking function in the area of mental activity, and a strong control over one's own impulsiveness. These signs also indicate inflexibility, rigidity, extreme adherence to principles, reduced spontaneity and difficulty in adapting to change.

The relative graphic indicators are:

- *Parallel*
- *Pedantic*
- *Planted on the line*
- *Squared (or Strongly Designed)*

It is not necessary to find the whole cluster of signs in a handwriting sample, because each sign alone is already highly indicative of some characteristic of type One. At the same time, a marked presence of these signs can lead us to exclude with reasonable certainty other enneatypes. In future articles, when other types are discussed briefly, it will become obvious how the psychological mechanisms implied by these signs are completely incompatible with, for instance, type Twos, Fours and Sevens, although each sign may very well have characteristics in common with other types.

The sign *Parallel* is present when all the letter axes show the same angle of slant. The positive sides of this sign are precision, order, scruples, respect for the rule of law and strong self-control. On the negative side, it may indicate a lack of emotional flexibility, mental schematism, and a rigidly conventional attitude towards rules.

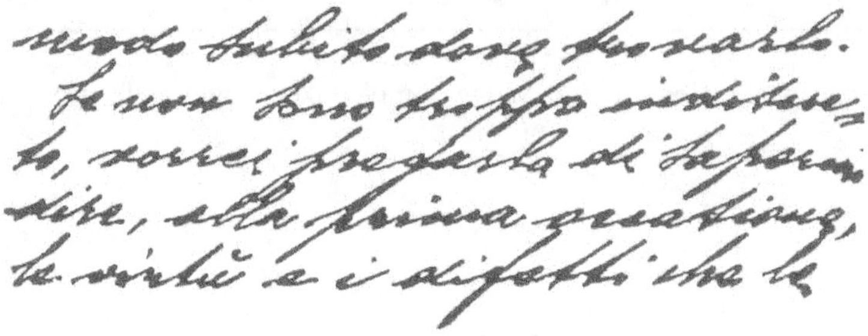

Sample 20

Sample 20 If we try to contemplate this handwriting, we can perceive the liveliness subject to constraint of the rhythm of movement. In the handwriting sample anger is very deep and unconscious to the writer and its expression is strongly repressed.

In the sign *Pedantic*, the graphic movement lacks flow and elasticity. Exasperating attention is given to the rhythm of the pressure of the strokes that are made to alternate between light and strong as in calligraphic writing. At the neurological level, more pressure is normally exerted on the descending strokes and less pressure in the ascending ones. But spontaneity implies that the writing has many nuances and variations in ink flow. The pedantic rigidity does not allow this natural tendency to move easily. Psychologically there is a mental attitude lacking of ductility, a strong sense of duty bound by conventions, a tendency to be a stickler for detail and dogmatic. Under the sign Pedantic, rules must be respected to the detriment of pleasure or letting one's self go. The writing lacks genuineness and feels as if it was drawing self-esteem from its own contrived and stiff perfectionism and exhibits a need to parade ostentatiously (See **Sample 21**, from Palaferri N., op. cit.).

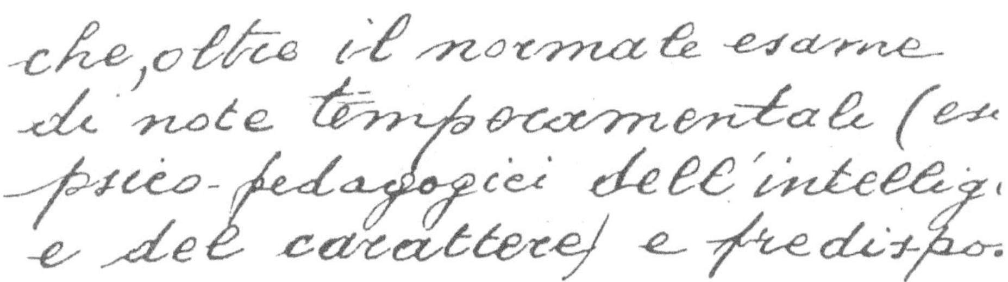
che, oltre il normale esame
di note temperamentali (es
psico-pedagogici dell'intellig.
e del carattere) e predispo.

Sample 21

The sign *Planted on the line* is formed by “lined up” elements that seem prefabricated elsewhere and then squatted on the text baseline. The *Planted on the line* sign renders the graphic movement cold and rigid, and lacks in fluidity and expansiveness in making the strokes that create the letters and words.

Such a personality is most likely dominated by the thinking function, fond of precise planning, consistent and reliable by nature, strong of character through its good control over its own impulsivity, with an underlying hue of superiority and toughness.

On the negative side, the sign *Planted on the line* shows a personality that could have a lack of flexibility, that is attached to conventions, that has a low level of spontaneity, that demonstrates a subjective insistence on righteousness of its own opinions as well as a formal courtesy, and, above all, is prone to intense outbursts of anger when suppressed emotions are released (See **Sample 22**, from Palaferri N., op. cit.).

il nostro rapporto che mi sembrava decisamente pi
maturo, soddisfacente e ben avviato .
Unico neo l'affiorare da parte sua di dubbi nei m
confronti a cui io non avevo dato importanza tov
mi parevano assurdi, e che avevo motivato con
mancanza di sicurezza dato il periodo di lontan
Da qui una serie di eventi in rapida successio
quali :

Sample 22

The sign *Squared* is indicated when the letters or the connecting strokes between letters are square-shaped and the words appear like rows of polygons.

The main psychological meaning of the sign *Squared* is seriousness, strength of will and a personal sense of distinction. The personality doesn't like to be overly influenced in it its decision-making process, especially in matters of feeling and emotions. There is a certain lack of spontaneity and its amiable expressions and availability are somewhat controlled (see **Sample 23**, female, probably with a Two wing).

There are days when everyone I meet appear as
symbols, and individually or together they form a prophetic
or occult writing that describes my life in shadows. The
words I exchange with familiar or unfamiliar faces are
phrases for which I have no dictionary, though I have
an idea of what they mean. They speak, they express,
but it's not of themselves that they speak, nor to

Sample 23

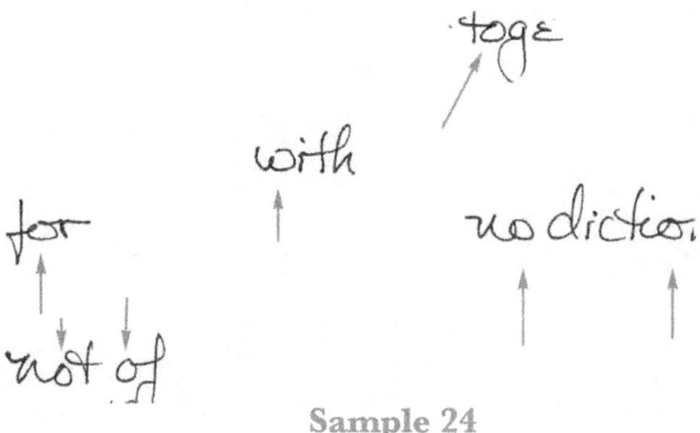

Sample 24

Sample 24 Excerpted from sample 23 above, shows Squared shapes. The movement of spontaneous handwriting indicates an original and organized personality that presents itself with amiability, indicating a type One with a Two wing. Nevertheless, this personality sometimes manifests a surprising degree of inflexibility.

Keep in mind that positive or negative meanings of signs depend on both the "degree" of a specific sign, and the presence, or absence, of other signs which either reinforce or moderate the psychological implications of the sign being examined.

The graphological signs *Squared, Parallel Pedantic, Planted on the line* which are so common for the type One personality, are rare in other Enneagram types; although, they may be present in a limited way. These four signs, so prevalent with type Ones, are almost impossible to find in the handwriting of Twos, Fours, and Sevens.

Two more graphological signs, *Meticulous* and *Minute*, need to be included among those signs that reflect the type One personality. The basic meaning of these two signs relates to perfectionism, tidiness, a sense of duty, scrupulousness, a tendency to criticize all and sundry, as well as a predisposition to bicker over minutia and to be distrustful.

In the sign *Meticulous* the vertical dimension of letters is rather contained and there is a lack of fluidity in the progress of the movement of spontaneous handwriting. The basic psychological implication is one of worry and anxiety caused by a difficulty in seeing the overall picture of situations. Perfectionism requires a rigorous compliance to rules. There is a pre-existing expectation of how things should be, and subsequently, a constant state of irritation over the imperfect reality. This state of unfulfilled expectation results in the inflexibility which causes the lack of fluidity in the handwriting.

The sign *Meticulous* indicates also a tendency to jealousy due to a difficulty in adapting to the complexity of feelings (See **Sample 25**. From Palaferri N., op. cit.).

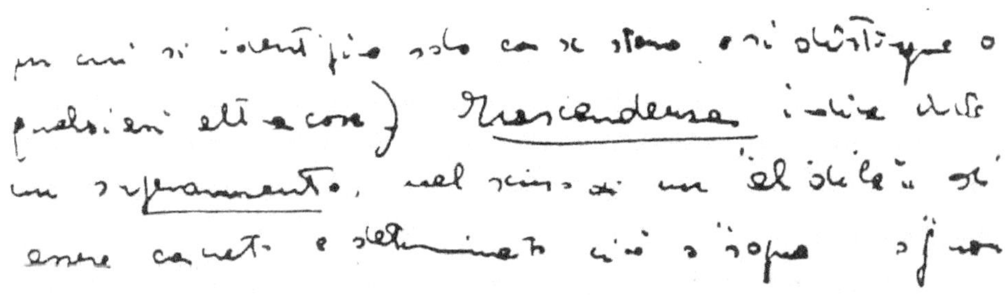

Sample 25

The sign *Minute* is exemplified by small writing, but unlike the sign *Meticulous*, there is fluidity in the handwriting.

The basic psychological meaning of the two signs is somewhat contiguous; in fact, those who exhibit the sign *Minute* in their handwriting, when stressed, can shift to *Meticulous*, but do not normally feel constantly irritated by people and situations. The sign *Minute* also indicates a strong sense of duty, self-control, containment in the communication style, and fluctuation between adaptability and inflexibility (See **Sample 26**. Minute, Palaferri N., op. cit.).

questa missione è stata trasferita in un'altra comunità.
Finalmente, dopo sette anni di vacanza (sarebbe troppo lun=
go specificarne le motivazioni che sfuggono anche a me),
di cui non mi sono mai saputa adattare e da cui so=
no rimasta letteralmente shockata, la Provvidenza mi
ha aperto una strada del tutto inattesa...

Sample 26

Ci sono giorni nei quali ogni persona
che incontro è, ancor più le persone abituali
delle mie convivenze obbligate e quotidiane,
assumono aspetti di singoli e, isolati o
fra loro connessi, formano un alfabeto
profetico occulto che descrive in ombre la

Sample 27

Samples 27-28 Female. The handwritings show the sign *Minute*, but in a context of carefulness, with a tendency towards perfectionism and being critical. The sample below, was written 30 years earlier (the writer is now 65 years old) and appears very rigid. Over the years, the graphic gesture has softened remarkably. The writer recognized that anger has been the pivotal emotion of her personality.

Sant'arte divina
Tu le percorri
or silenziose
dove i crociati
facevan fracasso
con le armature
e i loro destrieri
e tu ripensi
in tanta bellezza
ai tempi passati
alle gesta
agli eroi

Sample 28

The signs *Meticulous* and *Minute* can both be pertinent to type Five (many Enneagram authors point to similarities between both Ones and Fives), but we would need to look at the entire graphic spectrum for guidance in discriminating between Ones and Fives. We could start by considering that a One operates from the gut, while a Five is head-based. The Five's handwriting will have an overall flavor of dryness, while the One's will manifest an attitude of self-control. In this case, the graphic pressure will help us make a distinction between these two types. The pressure will be more intense in the One's handwriting, while the Five's graphic movement will be much lighter; but both types could be described as "meticulous and restrained."

One last graphological sign we can find in the handwriting of Ones, though it is neither typical nor exclusive to this type, is the sign *Twisted.* It consists of a sharp and sudden folding back of the letter axes, as if they were clashing against each other.

Psychologically, these subjects are constantly tense and get offended and irritated easily. They observe other people's behavior and can't help themselves—almost automatically they nit-pick everything they perceive as wrong.

The abrupt folding back of the letters' axes indicates an absence of calculated behavior. For instance, it would be pretty difficult to be manipulative in the fashion of a type Two while in the throes of intense reactivity. (The Two is reactive as well, but with the Two, the folding back of the letter axes will be less sharp).

The sign *Twisted* sign indicates characteristics of honesty and openness. However, those with this sign in their handwriting are notoriously unable to let go of any imperfections. They tend to be compulsively hypercritical, both at the verbal and non-verbal levels (See **Sample 29**. Twisted, from Palaferri N., op. cit.).

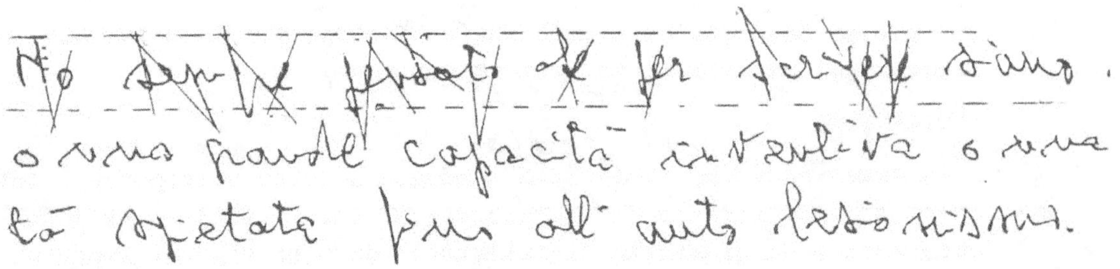

Sample 29

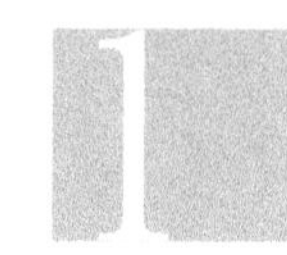

The direction of integration for the type One is toward Seven, which implies essentially a reduction of tension and more freedom in the One's orientation toward life. **Sample 30** is from a One who has made her own way to Seven.

Ci sono giorni nei quali ogni persona
che incontro è, ancor più le persone
abituali della mia convivenza obbligata
e quotidiana, assumono aspetti di simboli.

Sample 30

Sample 30 Female, defines herself as: "a One who is happily on my way toward Seven". This handwriting mirrors very clearly the self-perception of the writer - as if she were in the midst of change between compulsive self-control and spontaneity. The handwriting is *Careful,* with the sign *Straight Extension, Stable Baseline,* and *Strokes of Subjectivity,* the slant is mainly *Upright.* Nevertheless, we can notice a bit of expansion and smoothness; for instance, in some words the Space between letters increases, some final strokes are more *Curvilinear,* and the slant becomes *Rightward.* The writing would like to relax, but she is afraid of the expression of her emotions, including anger.

Her handwriting still has the rigid basic frame of a One, including *Upright, Straight Extensions,* and *Careful,* but also, there is some smoothness. In some words, the movement of spontaneous handwriting (MSH) increases the rightward slants, and the space between letters. It becomes more thrusting, and, as a whole, more curvilinear.

When Ones feel stressed, they tend to go towards type Four. It is rather a release of an emotionality that heretofore was hyper-controlled. In handwriting, suppressed impulses show up as "accumulations" of energy; for example, as expressed by the clumsy, but accurate graphological term *Thickened Type II, w*hich often indicates anger that transforms and becomes intense anxiety when a One goes to Four. Ones may try to control the expression of this anger or even turn it against themselves.

Thickened Type II happens when the stroke suddenly thickens and then rapidly takes back the habitual flow of ink in the pressure. It is a sort of spasm.

Impressionability rules the psychic life of those who exhibit the sign *Thickened Type II*. This impressionability causes the One's impulsiveness to be dominant and hence to lose control of rationality; imagine how destabilizing that could feel to the type One.

Ones lose the feeling of coherence towards their environment because their behaviors are influenced by sensations and moods which may run contradictory. There is a loss of serenity and composure. When impressions are particularly intense, they get restless, anxious, and worried.

In extreme situations, they can fall prey to a persecution complex; religious or political engagements can turn into fanaticism, sexual rupture can become passionate morbidity (when Ones move towards Four, they assume some similarities to Six).

Finally, Ones going to Four with *Thickened Type II* in their handwriting, find it difficult to maintain a balance in their vital expressions. Their main mechanism of defense, the reactive formation, becomes less effective, and they lose the ability to control the spontaneous manifestation of their real feelings.

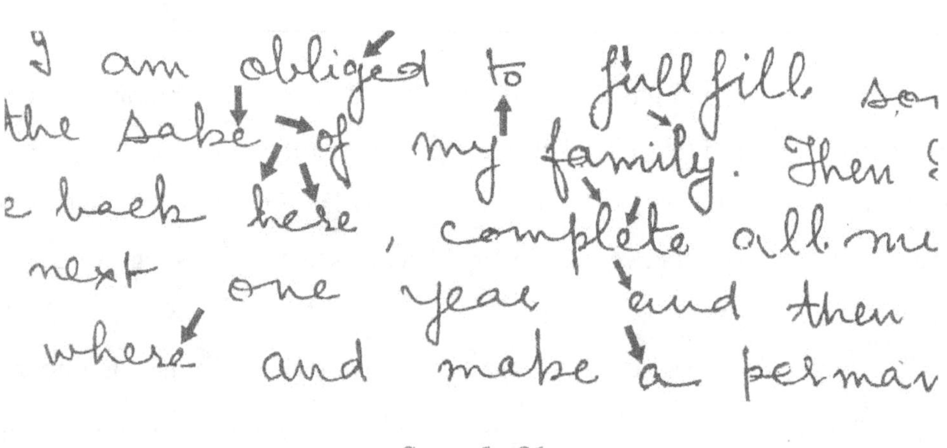

Sample 31

Sample 31 *Thickened Type II* from: De Petrillo V. – Millevolte A. in *The Application of the G. Moretti Graphological System*, p.44, Roma, Brain Edizioni, 2000.

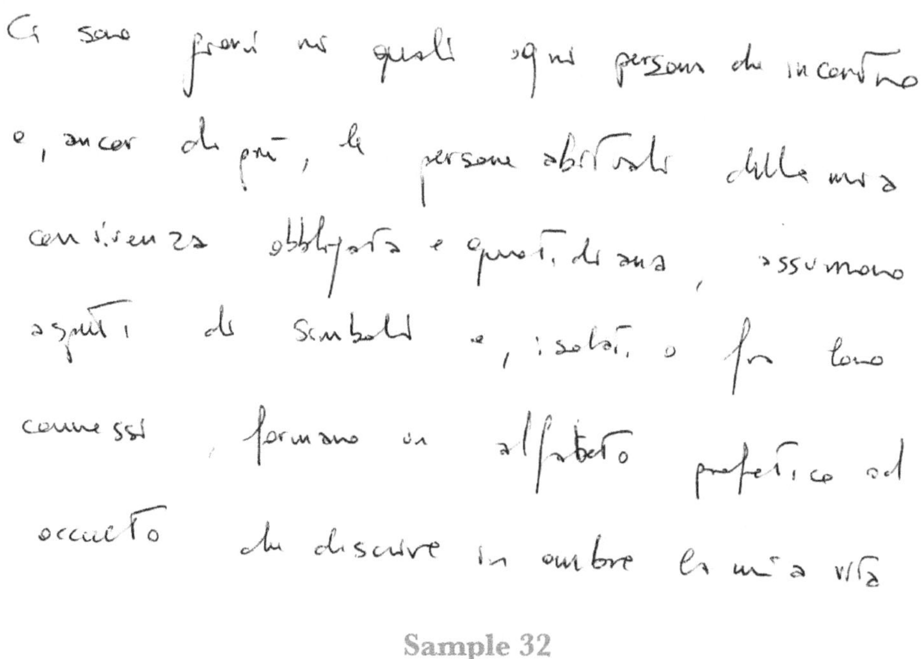

Sample 32

Sample 32 Female – Enneatype One in a period of stress. This printed image does not fully show the high degree of *Thickened Type II*. The sign *Meticulous* in this handwriting indicates a strong perfectionism, and consequent anger. The handwriting is lively, but the hypercritic is powerful (signs: wide S*pacing between words* and *Disconnected*). The rhythm of the connections between letters is not homogeneous: in some words the letters are bonded, in other parts of the handwriting they are disconnected, and, quite the opposite, there is a wide space between the letters. So, graphologically speaking, we say that the rhythm of the connections is not harmonious. Here hyper-critic transforms into self-critic, and self-blaming (signs: *Descending line*, and *Thickened Type II*). Tension due to perfectionism becomes discontent, which diminishes efficiency and the characteristics of the type Four surface.

This article concludes the graphological characteristics of the enneatype One. It contains a general idea of the connections between the Enneagram and handwriting analysis, emphasizing some dominant features. The signs characteristic of type One examined here certainly are not exhaustive of the plurality of the dynamics of the type.

Finally, I will show three samples, the first one representing enneatype Two, the second one enneatype One, and the third one the enneatype Nine. I hope that readers can intuitively perceive the differences of the *Spontaneous Movement of Handwriting.*

L'immaginazione è un
modello conoscitivo che affonda le sue radici in
molte di quelle tradizioni,
soprattutto orientali, che
hanno coltivato più la conoscenza della mente di

Sample 33

Sample 33 Type Two.

There are days when everyone I meet appear as symbols, and individually or together they form a prophetic or occult writing that describes my life in shadows. The word I exchange with familiar or unfamiliar faces are phrases for which I have no dictionary, though I

Sample 34

Sample 34 Type One.

Ci sono giorni nei quali ogni persona che
incontro e, ancor più, le persone abituali
della mia convivenza obbligata e quotidiana,
assumono aspetti di simboli e, isolati o
fra loro connessi, formano un alfabeto profetico od occulto che descrive in ombre la
mia vita.

Sample 35

Sample 35 Type Nine.

The following texts were used for the meaning and definitions of the signs:
PALAFERRI NAZZARENO, *L'indagine grafologica e il metodo morettiano*, Istituto Grafologico Moretti, Urbino, 1986.
PALAFERRI NAZZARENO, *Dizionario Grafologico*, Libreria "G. Moretti, Urbino, 1993.
TORBIDONI-ZANIN, *Grafologia* (testo teorico pratico), IV ed., Editrice La Scuola, Brescia, 1986.

HANDWRITING AND ENNEATYPE TWO

2

In *Character and Neurosis* Claudio Naranjo states, "The body build of ennea-type II is typically more rounded than ennea-type I and also softer than ennea-type III, and so it is possible to think that a genetically determined endomorphia supports the viscerotonic need for affection" (p. 192). We can start right from this point in order to understand the graphological characteristics of type Two. These characteristics are particularly striking if compared to handwriting samples of type One in the previous articles. And since the specific properties of the *Movement of Spontaneous Handwriting* (MSH) are nothing less than the manifestation of neurological, psychological and physiological peculiarities, they must include considerations of the constitutional components of the writer.

I don't want to oversimplify and say that the handwriting of the Two will be more rounded than that of type One, but as a general rule we can say that an important feature of type One is *rigidity*, manifesting in different ways; while for the Two it is *flexibility*, expressed in thinking, emotions, affectiveness, and physical processes. Naranjo calls the Two anti-rigid.

There is a marked difference in posture, muscular tone, and in the style of approaching another person between types One and Two. The One emanates a sense of control, of constraint, and is respectful of special boundaries. The Two conveys a sense of expansion, of stretching out toward the other, at times to the point of becoming intrusive. The type One's gestures may seem stilted with movements that include straight lines. Type Two is more 'flexuous', with spiraling movements that seem to entice, allure, and catch attention. If these differences are plausible, they should be mirrored in the handwriting.

To illustrate these clear differences, see Sample #1 (a type One) next to Sample #2 of (a type Two).

2

Se penso all'anno trascorso credo, in coscienza, che
abbiamo fatto un buon lavoro.
Siamo riusciti, ancora, a conciliare l'interesse della
nostra impresa con la domanda del Paese, proseguendo
un grande sviluppo nel quadro di un attento equilibrio
con le nostre risorse.
La crescita del numero dei comuni in concessione e
degli utenti gas, l'espansione nel settore idrico, l'attiva
presenza all'estero, si sono accompagnate infatti con
una accresciuta forza economica e finanziaria.
Abbiamo avuto come sempre punti di riferimento
precisi: i nostri azionisti, i comuni concedenti,
gli utenti.
In questi anni siamo stati determinati nello
sviluppo ed attenti a conservare le condizioni
che lo hanno permesso.
Siamo consapevoli di essere un Gruppo che ha fatto
e farà molto perché continueremo ad essere
una squadra motivata ed unita.

Sample 1

Sample 1 Male type One - for the description of this sample see article about Type ONE.

L' Enneagramma è un
modello geometrico che affonda le sue radici in
molte di quelle tradizioni,
soprattutto orientali, che
hanno coltivato più la conoscenza della mente che
quello del mondo.

Sample 2

Sample 2 Male, age 50 type Two. Very illustrative handwriting shows, in a marked way, the signs *Flexuous*, *C Angles*, *Loops*, *Regularly Alternating Inclination*.

We notice in the Two's handwriting a sort of "dilated self-image" that contrasts with type One's formalism. In fact, type Two invades the graphic space, takes possession of it and expands on it with ease; in contrast, the type One's handwriting feels forced to respect both margins and shows a general carefulness of movement.

Moreover, the handwriting of the Two markedly shows the sign *Flexuous*, which is defined, in Moretti's graphological system as: "…spontaneous movement that is basically curvilinear (means a predisposition to adaptability), and that gives to the strokes, to the letters, and to the connections among them, soft, almost elegant folds, sometimes even showing a sinusoidal shape."

Flexuous is a handwriting that flows on the baseline with much suppleness and lacks rigidity, strictness, and sharp angles.

2

We have to keep in mind that the meaning and the strength of each graphological sign must be taken in context, considering both the degree of its intensity, and the presence of the other signs.

When the degree of *Flexuous* is not very high, it indicates a pleasant personality, a deep sense of adaptability, and especially a sympathetic attitude and willingness to help others.

If we see *Flexuous*, as well as the sign *Regularly Alternating Inclination* (this will be defined below): "it adds intuition and deepens the ability to understand and to get involved in a supportive and helpful way with others."

A moderate presence of this sign in the handwriting indicates a balanced tendency towards altruism and generosity, traits that cannot yet be considered "compulsive" as described in Enneagram literature when referring to an unhealthy type Two.

But if the sign *Flexuous* appears to a high degree (*i.e.*, when it manifests in most letters of a script), along with other signs—like *ample starting* or *final curvilinear strokes*, which stress "the external manifestations of generosity"—it implies automatism and a self-serving form of altruism. Such altruism may be driven by a desire to gain confirmation of one's own identity through the compulsive satisfying the other's need, and does not necessarily stem from an opportunistic and manipulative attitude.

As is the case for all personality traits, what makes the difference is their degree of intensity and quantity.

In some handwriting, especially those containing *Loops* (to be defined further on), the sign *Flexuous* can indicate the need to be admired, and a drive to show off. In graphological literature, when this sign is present to a high degree, it means: "Egocentrism and selfishness that manifest with affectation, using seduction in order to gain an advantage" and "Psychophysical mannerisms that are refined and rather artistic but designed to bring self-serving results."

People with the sign *Flexuous* can tune in and feel an emotional resonance with others - in contrast to those who show rigidity in their handwriting, which inherently implies an inability to vibrate with different and multiple frequencies. Nevertheless, this empathetic characteristic of the Two can turn out to be deceptive and temporary.

Flexuous implicitly includes traits pertaining to the graphological index technically defined as *C Angles* - handwriting that shows "flowing, curved, and elastic movement; most of the angles are rounded, some letters have beautifying embellishments, and there are only a few sharp angles here and there." (De Petrillo V., Millevolte A, *The Application of the G. Moretti Graphological System*, Brain Edizioni, Roma, 2000).

C Angles indicate savoir-faire at the practical, mental, and emotional level. Taking each element of this sign separately:

- The smoothed angles show tenacity and balanced self-control (but not tense and rigid as for type One).
- The flowing and elastic movement implies social adaptability and a charming naturalness that makes others comfortable.
- The letters with beautifying embellishments (but without exaggeration) indicate amiable manners.
- Some sharp angles here and there show the ability to conceal strong resentment (these sharp angles, indexes of an emotional reaction, are not clearly visible in such a graphic context, and the same happens in the personality).

Two pupils of Moretti, Prof. Torbidoni and Prof. Zanin, say that those who show *C Angles* in the handwriting "...are willing to make sacrifices in order to get their aims met, but they do it in a way that makes their sacrifice visible to others. They discreetly earn the sympathy of others by expressing interest and understanding for their feelings; then, if they encounter resistance, they can back off strategically until another opportunity comes along." (p. 63).

If this sign is present to a high degree, *i.e.*, when the sign C Angles manifests with the presence of all the four elements that compose it, the psychological meaning changes: "The sense of opportunity becomes opportunism, the attention given to people turns to exploitation, the subtle and refined self-control is transformed into a lie and amiability becomes a way to manipulate others."

The sign *Loops* refers to each stroke drawn with a spiral movement (garland movement, double eye inside the oval, far-fetched movement in the starting stroke of letters, for instance in the letter c).

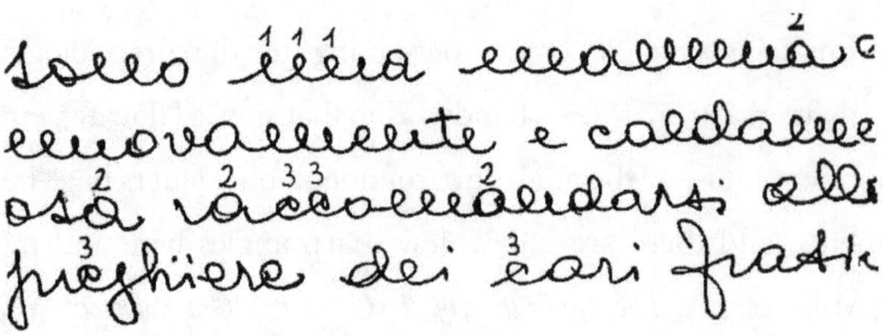

Loops

The psychological meaning of *Loops* is an amiable, adaptable and lively personality, but somewhat insincere about their underlying motivations.

A last, very meaningful, sign is ***Regularly Alternating Inclination (RAI)***. This refers to letters leaning alternately slightly to the left and then to the right, winding as if in a serpentine manner—in other words "a slight and harmonious oscillation of the letter-axes, so that their projections meet far from both the upper and lower vertexes of the letters."

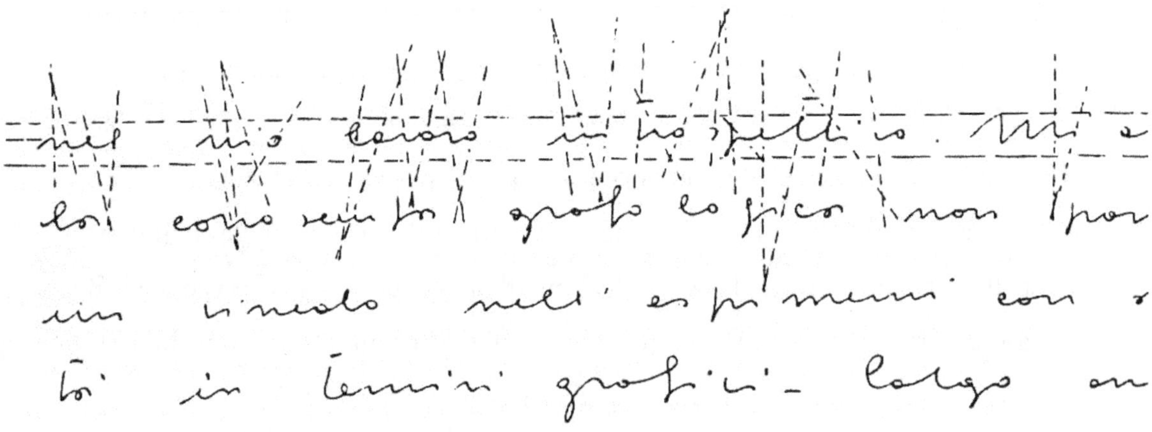

Regularly Alternating Inclination (RAI)

"From a psychological point of view *RAI* indicates a flexibility that enables the writer to gain a deep understanding of people and situations, and to read between the lines." (De Petrillo V., Millevolte A, *The Application of the G. Moretti Graphological System*, Brain Edizioni, Roma, 2000).

These four graphological signs—*Flexuous, C Angles, Loops,* and *Regularly Alternating Inclination (RAI)* on the one hand imply the simultaneous presence of other indexes with a compatible psychological dynamic; while excluding other signs. Space does not permit more detail, but the point is simply that mutually exclusive signs make no sense in the same HW, just like we can't have square circles or round squares.

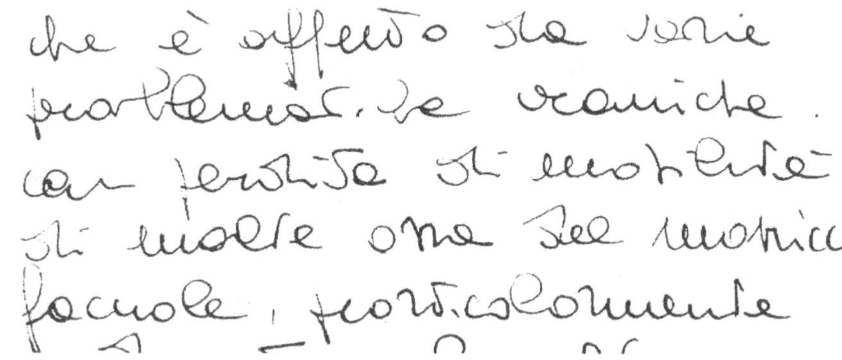

Sample 3

Sample 3 Male age 45, type Two. Script with the signs: *High middle zone, Narrow spacing between words, Mellow pressure* (symbol of being a nourishing person), *Curved, Flexuous, Loops.*

Esta mente pura que es la fuente de todo brilla por siempre sobre todo con el brillo de su perfección, pero la gente no está despierta a ello, considerando solo como mente aquello que ve, escucha, siente y sabe. No perciben el brillo espiritual de la sustancia fundamental. Si solo eliminasen todo pensamiento conceptual, esta sustancia fuente o fundamental se manifestaría como el sol que todo lo ilumina

Sample 4

Sample 4 Female age 40, type Two / Sexual subtype. The script is very *Flexuous*, with *C Angles*, *Loops*, *Regularly Alternating Inclination*, *Narrow spacing between words*. The *Pressure* is mellow and fluent.

We assume that flexibility, adaptability, intellectual and emotional agility, and a tendency to expansiveness rather than contraction are common characteristics of type Two. If our assumption is correct, it is plausible that signs indicating dryness, control of impulses, a restrained attitude, inhibition, hypercriticism, scientific analytical tendency, slowness, absence of adaptability, roughness, marked introversion, authoritarianism, and dogmatism, are *incompatible* with the personality of the Two.

Consequently, when a handwriting contains the signs listed below, it is unlikely that the writer is a type Two:

- *Bristling*: script with very pointed letters and reduced horizontal expansion = exasperatingly hair-splitting attitude.
- *Austere*: script with rigidly strict strokes and letter endings = rigid adherence to traditions, soberness in expression, and steadiness of conviction.
- *Extension concave to left*: script where letter extensions (t, d, l, g, h, f, p) show concavity to left = inability to be satisfied, easily repulsed, mistrust, prejudicial denial.

- *Gross*: script with a very marked pressure, sloppy and coarse = coarseness which manifests in thoughts, feelings, emotions and actions.
- *Slow*: script that advances in a lazy, and phlegmatic way, due to a lack of dynamism = Unwillingness to take on responsibility. Sluggish in mind and action, laziness, lack of interests.
- *Meticulous, Parallel, Pedantic, Planted on the line*: these signs, peculiar to type One, and incompatible with type Two, were described in the article about type One.
- *Sober*: small, plain writing with simple, basic letter forms lacking any additional strokes = conciseness, laconic in speech and action, dislike of the superfluous.
- *Truncated*: script with clean-cut strokes, sudden brakes, letter and word end-strokes are broken off vigorously = resolute attitude. Essentiality.
- *Dry*: very angular writing; tight letters, no end strokes and narrow spacing between letters; simplified forms, small in size = moral, intellectual, affective and material stinginess.
- *Skimpy*: very angular writing; disconnected, with straight rigid extensions; tight letters with narrow spacing between letters; the stroke seems devoid of ink = stunted constitution with weak muscles and bones. Also held back and contracted psychologically.
- *Disconnected*: script with letters that are detached from each other within the same word = analytical mind but lacking cohesive vision, tendency to get lost in details, lack of interpersonal skills.
- *Regular*: script of even and consistent size, slant, spacing and letter-formation; monotonous rhythm = need for schematic arrangement, dislike of change and new experience, little ability to adapt.

The signs we are likely to find in the handwriting of a type Two would contain indications of:

Gentleness; dependence; sociability; malleability; being easily influenced; excitability; physical agility; open seductiveness; histrionic personality; strong suggestibility; emotional lability; little interest in rigorous analytic thinking, but often very creative and imaginative; emotional readiness to feel others' needs; seductiveness; responsiveness to body contact; intrusiveness; hedonism; little tolerance for routine; incessant drawing of attention to oneself; superficiality;

changeableness; instability; amiability; cordiality; helpfulness; lack of inhibition; euphoria and exuberance; impulsive egocentrism.

These characteristics are of course not exclusive to the Two. Naranjo writes: "Points Two and Four stand in opposite positions in regard to point Three, and involve internal gestures of expansion and contraction of the self-image, respectively" (p.176).

This observation leads us to infer that some of the same graphological signs can also be found in the handwriting of type Four (*C Angles, Loops, Flexuous, Regularly Alternating Inclination*), because both are emotional types who share many psychological characteristics—specifically a problem with the stability and definition of their self-image.

Type Two is more extroverted and internally happy than the Four and also less "intellectual" (the Four may be influenced by the Five wing, the mental center; while the Two is next to the One, in the instinctive center). One of the main differences between the handwriting of these two types is the dimension of the letters of the middle zone (a, o, e, u, etc.). Twos make the middle zone letters larger than do Fours. Technically this is called *High Middle Zone.*

In my experience, I have rarely seen handwriting of a Two with a *Small Middle Zone*. Considered in a specific graphic context, the *Small Middle Zone* indicates a reduction of expansiveness, dissatisfaction, lowering of libido, meticulousness, reduced adaptability, tendency to isolation, and pessimism.

In general Twos show either a *High* or average *Middle Zone*, which points to characteristics of vitality, exuberance, extroversion, expansiveness, sociability, dynamism, self-confidence, "pride," optimism, vibrant feelings, generosity, need to attract attention, exhibitionistic tendencies, vanity, and a need to be held in high esteem by others. Naranjo calls it "pride considered as an enlarged self-image."

without waking up. The hard part was the three hour layover in London. I wasn't hungry and the wait was long. The trip from London to Milan was also

Sample 5

Sample 5 Female age 60, type Two. For a long time, this woman thought of herself as a Four. Recently she discovered she is a Two, and the handwriting totally confirms this new perception. The script is *Flexuous*, with *Regularly Alternating Inclination* and *Narrow space between words*. A typical sign here is *Open*, in which the letters "a" and "o" are open at the top, a strong identifying mark for type Two; indicating receptiveness, openness and responsiveness to stimuli, impressions or suggestions; a tendency to be easily moved; yielding in terms of affection and sexual drive; tendency to express emotions and feelings rather impulsively. It belongs to a very warm personality. The sign *Open* is in some ways the opposite of the sign *B Angles* (see article on type One in previous issues), because not closing the top of the ovals means "being influenced by feelings," and not always having the tenacity to stand up for one's own position.

2

There are days when everyone I
meet appear as symbols, and individ-
vally or together they form a
prophetic or occult writing that
describes my life in shadows. The
words I exchange with familiar

Sample 6

Sample 6 Female age 53 type Two. The script has the signs *High middle zone*, and *Narrow spacing between words*. The signs *Flexuous*, *Regularly Alternating Inclination*, and *Curved* are present, but *Not homogeneous* in their manifestation. Also the *Slant* is not homogeneous. Here the emotions are very powerful, influencing the well-being and self-image of the writer. But in this case the non-homogeneity implies that the person is friendly and warm towards others due to her spontaneous non-judgmental attitude.

In conjunction with the *High Middle Zone*, we find that Twos often use *Narrow Spacing Between Words* (precise technical criteria for measurement of this sign exist, but a description would be too detailed for the scope of this article).

In short, the spacing between words is equivalent to the lapse of time—translating into space—that the writing gives to each concept before expressing it on paper.

Disproportionately large *Spacing Between Words*, especially when joined with a *Small Middle Zone*, indicate a severe and meticulous critical attitude that can develop into hypercriticism, doubtfulness, wariness, strict self-control, introverted tendencies, sense of isolation, dissatisfaction, and melancholy.

In contrast, *Narrowness of Spacing Between Words*, especially in conjunction with a *High Middle Zone*, indicates spontaneity, generosity, a thinking process based mainly on intuition rather than scientific criteria. It also points to imagination, impulsiveness, lack of stability and autonomy in judgment, difficulty in discriminating clearly between inner and outer stimuli.

There are days when everyone I meet appear as symbols, and individually or together they form a prophetic or occult writing that describes my life in shadows. The word I exchange with familiar or unfamiliar faces are phrases for which I have no dictionary,

Sample 7

Sample 7 Female age 47, type Two / Sexual Subtype. Script with signs: *Flexuous, Regularly Alternating Inclination, C Angles, High Middle Zone, Narrow Spacing Between Letters, Curved.* Here, clarity of mind arises from carefulness rather than critical judgment. The sign *Careful* reflects a sort of preoccupation with judgment by others. The writing seems to be attentive to others' feedback. Thus, clarity of mind is a consequence of preoccupation, rather than of reflection. True critical ability, and the consequent depth of mind, are manifested by *Balanced Triple Width*, that is, from the balance of *Letter Breadth*, *Space between Letters*, and *Space Between Words*. We will analyze this sign in the next article.

These last characteristics fit a type Two very well, but would be totally incompatible with:

- Type Five, who gives more space to reasoning,
- Type One, who is more stable, self-controlled, and less spontaneous,
- In part, Type Three, who is more mentally organized, and less impulsive,
- Type Four, who is more introspective.

There may be some similarities with the other types.

- For example, the characteristics described above can coexist with type Nine, who could look like a type Two regarding generosity and adaptability. The Nine is less impulsive, however, and the handwriting flows with less impetus.
- Type Eight, though impulsive, is more direct than type Two, and does not need, and even rejects, the psychological characteristics that go along with smoothness and savoir-faire.
- Type Six often shows a *High Middle Zone*, but this type's doubtfulness and suspiciousness towards others' intentions prevents the handwriting from being as fluent and agile as that of a Two.

• Type Seven manifests the same vitality and exuberance as type Two, but the handwriting is less curvilinear. While the Seven is mentally agile and impulsive, this type doesn't have the compulsion to satisfy others' needs in order to raise his self-esteem. Also, the Seven doesn't show the typical emotional receptivity (*curvilinear handwriting*) of type Two.

A common characteristic of type Two's handwriting is the sign **Extended**, when the ovals are more extended horizontally than vertically.

Moretti regards this as a sign of vanity: "An exaggerated expansion toward others, with a simultaneous need to be considered a person who is motivated by a deep love for people…a sort of hypocrisy."

The sign *Extended* is the opposite of the sign *Angles*, which generally are found at the bottom and top of the oval letters. As described in the previous articles, *Angles* indicate the ability to affirm and defend our own sense of identity.

When *Extended* is present to a moderate degree—*i.e.*, only a few ovals are extended—it is a positive sign, provided the graphic context gives evidence of genuine openness and empathy.

But if most ovals are extended and especially overly extended, the personality manifests excessive profusion, and is at high risk of dispersion of the identity (plurality of the Egos), with consequent compensation that tends to be hysterical in nature.

diventano aspetti di simboli e,
isolati o fra loro connessi, formano
un alfabeto profetico od occulto
che descrive in ombra la mia
vita.
Da quando il caldo necessario
e la prima leggerezza della pioggia è cresciuta fino a farsi
sentire, nell'aria è rimasta una

Sample 8

Sample 8 Female age 50, type Two. The sign *Extended* is strongly evident, mainly because it is accompanied by a marked *Non-homogeneity*, *Curved*, and *Narrow space between letters*. Although the writing shows that she is generous and available towards others, it also shows that she has difficulty expressing her need for approval and support. This characteristic is reinforced by her lack of critical discernment. For example, she'd be capable to totally devoting herself to family, or to comply with others' needs (*Extended*), forgetting her own.

Da quando il caldo é cessato e la prima
leggerezza della pioggia é cresciuta fino a
farsi sentire, nell'aria è rimasta una
quiete che l'aria del caldo non aveva,
una nuova pace a cui l'acqua dava
una sua brezza. Fernando Pessoa. -
'Il libro dell'inquietudine".

Sample 9

Sample 9 Female age 50, type Two/Social subtype. The script shows the signs *Flexuous, C Angles, and Regularly Alternating Inclination.* But it is the sign *Extended* that is most relevant, indicating an adaptability so excessive that it is likely a form of ego compensation. She gives more than she would like to.

Finally, one last sign of the Two's handwriting, though there are many more: *Not Homogeneous*, which indicates the opposite of regularity and stability in the writing.

This sign is characteristic of agitation, hyper-emotionalism, hyper-sensitivity, inconsistency, and instability.

Not Homogeneous handwriting can manifest in different ways: in the space inside the ovals, spacing between letters and between words, in the variability of pressure, the dimensions of the letters, the speed, the slant of the letter axes, and more.

Variability of handwriting is the direct result of the influence of emotions, expressive of an inner richness. But often it also indicates a personality that is easily influenced and then behaves impulsively. It points also to a passionate and dependent nature, capriciousness, changes of mood, mental processes that are sometimes meticulous and sometimes sloppy

Naranjo refers to: "High excitability, with sudden shifts in enthusiasm; a simultaneous presence of tenderness and aggressiveness; impulsiveness; intolerance of limitations and deep inconstancy."

In contrast, *Graphic Homogeneity* does not mean rigidity or monotony in handwriting, but rather a well-proportioned harmony that includes variations in all its components. The presence of *Homogeneity* indicates a psychological structure characterized by stability in all aspects of the personality, especially emotional stability.

Can we say, in general, that our generous and friendly type Twos live up to those characteristics?

Os budas e os mestres de todos os tempos
e lugares só emergiam pela busca
da verdade e os buscadores de hoje
também vão atrás da verdade.
Somente quando você chegar a
verdade se sentirá completo. Sem
ela repetirá sua forma de ser antiga. De que verdade estou falando

Sample 10

Sample 10 Male type Two / Social subtype. The handwriting expands on the graphic space, showing the signs: *C Angles, Flexuous, Loops, final Strokes of Affectedness, Curved*, and a widespread *Non-homogeneity*.

Enquanto os mestres e iluminados de todos os tempos imergirão pela busca da
verdade e os buscadores de hoje também
vão atrás da verdade. Somente quando
você chegar a verdade se sentirá completo. Sem ela repetirá as suas formas de

Sample 11

Sample 11 Female type Two / Self-preservation subtype. Of all types, the handwriting of the Self-Preservation Subtype is generally more static than the Sexual and Social subtypes. This handwriting shows a high degree of the sign *Curved, Narrow space between words, Careful, Loops, High middle zone.*

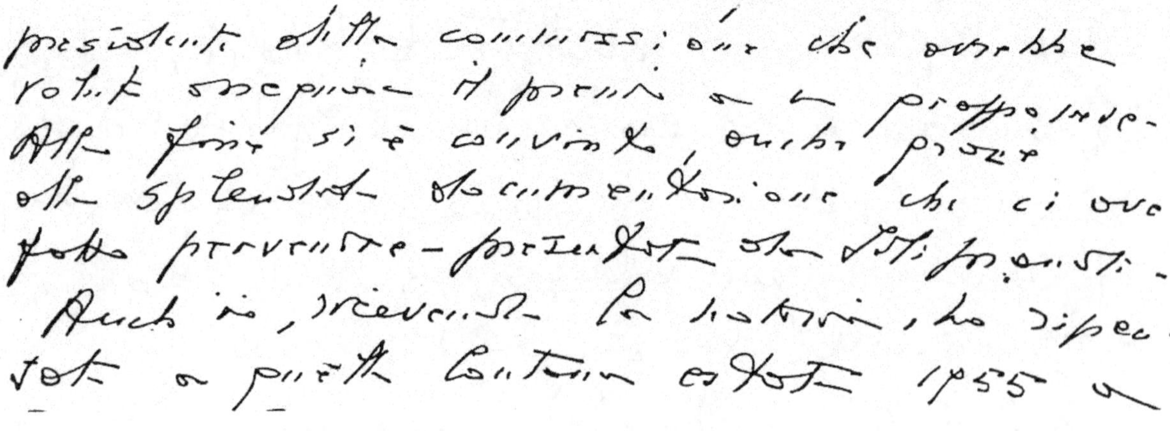

Sample 12

Sample 12 Female age 80, Rita Levi Montalcini, a famous Italian Nobel Prize winner for medicine, and probably a pure Five. The totally dominant sign is *Disconnected*, which even manifests in each small stroke of letters *m* and *n*. This indicates a mental process "extremely" rigorous and analytic. Talented in research.

Samples 10 and 11 are the handwriting of an average type Two, and Rita Levi Montalcini the Italian Nobel prize winner for research on the nervous system, in all likelihood a Five.

The point is to highlight the difference in the handwriting of a Two with a generous and perceptive intellectual process—neither too critical nor self-critical—and generally available to others (*Curved, Narrow space between words, High middle zone*; the shape of the letters is quite overblown; and a highly developed type Five, with a mental process that is rigorous and thorough; intuitive, but also capable of analyzing concepts and situations with the precision of a microscope (*Disconnected*, *Small Middle Zone*, *Sober*, *Homogeneous*, *Wide Space Between Words*. The shape of the letters is essential).

We can understand why the Two is described by Naranjo as the anti-intellectual, or, graphologically speaking, "a thinking process lacking in scientific criteria."

I ask the readers to excuse me for having used such an extreme example and comparing the handwriting of a famous scientist, who has devoted all her life to research, with an average type Two. My intention was to make graphological characteristics better understandable.

le storie continue come non mi aspettavo, ci siamo visti a Parma una giornata e la prossima settimana starò 2 giorni via a metà strada (io anche) e un corso organizzato da. non sono abituata alle cose belle e facili non mi sembra possibile e vero, forse anche perchè queste storie so che non potrò mai essere più di così - intanto mi telefona ogni giorno e dice di fare queste cose per le 2 volte in vita sua - spero davvero che passi velocemente questo mese e che potremo presto stare un po'

Sample 13

Sample 13 Female age 45, type Two, wing One. In her handwriting coexist both graphic signs indicating smoothness (*curved final strokes - ovals rather curvilinear*), and other signs demonstrating self-control and rigidity (*Upright, Extensions concave to left*).

Da quando il caldo è cessato e la prima leggerezza della pioggia è cresciuta fino a farsi sentire, nell'aria è rimasta una quiete che l'aria del caldo non aveva, una nuova pace a cui l'acqua dava una sua brezza -

Sample 14

Sample 14 Female type Two, wing 3. The signs are: *Curved, High middle zone, Narrow space between words,* hints of *Flexuous, Upright, Clear, Homogeneity*. This handwriting shows preoccupation and uncertainty about her self-image (sign: *Careful*). Notice the greater expansion compared to Sample 13. Nevertheless, this script (type Two, wing Three) shows a *High Middle Zone*, with a graphic space less airy than type Two, wing One. It remains a type Two due to the high degree of the sign *Curved* (there is more interest in adaptability than efficiency). Nevertheless, we can't say that the handwriting is completely spontaneous (sign *Careful*).

sto dicendo, solo per essere scaturito
da un incontro in un ambito ben più
profondo. Mi sono appena svegliato e
sto mettendo giù frasi a ruota libera
senza riflettere troppo e con gli occhi ancora socchiusi! mi hanno detto che la perizia
calligrafica non tiene conto della bella
grafia, ho solo messo il foglio su un qua-
derno rigato tanto per seguire la traccia
se no, temo, ti avrei costretto ad un terribile

Sample 15

Sample 15 Female age 48 type, Two wing Three. The handwriting shows the sign *Careful* (influence by type Three), *Narrow spacing between letters and between words*, *High Middle Zone*. Here the adaptability is only for appearance (*curved* but with *narrowing spaces*). Narcissistic and manipulative tendencies, which impose their whims (*t-bar super-elevated*). Stubbornness. She has a good intuitive sense of where others stand (*curved Flexuous*, *C Angles*). According to Moretti, this handwriting is most typical of PRIDE.

I love California!
The air is so very
sweet smelling! The
flower scent permiates

Sample 16

Sample 16 Female age 57, type Two wing Three. In my opinion, this handwriting speaks by itself without need for comment. Notice how it takes possession of the graphic space.

For graphological definitions and interpretations I used the following texts:
PALAFERRI NAZZARENO, *L'indagine grafologica e il metodo morettiano,* Istituto Grafologico Moretti, Urbino, 1986.
PALAFERRI NAZZARENO, *Dizionario Grafologico,* Libreria "G. Moretti, Urbino, 1993.
TORBIDONI-ZANIN, *Grafologia* (testo teorico pratico), IV ed., Editrice La Scuola, Brescia, 1986.

For descriptions of Enneagram type characteristics:
NARANJO CLAUDIO, *Character and Neurosis. An Integrative View*, Gateways, Nevada City, CA, 1994.

HANDWRITING AND ENNEATYPE THREE

3

According to Claudio Naranjo (see *Character and Neurosis*) the **Three** is constitutionally somatotonic and as such has a good dose of mesomorphic traits. After the type **Eight** and the **Counterphobic Six**, the **Three** is the most energetic type—that includes an active character as well as a physically athletic disposition.

This understanding is useful when considering the Three's traits since "energy and vitality," although hard-wired to the temperament, do influence the personality in all its aspects; intellectual, emotional, physical, as well as sexuality and aggressiveness. Obviously, this psycho-physical structure is also expressed in the handwriting.

Furthermore, recognizing these Three's character traits can help us exclude other types. For example, "energy and vitality" are not likely to be the foremost traits in the handwriting of **Fours**, **Fives** or **Nines**.

Naranjo specifies that:

• Type **Four** has an ectomesomorphic physical constitution (that is not fully ectomorphic like the type Five, nor mesomorphic like the Three).

• **Fives** are the most ectomorphic of all Enneagram types, thus Fours and Fives are rather cerebrotonic and their energy is predominantly mental.

• **Nines** are distinctly the most endomorphic type of the Enneagram. Type Two is also quite endomorphic but less so than the Nine. Nines are also the most ectopenic (low in ectomorphia), which give them the characteristic loss of interiority. **Eights** too are low in ectomorphia.

It is rather interesting to note that while types **Three** and **Eight** both are quite active and actually get charged up through effort, it is the type **Seven** that according to Naranjo is tireless. Based on Sheldon's typology, the Sevens are primarily ectomorphic and secondarily endomorphic; but seen as a whole, they appear to have the most balanced distribution of all three characteristics.

Having said that, we know that it is type **Three** who is best able to focus and to concentrate on one task, while the **Seven** tends to dissipate. Type **Eight** too has the "impact" force of the Three (the Eight is constitutionally the most mesomorphic), but due to a lack in cerebralism, has a hard time focusing on a single task for very long.

3

Finally, type **One** is considered to be meso-endomorphic and more often than not low in ectomorphia (a characteristic shared with the **Nine** and **Eight**) that give the One a certain constitutional rigidity.

Back to type **Three**, we can assume that the above mentioned characteristics will appear in the handwriting (HW) making it agile, dynamic, rushed, energetic, relatively fast and without too much fluctuation in the rhythm—all in all, functional and efficient.

Recapping very briefly we could say that the Three's HW is:

- Less rigid than the One's
- More homogeneous than the Two's
- More incisive than the Four's and Five's
- More confident and less wavering than the Six's
- Less dispersive than the Seven's
- Better organized than the Eight's
- Faster and more dynamic than the Nine's

The Three's "tendency towards action" is a very positive aspect in that it enhances the function of the personality. It boosts initiative, enterprise, independence, self-assuredness, and mastery over situations and reinforces the will—this coincidentally lessens the susceptibility to mental and physical illness.

Theoretically these characteristics do not appear to have a negative side. However, when overdone, they can suck the spirit too much into indulging in external activity at the expense of an internal life. Hyperactivity diverts energy outwards and the individual becomes addicted to action.

There is no specific graphological sign that by itself indicates "action" or one that makes a clear distinction between an active and an inactive individual.

Good indicators for action are:

- A 'clean' pressure with adequate 'inking,' modulated, neither too dry or light, nor lacking in uniformity. The neuro-muscular mechanism of tension-relaxation that happens with the up and down-strokes, needs to be effortless, without impediments or slowing down (sign:*Thickened type 1*, *Precise*)
- A sustained and lively rhythm (signs: *Fluent*, *Springing Rapid*)
- A good graphic structure that derives from a steady movement, order,

dynamism, agility and homogeneity (signs: *Orderly*, *Homogeneous*, *Dynamic*)

• Tension and energy: the three main signs in Moretti's system indicating these qualities that we could synthesize as "steadiness" are: *Angles B*, *Straight Extensions* and a *Stable Baseline* (see previous articles). These three signs are also common in type One since both types have a distinct leaning towards activity.

• A well-formed *Triple Width* (will be addressed later)

• An appropriate size of HW that fits with the rhythm and degree of orderliness is a good indicator for activity; then, the *middle zone letters* are neither too big nor small.

• Simply formed letters but neither dry nor incomplete.

• The lower extensions need to be appropriate in length, not too short or retracted; they need a healthy dose of energetic impulse, and an acceleration of the movement, otherwise, a writing that slows down usually makes the lower extensions shorten and soften.

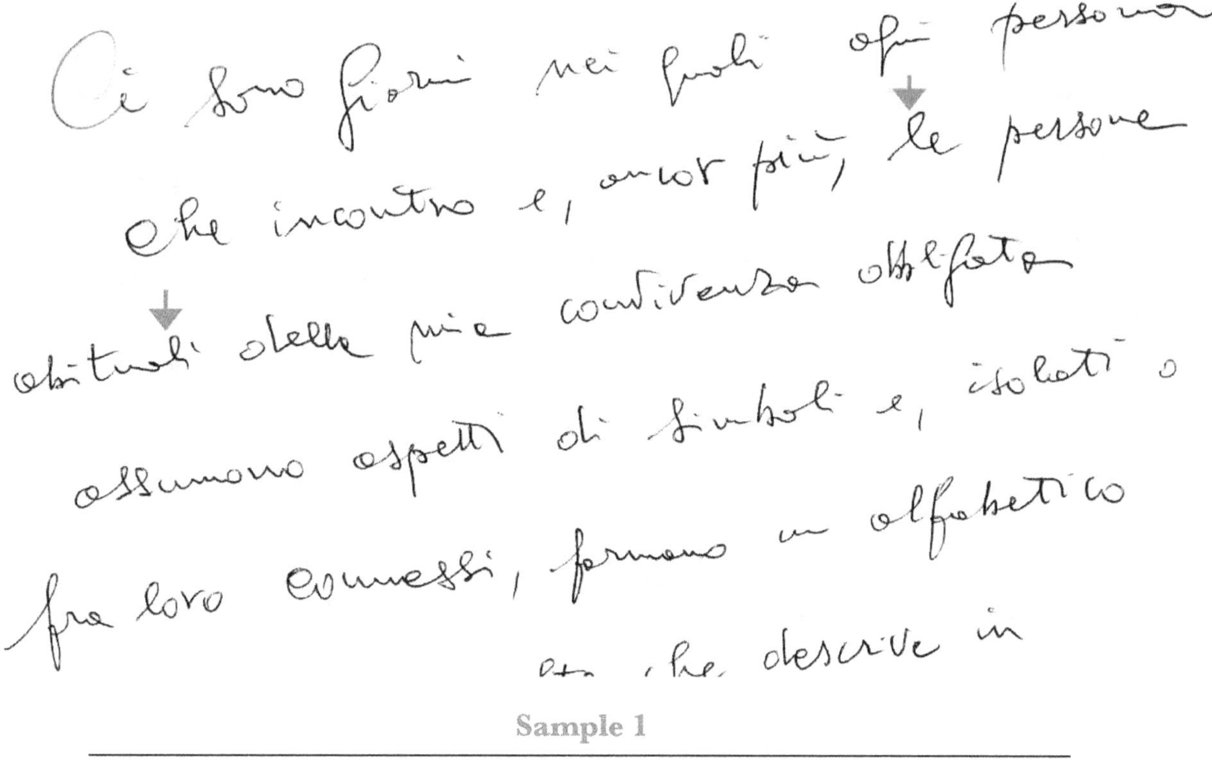

Sample 1

Sample 1 Male age 50 - Type Three, Social. Handwriting showing a lively *rhythm*, and the signs: *Rising*, *good Triple Width*, *tension* and *energy*, *prolonged lower strokes*, *Dynamic*. Sometimes tension is excessive and it transforms into anxiety and hyper-tension, expressed mainly through the *bi-angular movement of buttonholes* (see arrows), which normally should be curved. This is a signal of strong physical, mental, and emotional tension. Moreover, in some places the stroke is not elastic.

The positive aspects of the energetic qualities give Threes the ability to perform tasks fast and accurately; they know how to pace themselves at an elevated rhythm while maintaining efficiency. Threes have a built-in thrust towards seeking results, being competitive and are gifted with organizational qualities. The Three's thinking tends also to be clear, systematic, competent and oriented towards success and pragmatism.

We will limit ourselves to examining only a few of the above mentioned traits associated with positive action, as they appear in the handwriting. The HW should always have a good pressure and a fluent movement. We would look for the signs:

- *Thickened Type 1*, where the downstrokes are thicker than the upstrokes, which is one of the essential graphological signs indicating vitality, energy and activity.

Ci sono giorni nei quali ogni persona che incontro
e, ancora di più, le persone abituali della mia
esistenza obbligata e quotidiana, assumono
aspetti di simboli e, isolati o fra loro connessi,
formano un alfabeto profetico od occulto che

Sample 2 Female age 46 – Type Three, Self-Pres.

Samples 2-3 Handwritings with a good pressure (*Thickened type I*). The descending strokes of letters are more marked than the ascending ones. The HW manifests an effective orientation and organization of energy. The ovals are nor excessively angular nor rounded.

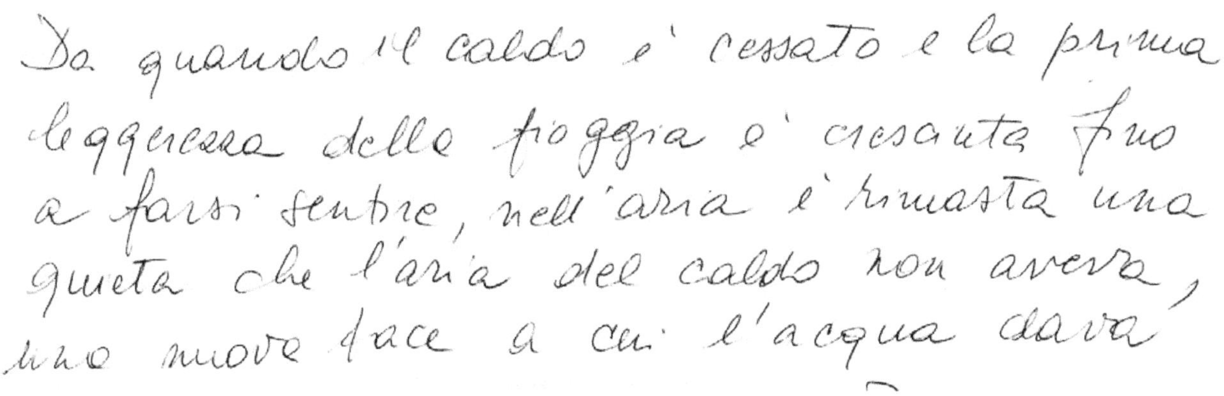

Sample 3 Female age 50 – Type Three, Self-Pres.

- ***Fluent***, supple writing that proceeds smoothly, indicating agility of mind, power of synthesis, intuition, adaptability, and interpersonal skills.
- ***Dynamic***, writing which progresses very easily with spirally and personalized inter-letter links; some simplified and skeleton letters; vivacious movement = quick intuition, original associations of ideas, skills in summarizing, economy in planning and implementation, mental and practical organization that wastes no time and energy.
- ***Homogeneous***: writing which presents evenness throughout; all the graphological signs in the script occur with the same intensity of degree = consistent behavior, stable disposition.

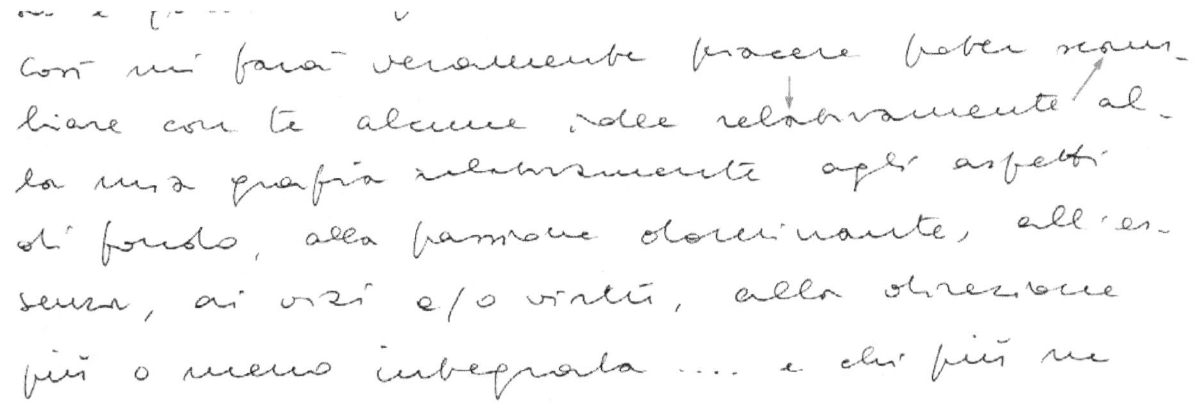

Sample 4

Sample 4 Female age 50 – Type Three, signs: *Fluent*, *Homogeneous*, *Dynamic*, and a very balanced *Triple Width* (the arrows show the signs of dynamism).

El maestro les dijo: Todos los Budas
y todos los seres conscientes no son más
que la mente única a parte de la cual
no existe nada. Esta mente que no tiene
comienzo es no nacida y es indestructible.
No es verde ni amarilla no tiene forma

Sample 5

Sample 5 Female – Type Three, Self-Pres, signs: *Fluent*, *Homogeneous*, *Dynamic*, *balanced Triple Width*.

- *Rising*: script in which the lines progressively rise upwards as they approach the right margin = excitement, enthusiasm, feeling of the need to do one's best, self-confidence, presumption and conceit (excessive appreciation of self).

There are days when everyone I meet
appear as symbols, and individually or
together they form a prophetic or occult
writing that describes my life in shadow
The word I exchange with familiar or
for which I

Sample 6

Sample 6 Female age 60 - Type Three, signs: *Rising*, *Fluent*, Dynamic, *balanced Triple Width*. The lines have been added afterwards, in order to measure the degree of the sign Rising.

Distinct: is a sign that includes:

• Letters are clearly distinct from each other.

• Descending and ascending extensions, so as essential strokes and accessorial ones are clearly separated within the individual letters.

• The spacing is well defined and organized so that the occasional disconnections between letters cannot be mistaken for a space between words.

• The lines are sufficiently separated to avoid tangling up or causing confusion by linking between lines.

Psychologically, the sign *Distinct* indicates a high level of mental discrimination, clarity of thought and a scientific or practical ability.

El maestro me dijo: todos los budas y todos
los seres conscientes, no son más que la mente
única aparte de la cual no existe nada.
Esta mente que no tiene comienzo es no
nata y es indestructible. No es verde ni
amarilla ya que no tiene forma ni apa-

Sample 7 Female – Type Three, Self-Pres.

El maestro me dijo:
Todos Los Budas y todos los seres conscientes
no son más que la mente única aparte de
la cual no existe nada. Esta mente

Sample 8 Female – Type Three, Sexual

Samples 7-8-9 Handwritings with the signs *Distinct* and *Precise*. Sample 8 shows also the sign *Rising*. In sample 9, marked by the arrow, we see the sign *Dynamic*, which in this context, takes on a significant value of the capacity of organization of the writing.

Handwriting analysis is fascinating and I am very curious to see what you will say about my handwriting. I am an Enneagram Four but now I am wondering maybe I am a One. This

Sample 9 Male age 35 – Type Three

Precise: is when:

- The strokes are clearly defined, sure and steady. All edges are clean and decisive.
- Letter shapes are well defined, precise and fluid.
- The general impression is that of confidence, order and the strokes are laid down in a determined manner.

This sign indicates vitality, strength of convictions, organizational qualities and self-assuredness. On the mental plain it shows a capacity to approach problems with clarity and find practical solutions. The negative aspect may be an overly superior attitude, absence of spontaneity and coldness regarding expressing one's own feelings.

It is actually from signs indicating a good mental setup that we can with reasonable certainty, graphologically single out a Three from all other types.

Naranjo as well as most enneagram authors agree that: "Threes (contrary to their neighbors who are decidedly emotional) are typically and systematically oriented towards rationality and things; intellectually as well as practical, and that includes a high level of self-control." In the Moretti system the sign *Triple Width*, when balanced, seems tailored to capture exactly these traits of Threes.

Triple Width is a graphological sign that comes from the genius of Moretti and is composed of three different signs, which together form a distinct and new sign that is the benchmark for measuring the level of integration in a person.

3

The balance between these three signs needs to be taken as an "interactive whole" in order to assess the following qualities:

1. The breadth and depth of the intellect, its ability to understand, perceive and receive stimuli.
2. The intensity, openness or closure of the feeling function associated with evaluating subjective aspects of others that are not based on reason alone.
3. The development of penetrating reason and refinement of our critical judgment

In order to have the balance of the *Triple Width*, these three factors have to be simultaneously present:

1. A proper *Letter Breadth* (mainly seen in the shape of the ovals which should be neither too narrow nor too round) is a sign of a mind that is neither restricted in its ability to comprehend, nor overly vague to the point of losing definition and precision.

2. A proper *Space between Letters*, so that the higher judgement is neither restricted by pettiness nor untrammeled by placing too much weight on impulsiveness, feelings and subjective sentiments.

3. A proper *Space between Words*, indicating the critical function and level of reasoning, abilities that prevent naive acceptance of things, as well as an overly obsessive or sophisticated pursuit of knowledge.

The space between words is symbolic of the amount of time the writer dedicates to examining individual concepts before putting them "to paper." It shows us the 'habitual' level of thoughtfulness the writer invests before acting.

Triple Width is a framework that includes characteristics of energy, mind, emotions and reasoning. In other words, *Triple Width* is the yardstick that measures the state of balance and the organization of the mental processes.

In this context it would not be possible to get into all the psychological variations that can be seen from examining the three signs that make up *Triple Width* individually.

3

S.b.L. = Space between Letters

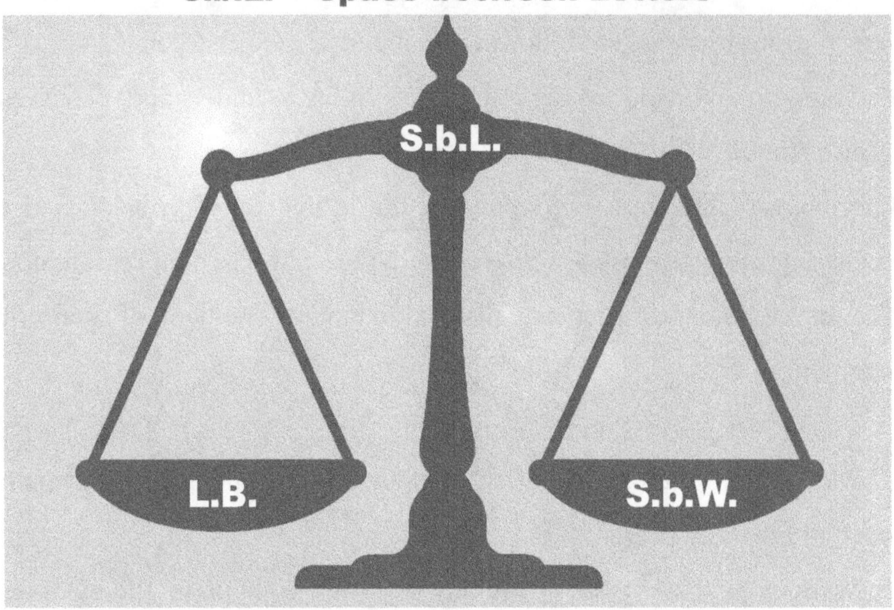

L.B. = Letter Breadth/S.b.W. = Space between Letters

We could visualize it like a scale where three factors need to be considered. The tipping point (*Space between Letters*), which represents the equanimity of judgment based on subjective feelings, then, one tray holding the ability to understand (*Letter Breadth*), and the other our critical faculty (*Space between Words*). Without a just proportion between these factors, we can have neither an intellectual nor emotional balance.

Triple Width can be balanced or not, homogeneous or not. It is balanced when the *Letter Breadth*, *Space between Letters* and the *Space between Words* is neither too tight nor too loose.

Should two of these three signs be well proportioned, but one sign was lacking, we could not call that personality balanced. It takes all three factors in the right proportion to indicate a balanced mental organization.

For example, if the ovals are very rounded, i.e. high degree of *Letter Breadth*, but the *Space between Words* is tight, it would indicate that the otherwise good ability to perceive stimuli and to understand is not supported by an adequate critical ability. This could be a recipe for superficiality.

If on the other hand, the ovals are tight, i.e. *Narrow Letter Breadth*, but the *Space between Words* is ample, it could mean that the writer is likely to focus on situations in a compartmentalized or sectorial way; this may lead to be somewhat absolutist about one's own point of view, hypercritical and detail oriented at the expense of a broader view.

In this group, the *Space between Letters* is the factor most closely linked to one's personal emotional world and past conditioning by life experiences. We could say that the *Space between Letters* portrays our predisposition towards opening up or closing down, which in its turn marks the balance between perception and reasoning.

Thus a person with a very narrow *Space between Letters*, even if the *Letter Breadth* and *Space between Words* were balanced, will always be restrained in their show of feelings, and that will also constrain their intellect and reasoning. Indeed, such a person might "feel" that others are never to be trusted and have that as a built-in precondition coloring their perceptions and attitude.

Triple Width is balanced when the *Letter Breadth* and *Space between Words* are about equal in their degree (neither too wide, nor too narrow) and the *Space between Letters* is average (objective relationship with feelings).

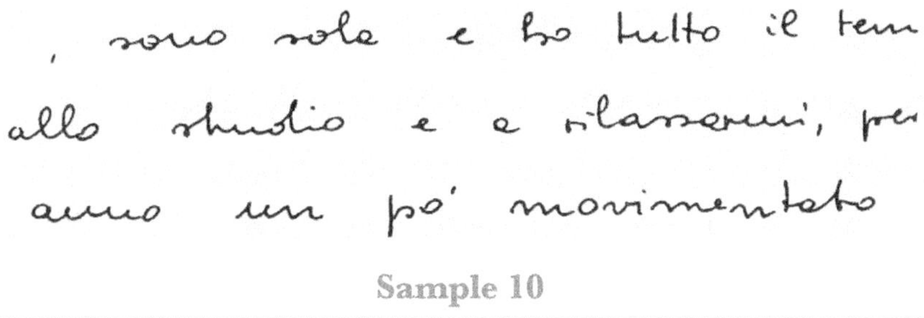

Sample 10 *Balanced Triple Width* = intellectual and emotional balance, breadth of vision, organization and steadiness.

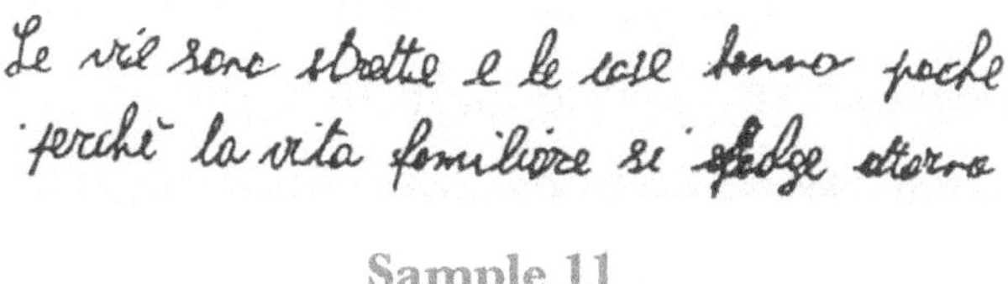

Sample 11 *Below Average Triple Width* = narrow-mindedness, introversion.

Triple Width is homogeneous when in all the handwriting the degree of the three signs is consistently stable but not static. Such homogeneity is rather typical for the type Three and is a very positive indicator of good mental organization, practicality and steadfastness.

Absence of homogeneity of *Triple Width* is common among type Six, and indicates an inconsistent way of dealing with situations and people. The ability to adapt and to tune in with the feeling tone is hampered and oscillates between lapses in critical judgement and captious attitudes, between dependency and autonomy.

Ma io non ci capisco
niente. In ogni caso
questa settimana è stata

Sample 12

Sample 12 *Not Homogeneous Triple Width* = incoherence, inconsistency, lack of organization. (sample 10-11-12 taken by De Petrillo V., Millevolte A., The Application of the G. Moretti Graphological System, Roma, Brain Edizioni, 2000 p. 60).

We can see from various HW samples that type Three has a balanced degree of the *Triple Width*. This underscores the Three's ability to reach brilliance, efficiency, social graciousness, genuine self-control (not only the manipulative variety driven by a need to project a positive image), good judgment that is neither too impulsive due to the sway of emotions, nor too pedantic due to excessive attention to detail—a good combination for being pragmatist, competent and focused on the present.

Obviously, the above-mentioned qualities are desirable in the field of human endeavor; they can be seductive enough to absorb the Three in a protracted pursuit of success and excellence at the expense of an inner spiritual life.

While other types have a "harder row to hoe" in the practical arena, they benefit from their "failings" because such failings act as an early warning system. Threes are reputed to be so apt at balancing and hiding their flaws, that when they can't "hold it together" any longer, they tend to crash rather suddenly and hard.

It is not by coincidences that among spiritual seekers Threes are less likely to be seen than in business or corporate settings. Many introspective Threes complain of an inner void that was nagging in the background while they were successful in the outer world.

Here some differences in the expression and graphic organization of the *Triple Width*:

- Type **Three**: Balance and homogeneity among *Letter Breadth*, *Space between Words* and *Space between Letters*.

- Type **Two**: High degree of *Letter Breadth*, low degree of *Space between Words*, high degree of *Space between Letters* = superficial criticism, emotional evaluations.

- Type **Four**: Not homogeneous degree of *Space between Letters* = feelings (or mood) influence intellectual objective evaluation.

- Type **Five**: Low degree of *Space between Letters*, high degree of *Space between Words* = hyper-rationality influenced by restriction of feelings.

- Type **Six**: *Letter Breadth*, *Space between Letters* and *Space between Words* not homogeneous = dependence/counterdependence, trust/suspicion, dogmatic/heretic, fluctuation of intellectual and emotional evaluations.

- Type **Seven**: Too high degree of *Space between Letters* = unsystematic activity because too many stimuli catch attention.

- Type **Nine**: Static degree of *Letter Breadth*, *Space between Letters* and *Space between Words* = lack of dynamism.

- Types **One** & **Eight**: No fixed rule, but rigidity of One and impulsiveness of Eight influence the overall organization of situations. Type Three is more flexible, self-controlled and organized at the same time.

3

così mi farà veramente piacere poter scam-
biare con te alcune idee relativamente alla mia grafia relativamente agli aspetti
di fondo, alla passione dominante, all'es-
senza, ai vizi e/o virtù, alla direzione
più o meno integrata ... e chi più ne

Sample 13

Sample 13 Female age 50 – Type Three. It is the same HW of sample 4. I re-propose-it again, because it shows a very good balance of the Triple Width.

Os budas e os mestres de todos os tempos e
lugares só emergiram pela busca da verdade e
os buscadores de hoje também vão atrás da verdade. Somente quando você chegar à verdade se sentirá completo. Sem ela, repetirá seus

Sample 14

Sample 14 Female – Type Three Social. *Balanced Triple Width.*

fino a farsi sentire, nell'aria è rimasta
una quiete che l'aria del caldo non
aveva, una nuova pace a cui l'acqua
dava una sua brezza.

Sample 15

Sample 15 Male age 45 – Type Three Sexual. *Balanced Triple Width.* Notice the different stile between the text, which is very readable, and the signature, totally illegible.

Ci sono giorni nei quali ogni persona
che incontro è, ancor più le persone
abituali della mia convivenza obbligata
e quotidiana, assumono aspetti di simboli

Sample 16

Sample 16 Female age 53 – Type Three w4. *Balanced Triple Width.*

There are days when everyone I meet appears as
symbols, and individually or together they form a
prophetic or occult writing that describes my
life in shadows. The words I exchange with

Sample 17

Sample 17 Female age 48 – Type Three Self-Pres. *Balanced Triple Width.*

In my twilight vision, however I only vaguely
distinguish what these sudden glass panes
on the surface of things let show from the
interior which they veil and reveal.

Sample 18

Sample 18 Female age 63 – Type Three w4. *Balanced Triple Width* with a low degree compared to sample 16.

Esta mente pura, que es la fuente de todo brilla por siempre, sobre todo, con el brillo de su perfección pero la gente no está despierta a ella, considerando sólo como mente aquello que ve, escucha, siente y sabe. No perciben el brillo

Sample 19

Sample 19 Female – Type Three Social. *Balanced Triple Width.*

Is the type Three Emotive or not?

At this point the question arises both, from the Enneagram perspective as well as the graphological one: is the type Three a feeling type or not?

We know that the Three is at the center of the feeling/heart triad, but simultaneously represses the energy of this center; actually, is considered rather "cold and calculating," an "opportunist who is detached from emotions." Then, there is a large distinction in characterology between the emotive / "active" and "non-active." types.

The Non-emotive/Active types are relatively cold due to lack of emotionality; that goes with an inner feeling of emptiness which causes loneliness, which then is compensated by activity and multiple external relationships.

The Emotive/Active types are intensely emotional but in a controlled way. This goes with reflection, organization, farsightedness, internalized feelings and emotions, tenacity, will and a general state of stability.

The Non-Emotive/Active types are generally referred to as opportunists because their interests are predominantly material and concrete. Only facts are real, there is no interest in the inner world, theories or principles, or even truth.

3

Inner emptiness pushes this type to frenetic activity in search for gain or utility with emphasis on appearance rather than value. Such people embrace vanity and are comfortable in mundane situations.

The Emotive/Active types are emotional but controls feelings in a dynamic way, directing them towards action. They can use will to make their choices of action proportionate to their values. Not impulsive, because they do not give in to the first urge, they gear up once plans are made and goals are defined. Stable and consistent at pursuing an objective, they often become leaders who rally those around them. Gifted with abilities to convince others, rapid action, energy, organization and a sense of responsibility, they do not fear obstacles.

The intellectual process of the Non-Emotive/Active types is gifted of clarity of thought and practical rapid intuition, but without a true sense of creativity due to lack of emotions.

They are not very interested in theories but are more thought-sensation oriented, thus able to see things objectively and focus on the tangible and concrete. Their observation is pragmatic and almost exclusively focused on objective reality, not very influenced by personal feelings. Their vision is more synthetic than analytic. Their logic and reasoning are clear and crisp but based on evidence and facts.

The Non-Emotive/Active are always in tune with public opinions and aware of the collective mindset. They do not have a deep need to come up with a personalized logic and accept things as they are.

The intelligence of the Emotive/Active is intensely rational, deductive, rapid and intuitive but also practical (Jungian Feeling-Introvert, with auxiliary Intuition and generally a balanced Sensate function), with good memory and a sharp observation ability; methodical, orderly and systematic; deductions are logical, critical and complex; strength, cohesion of thought, stick-to-it'iveness in pursuing projects and precision.

Is the real Three Emotive/Active or Non-Emotive/Active? We can't talk about levels of development where we automatically assume that a Non-Emotive, who calculates coldly and is opportunistic, is to be considered as beneath the Emotive type— because we are talking about basic hard-wired character traits that are part of our innate temperament and thus hard to change.

The graphological answer in my experience is that there are two large groups of Threes. At the level of constitution, even before the differentiation into subtypes, I believe that Threes divide into two categories, the Non-Emotive/Active and the Emotive/Active.

Originally you did not
acknowledge that
innate knowing and
awareness are your
own Buddha, and so

Sample 20

Sample 20 Female age 57 – Type Three Social. Here the emotionalism is canalized through action (*Thickened Type I* of high degree - *Dynamic* -*Rightward Slant* - *High Middle Zone*). The HW is very lively and intense, but there is a good mental control of emotions (*balanced Triple Width*).

Ci sono dei giorni nei quali
ogni persona che incontro e, ancor più,
le persone abituali della mia
convivenza obbligata e quotidiana,
assumono aspetti di simboli e, isolati

Sample 21

Sample 21 Female age 50 – Type Three Self-Pres. The signs *Flexuous* and *Curved* indicates emotionalism, nevertheless there is self-control through *Carefulness* and balanced *Triple Width*.

Ci sono giorni nei quali ogni persona che incontro e, ancor più, le persone abituali della mia convivenza obbligata e quotidiana, assumono aspetti di simboli e, isolati o fra loro connessi formano un alfabeto profetico od occulto che descrive in ordine la mia vita.

Sample 22 Female age 33 – Type Three Self-Pres.

Samples 22-23 These two women are business consultants. The handwritings are very dynamic, and self-control is less effective if compared with the previous writings, because of impulsiveness. They are organized (*good balance of the Triple Width*), but also hectic in their behavior.

Ci sono giorni nei quali ogni persona che incontro e, ancor più, le persone abituali della mia convivenza obbligata e quotidiana, assumono aspetti di simboli e, isolati o fra loro connessi, formano un alfabeto profetico od occulto che descrive in ordine la mia vita.

Sample 23 Female age 55 – Type Three Sexual.

sempre al telefono.
Nella mia vita non mi manca niente, da chi le
vede dal di fuori, potrebbe proprio dire che
sto bene, ma io mi domando: "Perchè sono
sempre triste e depressa?"

Sample 24 Female age 28 – Type Three Self-Pres.

Samples 24-25 Here we could say that the writers, in some way, are basically not emotional. The *rhythm* is moderate, without any élan of the *Movement of Spontaneous Handwriting*. We find arcades, which psychologically mean a sort of emotional narrowness. This doesn't mean they are cold, but simply that their perceptions of stimuli is not vibrant. Anyway, they are very efficient and energetic people and being active is one of their main values in life. They have difficulty expressing emotions spontaneously.

Os sutras de todos os tempos e lugares, só emergiram
pela busca da verdade, e os buscadores de hoje, também
vão atrás da verdade, somente quando você chegar à
verdade se sentirá completo, sem ela repetirá suas
formas de ser antiga, de que verdade estou falando?

Sample 25 Female – Type Three Sexual.

Obviously, since there are no non-feeling individuals, we are talking about the intensity of reactions to feelings; a balanced reaction to feelings will influence our actions favorably.

A balanced emotionality depends on both, physiological factors as well as our way of processing thoughts.

The hyper-emotive is highly impressionable, excitable, variable in attitude and behavior, restless, prone to over-reacting and generally disorganized. These qualities are expressed in the *lack of homogeneity* of various graphic signs. The more pronounced and pervasive the disorder and variations, the non-homogeneity, and the disproportionality of the HW, the more a person is hyper-emotive.

3

Even minor but consistent signs of non-homogeneity point towards hyper-emotiveness: *variations in shape, pressure, slant, size of letters, rhythm, Triple Width, carefulness and spacing between the lines.*

We need to distinguish between the normal variations in rhythm from actual non-homogeneity in a HW that lacks harmony. The most common flavor of emotiveness influencing type Three is the complex of superiority given by the sign *Inflated* (letters, or part of them, showing a sort of amplification, both in the vertical and the horizontal dimension), or the cousin of frenzy, of throwing oneself compulsively into work.

Threes are not usually prone to exaggerated emotional reactions or to dramatization. Such expressions are more common with the **Twos**, **Fours**, **Sixes**, **Sevens** and occasionally **Eights**. **Fives** generally don't let their emotive reactions show, **Nines** are too narcotized to feel them, and **Ones** repress emotions until they blow up in anger.

Manipulation of Image, Disingenuousness and Deceit

Threes are prone to be obsessed with being evaluated by others. Sometimes this may become an all-consuming preoccupation that erodes their natural gifts of independence and spontaneity. Their fixation on making a good impression, attracting attention and avoiding failure, makes Threes so dependent on approval that they will sell out their values. In all likelihood this is due more to the pressures of the environment than innate temperament.

According to Moretti, an increase of control of the conscious over the unconscious brings a decrease in spontaneity and creativity. This too can add to the impression of dealing with a non-emotive person while in reality we are facing someone emotive, preoccupied and anxious. These underlying traits of the Three are expressed by a pronounced carefulness in the HW. Consequently, this indicates not only clarity of thought but also "preoccupation with effect." So, all the mental process can revolve around this fixation. Contrived carefulness can vary greatly in degree and is difficult to evaluate to an untrained eye. The clearest indication of this trend is the reduction of the spontaneity in the graphic movement.

Moretti added that the compulsion to "capture the attention" of others contains a core of deceit since overdone carefulness acts as a cover to hide true inner feelings.

Naranjo says that Threes "rather than a lack of truthfulness in regard to facts (they may be faithful and factual reporters) there is in vanity a lack of truthfulness in regard to feelings and pretense. (p.200).

Down slopes of summer grasses.
Then, when we find the place,
We can lie together,
Laughing in the sun,

Sample 26

Sample 26 Female age 30 – Type Three Social. The Handwriting is very accurate and the movement is a little studied. Projecting the "right image" is very important.

Credo che la grafologia possa essere una "scienza" importante, per poter conoscere meglio se stessi, per cui le auguro di ottenere un buon successo per la sua rubrica.

Sample 27 Male age 28 – Type Three.

Samples 27-28 The movement is not spontaneous, with carefulness in the letter formation. We find the graphological sign *Careful*. It is a sort of a mask, where the "Person," that is the role, is dominant. Concern with appearances. Ease in keeping emotions and reactions under control. In sample 28 we notice the difference between the "mask" expressed in the text, and the different personality that manifests in the signature.

Da quando il caldo è cessato e la prima leggerezza della pioggia è cresciuta fino a farsi sentire, nell'aria è rimasta una quiete che l'ansia del caldo non aveva, una nuova pace a cui l'acqua dava una sua brezza. Fernando Pessoa "Il libro dell'inquietudine".

Sample 28 Female age 25 – Type Three.

---

nel mezzo della notte
mi sono reso conto che
la coincidenza molto corta
mi avrebbe creato problemi
col bagaglio.

Sample 29

Sample 29 Male age 36 – Type Three. Here we can really say that "vanity" is an important trait of this personality. This is a self-seeking organization of personality, lacking of emotional transparency. The HW is *Careful*, *Flexuous* to a high degree. The person seems very amiable and available, but we find also a strong self-control (*Upright*). The scriptor is always very attentive to the effect he can win on others. It is an organized handwriting, but we cannot say that the letters are clear and well readable (ambiguity). Very clever (*good Triple Width*, and high energy), he does the right job: a diplomat.

Ci sono giorni nei quali ogni persona che incontro
e, ancor più le persone abituali della mia convivenza
obbligata e quotidiana, assumono aspetti di simboli
e, isolati o fra loro connessi, formano un alfabeto profetico
od occulto che descrive in ombre la mia vita _

Sample 30

Sample 30 Female age 32 – Type Three. Here the carefulness of the HW is not elegant, but rather awkward. The concern for the judgment of the environment inhibits spontaneity.

The preoccupation with appearing in a certain way creates a psychological tension that translates in over-preparing and elaborating one's attitude to present a "porcelain-perfect" face to the public, but without the warm-blooded truth. Graphologically this is seen in:

Strokes of Affectedness: script with strokes which are precise, artistically graceful, generally rounded, occurring at the beginning, middle or ends of words = tendency towards self-importance, charming and seductive manners; attention seeker, vanity, lack of sincerity. Together with carefulness in the HW these traits take the place of spontaneous expression.

Finally, we can notice that most handwritings samples in this article show the sign *Upright*: a common index among Threes, indicating a difficulty to surrender control of self as well as of the impression they want to make on the environment (when in combination with the sign *Careful*).

Ci sono giorni nei quali ogni persona che incontro, e, ancor più, le persone abituali della mia convivenza obbligata e quotidiana, assumono aspetti di simboli e isolotti e fra loro connessi formano un alfabeto profetico od occulto che descrive [illegible] la mia vita.

Sample 31 Female age 35 – Type Three Self-Pres.

Samples 31-32 Female age 30 – Type Three Social. The Handwriting is very accurate and the movement is a little studied. Projecting the "right image" is very important.

Three score and six years ago I arrived here. "Here" was a small town in northern Minnesota.

Sample 32 Female – Type Three Social.

One particular aspect that I noticed only in the HW of Threes regarding their expert "manipulating image" was alternating between *cursive* and printed words in the same text. I think this may be due to a sense of insecurity of which image to present - spontaneous or deliberate? - but also expressing the Three's agility and flexibility. To write fluidly in cursive or in print requires a high degree of graphic mastery. Many of the HW samples in these pages contain just that.

CI SONO GIORNI NEI QUALI OGNI PERSONA CHE INCONTRO
E, ANCOR PIU', LE PERSONE ABITUALI DELLA MIA CONVIVENZA
OBBLIGATA E QUOTIDIANA, ASSUMONO ASPETTI DI SIMBOLI E, ISOLATI
O FRA LORO CONNESSI, FORMANO UN ALFABETO PROFETICO OD

Sample 33

Samples 33-34 are two handwritings written by the same person, a male - age 38 - type Three. Usually he writes using an elegant block letters style, which is very fluent, and with a very well *balanced Triple Width*. I made an experiment asking him to write using the cursive style (In Italy most people write cursive), but we can notice that many letters have maintained the block capital style. Many of the handwritings of this article, show the same phenomenon, in my opinion connected with the capacity to manipulate self-image.

Ci sono giorni nei quali ogni persona che incontro e,
ancor più, le persone abituali della mia convivenza
obbligata e quotidiana, assumono aspetti di simboli e,
isolati o fra loro connessi, formano un alfabeto profetico od

Sample 34

come promesso ti mando un po' di cartaccia
dell'ILO, sperando che possa esserti di qualche
utilità.
Qualsiasi altra cosa del genere dovesse capitarmi,
spero di fartela avere prima che scadano eventuali
termini.

Sample 35

Sample 35 Male age 34 – Type Three. The handwriting is a mix of cursive and block capital style. *Balanced Triple Width.*

One final aspect associated pointing at "deceit with image" is a writing style where the signature is completely different from the general handwriting in the text.

fundemental. Si sólo eliminesen todo pensamiento conceptual, esta sustancia fundamental se manifestaría como el sol que todo lo ilumina sin impedimentos.

Sample 36

Sample 36 Female – Type Three Self-Pres. *Balanced Triple Width.* Cursive/Block Capital style. Notice the different movement of the signature, if compared with the text (for instance, the signature is *Rising*).

formas. No sabéis que deteniendo su pensamiento conceptual y olvidando su angustia el Buda se les aparecerá.

Sample 37

Sample 37 Female – Type Three Self-Pres with a strong Two wing. The handwriting emanates warm.

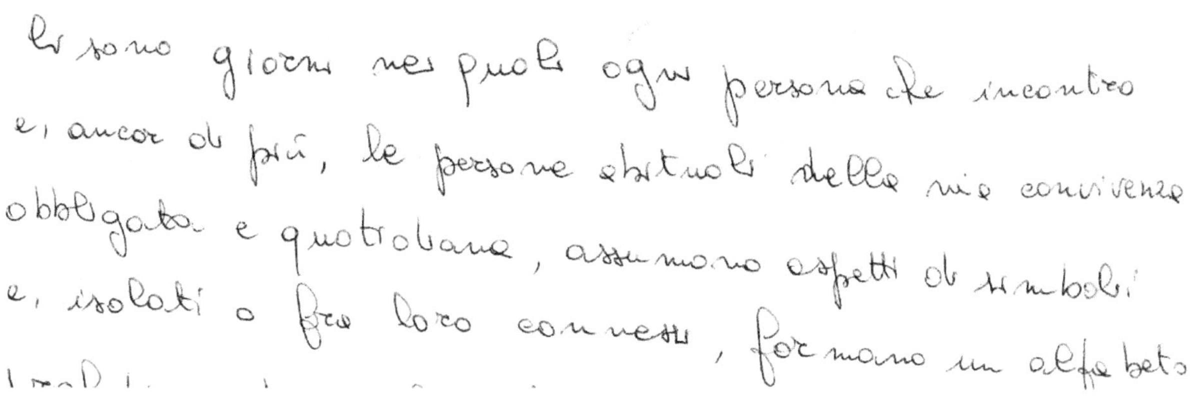

Sample 38

Sample 38 Female – Type Three with a strong Four wing. Notice the descending baseline. The handwriting is more restrained if compared to the sample of enneatype Three w2.

I started writing this article expecting it to be simpler to write about Threes only to find that the Three is harder to pin down graphologically than other types.

For graphological definitions and interpretations I used the following texts:

PALAFERRI NAZZARENO, *L'indagine grafologica e il metodo morettiano*, Istituto Grafologico Moretti, Urbino, 1986.

PALAFERRI NAZZARENO, *Dizionario Grafologico*, Libreria "G. Moretti, Urbino, 1993.

PALAFERRI NAZZARENO, *Tipologia umana, caratterologia e grafologia*, Libreria "G. Moretti, Urbino, 1999.

TORBIDONI-ZANIN, *Grafologia* (testo teorico pratico), IV ed., Editrice La Scuola, Brescia, 1986.

For descriptions of Enneagram type characteristics:

NARANJO CLAUDIO, *Character and Neurosis. An Integrative View*, Gateways, Nevada City, CA, 1994.

HANDWRITING AND ENNEATYPE FOUR

4

Imagine our graphological exploration of Enneagram types as a trip around the world. We depart in daylight with the sun high in the sky. First we meet type One. Their way of receiving and absorbing the sun's energy makes them capable of strength and determination. This causes Ones to feel justified in affirming opinions and defending their principles and ideals.

At times Ones identify with the sun's characteristics enough to feel like custodians of the laws of nature. This could make them presumptuous, rigid, and completely incapable of seeing their own point of view as merely relative - they react with anger when others refuse to concede this "right."

Strong of body—mesomorphic — to use a technical term — Ones are prone to action and expansion, while also needing more proximity to the sun than other types to justify claiming an official status as representatives of nature's laws. This impedes Ones from letting go into infinite space and playing. They tend to remain stiff like a parade soldier on guard duty.

Continuing our journey we encounter the type Two. Twos receive sun's energy with open arms and reflect it onto others. They seem to be pumped up and run hither and tither, playing, laughing, and joking. Twos can get so engrossed in this that they lose sight of any shadows.

The Two's shape is also pleasing: much rounder than the rigid One's, and softer than the restrained Three's. Twos seem to be born endomorphous with the tendency to be vivacious and joyful. Why ask questions - isn't it obvious that the sun would consult them on any question or need? Twos can be so convinced of their own role that they forget the sun is autonomous. And they get into an angry tizzy when the sun dares do something, say, an eclipse, without consulting them first - how dare the sun ignore ME!

Our voyage continues, and we are surprised to find these types so close together and yet so different.

Next, we encounter the Three who is also running back and forth breathlessly in an attempt to appear more radiant than all others. The Threes are terrified that their light would disappear if they stop. They can't understand that it is the sun's light they are reflecting, not a light generated by their effort.

Threes believe that it is through their doing that the sun will shine on them. They need to achieve something worthy of admiration and do everything they can to get into the limelight. Horror of horrors, failure would mean falling into absolute darkness; so they may even get pushy in their scramble to reach the front of the line.

Threes have a high degree of mesomorphism. This gives them athletic ability, endurance, and strength to sustain many activities. Tireless, they get too busy to notice when the sun sets and there is nobody left to appreciate their efforts—as far as they are concerned, it is their effort and skill that keeps the world organized and turning.

We now are leaving this luminous area and enter a twilight zone. This is the world of the Fours where light and dark interchange, now becoming one, now the other. Forms are vague and less defined, appearing, disappearing, now this shade, now that…

Fours are unsure whether the sun even wants to illuminate them. They sometimes hide in the dark to see if the sun will actually bother to seek them out and shine. They are not playful or joyful like the Twos, nor capable and determined like the Threes who will even stoop to being pushy in order to position themselves in the forefront.

The Four's constitution is delicate, technically ecto-mesomorphic, not as strong as the mesomorphic Three; but then again, not as dry and ectomorphic as their neighbor the Five, says the Four by way of consoling themselves.

The Four's vital force is active internally on the level of thought. This makes for a tortured inner process, envious of the exuberance, the practical sense, and the ability of others to act. It tears them up, but they can't help it and continue to ask themselves "am I worthy of being illuminated?"

With effort and pain, the Fours seek to come up with ever new and original hues and shades to attract the sun's attention. They do not realize that richness of nuances and colors is a reflection of the ever-present sunlight; and thus find themselves unable to fully appreciate this bounty, or have pleasure of its beauty.

From this little example, we can immediately distil several fundamental characteristics of Fours that will be reflected in the handwriting.

- not a high level of vital energy
- little expansiveness and a flooding back upon oneself
- non-conformism
- feeling different from others (they feel excluded and exclusive at the same time)
- original and creative
- lacking confidence in own qualities
- tortured, suffering, dark
- disoriented regarding existential identity
- discontented
- variable self-image
- internalization

These tendencies seem to be linked together and vulnerable only to a deep, soul-searching, development of spirituality that would bring about a sense of balance and peace with oneself.

The lack of vitality is mainly constitutional and makes it difficult for the Four to feel comfortable in their environment or to get deeply involved in activity. This causes a certain lack of basic trust and makes them feel different from others: ill at ease, pained, and out of sorts with life. This type of inner torment, however, stimulates creativity, originality, and non-conformism - which in their turn further reinforce the feeling of being different from others, thereby enhancing the underlying sense of discontent. The resulting isolation encourages self-absorption which coincidentally brings Fours in touch with their inner life, but makes action in the world harder.

This turning inwards into the (small) self-reinforces the feeling of lack of

4

vitality and the sense of distance from others. Thus the cycle continues until the Fours become aware of their own beauty and value, and render the past suffering meaningful in the search for the (large) self.

From a graphological point of view, the first thing that jumps out in the handwriting (HW) of a Four is a "re-elaboration" as it were of the school-taught writing style. This does not mean that the result is an aesthetic image of harmony and proportion, but merely that the HW is allowed to deviate further from the school-taught model than for example the handwritings of Ones, Threes, and Nines, who do not personalize their HW:

- Nines will not personalize their HW out of laziness, or out of fear that too much originality may be annoying.
- Ones are rigid, want to stick to ideal norms of perfection, and can't bring themselves to "play" with the graphic movement.
- Threes feel too much need to make a good impression and will make an effort to have a HW that is organized and pleasing but not very spontaneous.

Fours do not have the same urge as Threes to present their best image. They don't care as much about rules and conventions as the One (being too preoccupied with their own pain). They do not have the exuberance of the Two, nor do they have the apathy of a Nine, although they may resemble a Nine during passive periods of depression. Fours are not detached like Fives, nor ambivalent, preoccupied, and suspicious like Sixes. They do not have the positive impulsiveness of Sevens, nor the disruptive and somewhat rambling force of the Eights.

Fours feel different, mainly in the sense of being an individual "separate" from others. This sense of separateness causes deep suffering and loneliness and the HW will first and foremost express this aspect. This of course does not apply to integrated Fours who have learned to tap into their creativity and internal regenerative force. However, even evolved Fours show traces of not being completely free of torment; so that their HW, as creative and original it may be, almost always contains signs of internal suffering. The Fours will stand and face their demons for the sake of authenticity.

That's why Four's HW often has the sign *Spontaneously Careful*: that's an agile and flowing HW, without artificiality, rigidity, or excessive impulsiveness. Graphic elements appear to be orderly and harmonious.

Spontaneously Careful indicates essentially a rather differentiated personality that seems to have good communication going between the conscious and unconscious without too much inhibition or inclination towards avoidance.

In my twilight vision, however, I only
vaguely distinguish what these sudden
glass panes on the surfaces of things let
show from the interior which they

Sample 1

Sample 1 Female age 55 – Type Four. Handwriting showing the sign *Spontaneously Careful.*

The sign Spontaneously *Careful*, is often present in Four's HW, and embodies many of the essential qualities of this type that are very desirable. Above all it indicates a personality free of artificiality and with little or no preoccupation about impressing others. Psychologically it means an ability of depth and freedom of thought, combined with emotional honesty and a high level of sensitivity. This makes the Four able to construct and to maintain an authentic relationship between "me & you" where both are dignified equally and held in consideration.

In spite of this rare and precious quality, Fours tend to undervalue themselves, but that does not seem to impede the Four's ability to give others enough space in their consciousness. They are superb listeners. Such ability to hear is both wide and deep. They can open themselves to any and all aspects of humanness and rarely put barriers or censorship neither on their own subconscious nor that of others—you can talk to a Four about anything.

Fours are not fazed by human contradictions and are never tired of exploring and of seeking answers about their own and others' motivations. It is as if they instinctively can relate to all experience internally. Indeed, their inner dimension is almost tangible, so much so that the Fours are at risk to get imprisoned in that world.

Generalizations are abhorrent to Fours. They presume to be special or unique, but are also willing to extend the same courtesy to others, which of course is why they can be such good listeners—they do not just go through the motions of listening. Listening to the Four includes seeking a resonance internally with the experience of the other—they want to hear every hue and shade—and that confers a good dose of "humanity" to them.Habituated to an ongoing existential unease, Fours often manage to reconcile conflicting emotions that are at the root of personality.

The sign *Spontaneously Careful*, indeed is an indicator of the ability to harmonize the conscious with the unconscious; anima and animus, introversion and extroversion, egotism and altruism, self and other, matter and spirit, spontaneity and inhibition. Neither of these extremes is overly exaggerated or repressed and that is where the highest virtue of the Four comes from: equilibrium.

Two examples of how creativity manifests in a handwriting:

There are days when everyone I meet appears
as symbols, and individually or together they
form a prophetic or occult writing that
describes my life in shadows. The words I
exchange with familiar or unfamiliar

Sample 2

Sample 2 Female age 37 – Type Four, Sexual. A very rich and original HW that contains all three types of *Methodically Irregular*. This person has many talents, especially a narrative gift. She is well aware of it and although she dedicates a lot of time to writing, she frequently falls into periods of feeling discouraged and without motivation. She lacks discipline and stability. In spite of the strength of the graphic rhythm, we can see how the mid-range letters often become very small, closed, and inked up. This happens in moments of deep malaise which are somewhat typical for the type Four and connected to a fluctuating sense of identity. (I was writing theese words in 2005. Right now the writer is a Jungian psychoanalyst).

There are days when everyone I meet appear as symbols, and individually or together they form a prophetic or occult writing that describes my life in shadows. The word I exchange with familiar or unfamiliar

Sample 3

Sample 3 Female age 49 – Type Four, Social. This HW is also highly personalized, but less forceful, engaged, and "breathy" than the previous example. I believe she has a lot of creative potential, but was told that she never had any real opportunities to express her creativity.

Both handwritings are extremely rich and original although they resemble each other. Both contain signs of discomfort with realization of self-identity. We need to keep in mind that a high level of creativity can go along with an inability to find profound satisfaction - just as a type One who is excessively critical and perfectionist may become tense and anxious.

To quote De Petrillo and Millevolte: "The more a person can express individualism and originality, the more the graphic gesture is personalized, differing from what the person was taught at school and diverging completely from perfect regularity and monotony" (DE PETRILLO V. – MILLEVOLTE A., *The Application of the G. Moretti Graphological System* - Brain Edizioni 2000, Roma).

The sign *Methodically Irregular (M.I.)*, is present in samples 2 & 3 and refers to methodical irregularities that can be present in all aspects of the HW. The term *M.I.* was created by Moretti and he gave it a high analytical value. The renowned German Graphologist, Ludwig Klages, who has some theoretical differences from Moretti, described graphic rhythm saying that: "We never can draw, in a sequence, shapes of the same letter which are perfectly identical, nor can we (because of the dynamics of the graphic impulses) use a precisely equal speed reproducing the same letter. So, rhythm of the Spontaneous Movement of the handwriting consists of creating only similar shapes in similar frequencies of speed".

We can distinguish three principal types of M.I. :

1. *Methodically Irregular size of the middle zone letters*: wherein the dimensions of the

middle zone varies at regular intervals.

2. *Methodically Irregular in Axial Direction*: where the letters softly and rhythmically slant at different angles towards each other.
3. *Methodically Irregular in Springing*: the letters jump up and down in a methodical and rhythmic way above the baseline. (We find the sign Springing in "a script in which letters are at different heights on the baseline, but not in a methodical way).

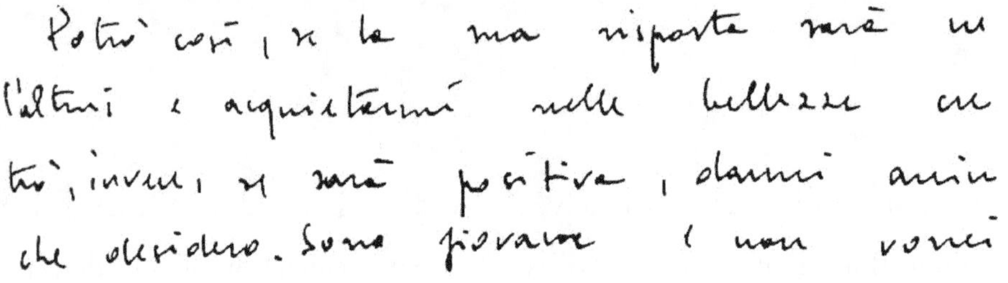

Sample 3a

Sample 3a This HW has a high degree of *Methodically Irregular in the size of the middle zone letters*. In diagram 3b and 3c we can see how the vital impulses of the rhythm modulate in frequency. (Graphics from PALAFERRI N., *L'indagine grafologica e il metodo morettiano*, Istituto Grafologico Moretti, Urbino, 1986, p. 166).

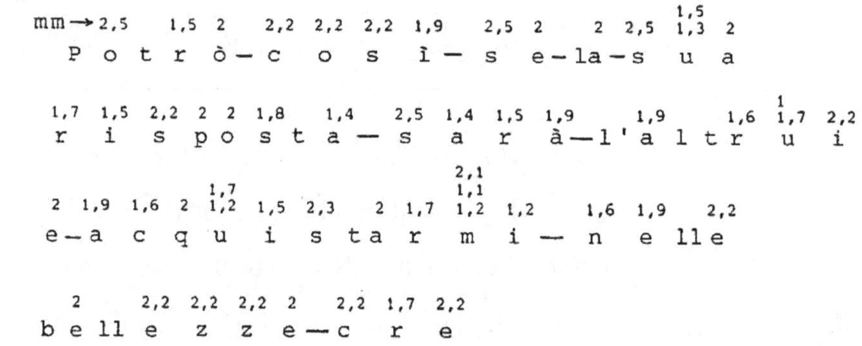
mm→ 2,5 1,5 2 2,2 2,2 2,2 1,9 2,5 2 2 2,5 1,5 1,3 2
P o t r ò — c o s ì — s e — la — s u a
1,7 1,5 2,2 2 2 1,8 1,4 2,5 1,4 1,5 1,9 1,9 1,6 1 1,7 2,2
r i s p o s t a — s a r à — l ' a l t r u i
2 1,9 1,6 2 1,7 1,2 1,5 2,3 2 1,7 2,1 1,1 1,2 1,2 1,6 1,9 2,2
e — a c q u i s t a r m i — n e lle
2 2,2 2,2 2,2 2 2,2 1,7 2,2
b e ll e z z e — c r e

Sample 3b

Sample 3b Measuring in millimeters of the middle zone letters referring to sample 3a.

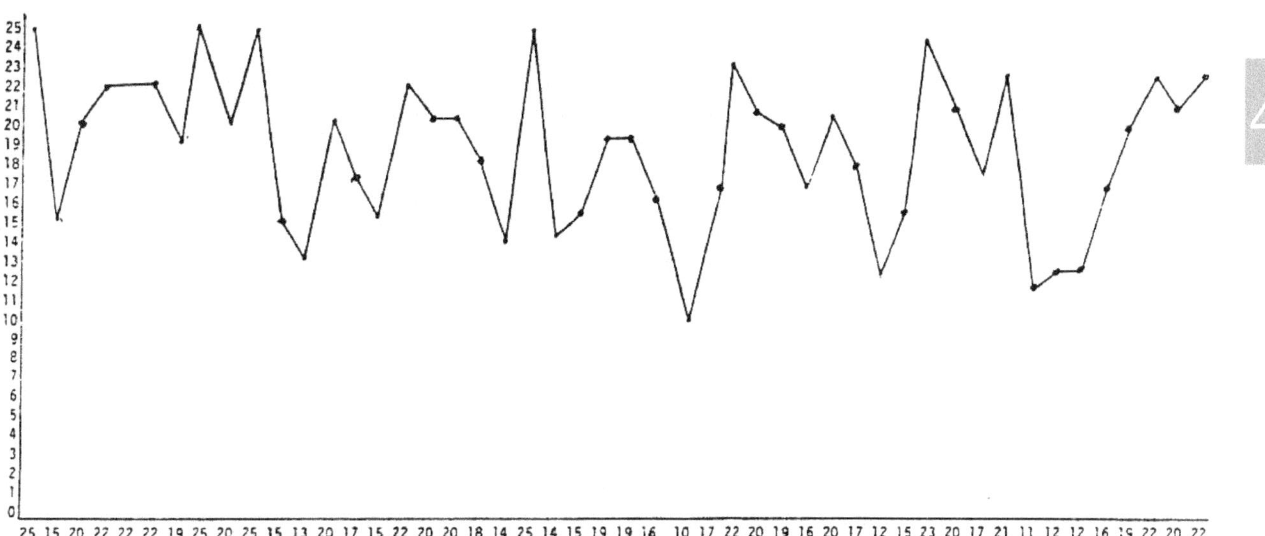

Sample 3c Diagram representing the measuring made in sample 3b.

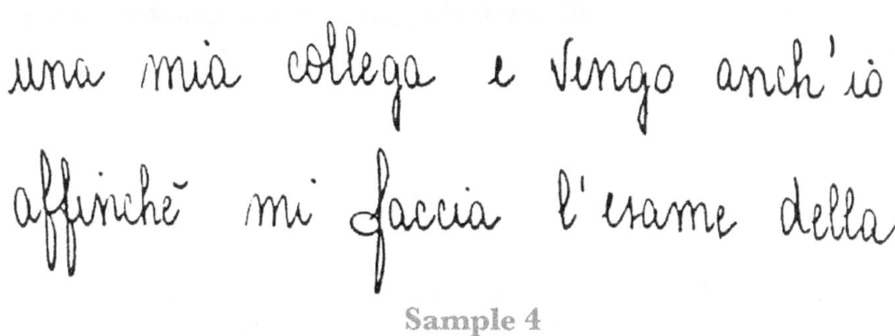

Sample 4

Sample 4 HW with a low level of *Methodically Irregular in the size of middle zone letters*, a slow and monotonous scrip, lacking in rhythm. The writer has a lymphatic temperament. Observe how the tops and bottoms of the mid-zone letters are often exactly on the same level (see diagram 4b). This indicates that the brain impulses driving the graphic movement are not very modulated and produce monotonous "cookie-cutter" style letters.
(Graphics from PALAFERRI N., *L'indagine grafologica e il metodo morettiano*, Istituto Grafologico Moretti, Urbino, 1986, p.168).

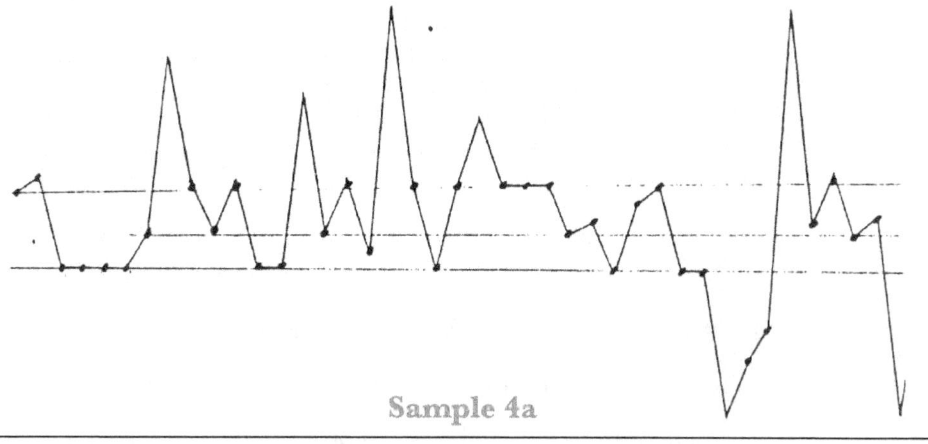

Sample 4a

Sample 4a Diagram of middle zone letters size referring to sample 4.

daily schedule? Am I being led by my
passion or my compulsion? Is it life
enhancing for me & for others? Do I make
... Do I ever

Sample 5

Sample 5 Male age 55 – Type Seven. HW presenting the sign *Not Methodically Irregular*. Variations are disorganized and stem from an impulsivity that is not well under control.

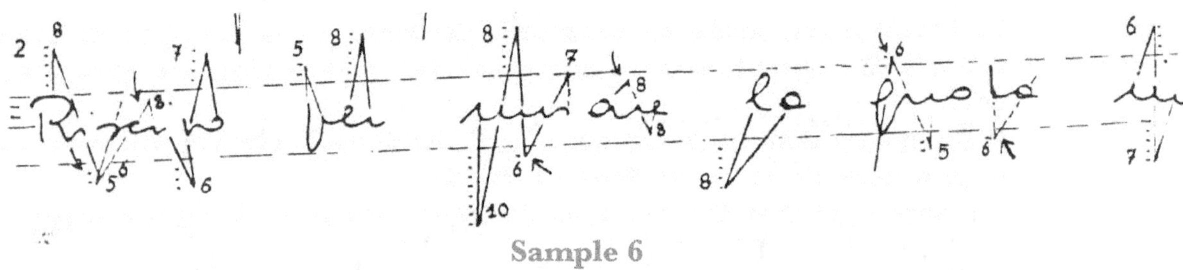

Sample 6

Sample 6 Writing showing Methodically Irregular in *Axial Direction* (the # correspond to the degree of inclination on a scale from 1 to 10) - (Graphic from PALAFERRI N., *L'indagine grafologica e il metodo morettiano*, Istituto Grafologico Moretti, Urbino, 1986, p. 150).

mm 0,7 1,5 0,7 0,3 1,8 1,4 0,7 1,4 0,4 0,7 0,9 0,4 0,4 0,4 0,4 0,5 0,4 0,3 1,2 1,4

Sample 7

Sample 7 Beethoven's HW. Showing a high degree of *Methodically Irregular of Springing*. The numbers are in millimeters measuring the distance of the letters from the baseline. (Graphic by PALAFERRI N., *L'indagine grafologica e il metodo morettiano*, Istituto Grafologico Moretti, Urbino, 1986, p. 154).

In this context, we will be referring to M.I. mainly as the *Methodically Irregular of size*. Graphologically this is an indicator of "primary creativity" which still would need discipline and method before it can become constructive. It is the vital rhythm that drives the creative impulse.

M.I. indicates absence of stereotypical mental attitudes and the presence of a capacity to “re-invent” existential schemes. It also means sensitivity, emotional richness, openness to many interests, vivid imagination, originality, spontaneity and a general inclination towards art. Not everyone with *M.I.* is an artist, of course, nor are all Fours. Moreover, the field (music, sculpture, painting) in which artistic talent could manifest depends of the presence of a few additional signs.

Other Enneagram types can certainly have *M.I.* but it is found most commonly in the HW of Fours, especially when conjunct with *Small Size of the Middle Zone Letters*. In fact, *M.I.*, when occurring along with *Small Size*, points to creativity that is mainly applied to the relationship with deeper aspects of inner life.

This sign also has some negative aspects, especially in the sense that it indicates a sense of uniqueness which causes difficulties accepting ordinariness in life and in relationships.

If we find all three types of *M.I.* and especially when *Fluent, Flexuous,* and *Balanced Triple Width* are also present, we get the sign *Elegant,* a truly rare and beautiful graphological sign that could indicate a highly evolved type Four.

Elegant means that the functions of perception, intuition, feeling, and thinking are well integrated and give a HW a general sense of harmony. It is a sign of profound overall balance, which is the Four’s highest virtue.

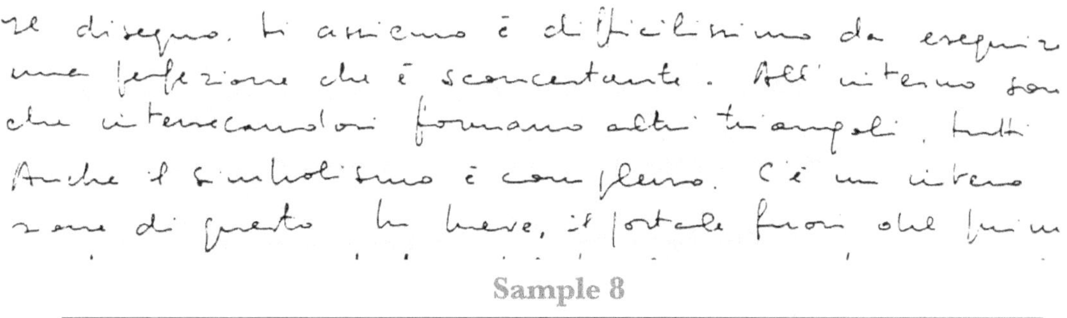

Sample 8 HW with a high level of *Elegant.*

In short, we could say that while *M.I.* is generally associated with type Four, *Elegant* is distinctly a sign of a highly developed Four. Both signs are closely tied in with the mind-set of originality, creativity, and anti-conformism of the Four.

Unfortunately, we have less integrated factors in the Fours.

At the level of bio-typology, *i.e.*, constitution, Naranjo says: "Ennea-type IV is most often ectomesomorphic in body build—neither as high in ectomorphia as type V nor as mesomorphic as type III" (*Character and Neurosis, p. 120*), and besides, their typical hypersensitivity and aloofness are in line with the cerebrotonic condition that is a complementary part of ectomorphia.

At a bio-typological level we have a nervous factor that is dominant (*i.e.*, with characteristics of sensitivity and restlessness) balanced with a bilious (tense-controlling) factor (that stems from mesomorphism and shows a degree of self-control). Constitutionally Fours are low in the lymphatic (heavy-passive-slow-stable) department, factor which brings stability (when the level is high); and particularly lacking in the sanguineous (buoyant-optimistic) one, which explains the tendency towards asthenia.

These factors together form the basic delicacy and sensitivity in Fours, which often can become into vulnerability and hypersensitivity.

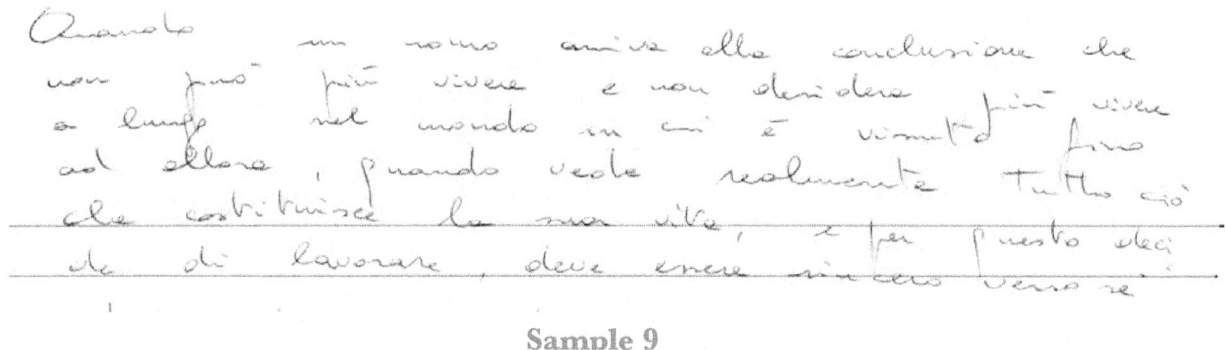
Quando un uomo arriva alla conclusione che non può più vivere e non desidera più vivere a lungo nel mondo in cui è vissuto fino ad allora, quando vede realmente tutto ciò che costituisce la sua vita, e per questo decide di lavorare, deve essere sincero verso se

Sample 9

Sample 9 Female age 34 - Type Four. This writing contains distinct signs of delicacy, deep sensibility, empathy and generosity (*Curved, Light, Small Size, Good Space Between Letters, Spontaneously Careful. Methodically Irregular*). However, there are also indications of vulnerability at the level of self-identity (letters rise, then drop down again onto the baseline). Instincts appear to be frail and there is probably envy towards those who are more exuberant.

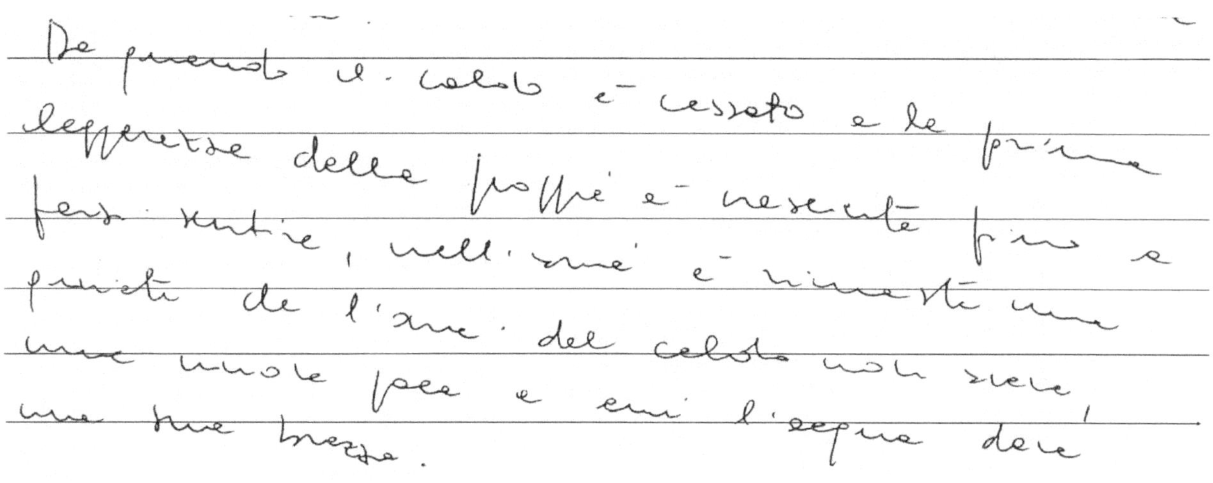

Sample 10

Sample 10 Female age 54 - Type Four. Similar signs as in sample 9, but differently proportioned. Dominant in this HW is the sign *Descending*.

Too much sensitivity, which is linked to lack of vitality, makes it hard to recharge energy. Impressions resonate strongly, are dramatized, and become draining. Graphological signs denoting this are:

Descending: "script which progressively falls downwards from the baseline as it approaches the right margin." The sign indicates shortage of stamina, risk of nervous breakdown and depression, neuroasthenia, lack of confidence, and an inclination towards feeling guilt, inferiority, melancholy, and hypochondria.

Light: "script with light pressure throughout." Low threshold in resisting life's stimuli, delicate, instincts that are in tune with feelings, intuition, and introversion. Also, inner suffering and restlessness, low level of vital energy, strong sensitivity towards other people's crudeness, tendency to withdraw when it would serve better to aggressively come forward, emotional vulnerability. Obviously this sign needs to be seen in the context of other signs; besides, sensitivity is a beautiful human quality, depending on how it is used.

Extensions Concave to Right: "script where letter extensions (t, d, l, g, f, p) show concavity to the right"; indicates a willingness to cooperate with and understand the needs of others. This goes along with a weak will only too often guided by feelings; tendency to dependency and depression (when combined with the sign *Descending*).

An interesting point is that type One tends to have a distinct and often excessive use of *Straight Extensions*; a sign showing steadiness and strong willpower—exactly what Fours need to develop in order to come out of their self-abandonment. But when *Extensions Concave* to Right are strongly present, the tendency is to drift towards surrender, to be overly influenced, and to depend on feelings; Fours then move towards Twoish inclinations and become dependent, clinging to a relationship.

Sample 11a

Sample 11a Type Four – Social, average level.

Sample 11b

Sample 11b Same person of as sample 11a -Type Four going toward type Two.

Sample 11c

Sample 11c Same person as sample 11a. Type Four going toward type One.

Samples 11a, b & c belong to the same person, a Four (male), taken from different periods in his life. 11a was written during a relatively "normal" period, not balanced, but rather his ordinary state.

Sample 11b comes from a very hard and painful time with a lot of suffering. The HW is breaking up, showing spatial disorientation on paper and hence in life. There is an increase of *Extensions Concave to Right* with four additional graphological signs indicating deep internal indisposition: *Arthritic, Laboured, Thickened Type II, Touching letters*.

Sample 11c is from a relatively serene period following some psychotherapy when he managed to resolve some problematic dependency issues with relationships. The HW in his sample is more confident, energetic and engaged. It is more expanded, with a higher degree of *Straight Extensions and Triple Width*. The baseline becomes *Ascending*—in brief, our Four acquired some of the positive qualities of the One: firmness, activity, and stability.

Returning to the previously mentioned signs, *Arthritic* means some letters are swollen and/or deformed. It's a sign of agitation in feelings, thoughts, imagination and activity. Such agitation nags day and night and is driven by conflicting desires, ambitions and mood. It is also a sign of obsessively fixating on ideas (it fits in with the Four's background of obsessiveness and rumination).

Laboured: "writing that proceeds with difficulty; spasmodic and congested pressure; sudden breaks in the texture of the stroke, recurrent blockages and contortions in the letter body" (DE PETRILLO V. – MILLEVOLTE A. *The Application of the G. Moretti Graphological System* – Brain Edizioni 2000, Roma).

In a very synthetic way we could say that Laboured is a sign of frustration of the instinctual drives, and of torment, conflict, and psychosomatic disturbance. It reveals a dissatisfaction that permeates the personality that then gets projected onto others, enhancing the sense of abandonment. It is also a sign both of anger at oneself and hatred of oneself, born of frustration (very common in Fours).

Sample 12

Sample 12 Male – Type Four, Sexual. HW showing the signs *Laboured and Arthritic*. Anger, guilt and self-loathing.

Sample 13

Sample 13 Female – Type Four, Sexual. HW with *Not Homogeneous of pressure* and *Thickened type II*. Anger and frustration.

Touching letters: "compressed script in which letters lean against one another." A sign of anxiety and anguish, a lack of breathing room and a blockage in the ability to move forward psychologically. These are warning signs the ego feels when danger is present—much more common in type Six, but also present in the Four.

Sample 14

Sample 14 Female age 42 – Type Four, Sexual. Handwriting with a good degree of *M.I.* - but showing also the sign *Touching Letters*. Anxiety.

Sword-shaped: "script in which the letter size progressively increases or decreases either in the body of a word or throughout the entire line." Indicates a person prone to experience ups and downs; variable feeling of personal well being (connected to the self-image); energy is not well channeled. This sign invalidates the *Methodically Irregular* sign because the handwriting shows only a sort of variation due to moodiness rather than a creative rhythm.

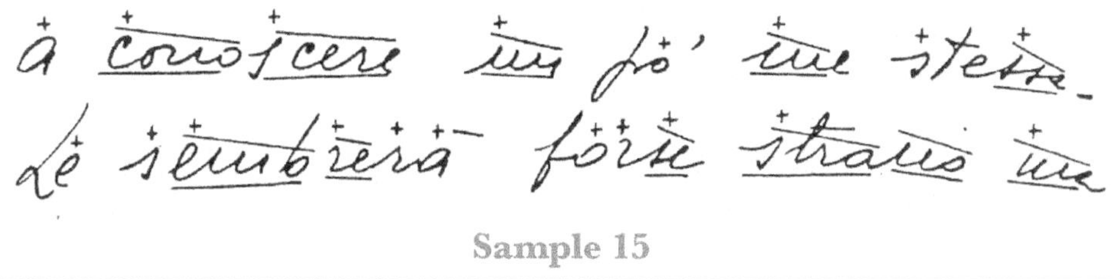

Sample 15 Handwriting showing the sign *Sword-shaped*.

Thickened Type II: we have already seen this sign in the One's HW. When unable to hold in anger, the One goes to Four. This is a "script in which the stroke shows sudden marks." It indicates hypersensitivity and excessive emotionalism permeating the personality both physically and intellectually.

These last signs are debilitating to the Four's creativity because they keep the Four in self-absorption, in their own world of feelings and rumination, and trapped in the past. All these signs impoverish vitality. Thus the Four can be in a vicious cycle in which emotional pain leads to passivity, which causes depression, regrets and sadness. That's why activity is considered so therapeutic to Fours: it prevents them from becoming isolated and stuck in their world of imagination, carrying on endless internal dialogues.

Considering Jungian function, it is not obvious where type Four fits in. Naranjo says that it's Intraverted (I) Feeling (F), while Riso leans towards iNtuitive (N) Intraverted (I). From a graphological perspective, the hypothesis of IN (which according to Naranjo in part fits type Seven) with Thinking (T) as the auxiliary function seems to be more fitting; even though IF certainly pertains to many traits of the Four.

4

This is not a minor differentiation, because the NI is low in F and Sensing (S); hence the lack of practicality. In addition, intimacy is a problem because the Four has never had intimacy and is continually searching for it but tortuously, by withdrawing.

In classic characterology the nervous-asthenic temperament goes with the Sentimental character, which implies emotionality, lack of action, and introversion. According to the graphologist Nazzareno Palaferri, this character matches the Jungian description of the NI.

J. Rivere describes the Sentimental type as: "the type who is most hurt by inner wounds; for whom the integrity and purity of the sense of 'I' is vital; and even though he is not the most introverted of all types, the introversion gives him a highly demanding and personal sense of self. It is the most self-referencing of all types, the saddest, the most lonely, the dreamer, the most regretful and in all probability the most unhappy of all." (J. RIVERE, *Graphologie du caractèr*, Mont-Blanc, Genève-Suisse, 1972, p. 87)

Among the most important problems a Four faces are lack of practicality (Jungian suppressed Sensate function) and self-confidence. Although Fours are often aware of this, they find it difficult to overcome such a limitation. Emotions get internalized so they can be re-lived longer, while externally Fours can look perfectly calm. But such internal tempests can set off psychosomatic problems.

Fours can get stuck in an unconscious pattern (for example an unresolved Oedipus complex) and lose sight of the fact that it is precisely their ability to relate to their unconscious at which they are better than any other type—that is their main resourse, and can bring out their self-renewal energy and creativity.

Because of their deep sense of dissatisfaction, it is hard for Fours to maintain a good attitude towards life. A series of signs goes with this mind-set:

- Lacking rhythm, looseness and fluidity in the HW (i.e., the abovementioned signs *Arthritic, Laboured, Descending, Touching Letters, Sword-shaped* are present);

- The graphic movement is restrained and poorly woven together (letters are contracted without adequate breathing room; the pressure and connections between the letters are not homogeneous);

- Introverted signs are accented, visible in reduction of the size of letters and tightening of the *Triple Width*);

- Contrast between the sense of order in the general appearance and the particulars: since Fours have difficulty being in touch with their instinctual side, their HW may present an overall picture of orderliness, but whatever aspects have been repressed and are causing anguish or malcontent will come our as tiny signs of contraction, agitation or out-of-sortness. Here again we have the outwardly calm surface with brewing turmoil underneath.

- Lack of power and tension will show in absence of decisive pressure and crisp strokes (sign *Precise*) as well as a lack of *Straight Extensions*, *Stable Baseline* and *B angles*—coincidentally signs that are typically found in the HW of Ones.

The Enneagram is as accurate as a mathematical formula when describing psychological development. The path of growth for a Four goes along with the development of self-discipline and increase in activity-once implemented, this little colorful planet on our voyage, will finally feel worthy of the sunshine and need not stay any longer hiding in solitude.

our new walk-in visitor center inside the Santa Monica
Place on the second floor. Our travel counselors can offer you
maps and brochures on retail, dining, and accommodation.
Housed in a fabulous architectural landmarks ranging from

Sample 16

Sample 16 Male age 58 – Type Four, Sexual. Good integration toward the characteristics of type One. The HW shows a high level of *M.I.*, but within a context of stability (*Stable Baseline, Straight Extensions, Angles A, Angles B*). The personality maintains consistency without falling into disorientation.

Da quando il caldo necessario e la prima leggerezza della pioggia è cresciuta fino a farsi sentire, nell'aria è rimasta una quiete che l'aria del caldo

Sample 17

Sample 17 Female age 39 - Italian handwriting of a Four w/5. The handwriting is *Spontaneously Careful*, with an average degree of *M.I.*, and the sign *Small Size*. There is however a marked increase in mental control over emotions: note the enlarged *Space between Words*.

of themselves that they speak, nor to themselves that they express; they give words and are not clearly indicative, but they allow glimpses. In my twilight vision, however, I only vaguely distinguish

Sample 18

Sample 18 Male age 55 - American handwriting of a Four w/5, Sexual. It is not easy to distinguish whether this is the HW or a Four or Five. The *size of medium zone letters* is very *small*. In the field below the baseline we see some regressive strokes towards the left (control of spontaneous expression of instinct). The inclination does not become *Methodically Irregular* because the *Axial Directions of letters* turn back "suddenly" one against the other (sign *Twisted*). Then we have several *sharp angles in the Ovals*. This person gives much mental space to analyzing feelings and is protective of privacy.

In my twilight vision, however, I only vaguely distinguish what these sudden glass panes of the surface of things let show from the interior th which they veil and reveal.

Sample 19

Sample 19 Female age 53 – Type Four, Sexual (in my opinion with a Three wing). The handwriting shows an average degree of *Methodically Irregular*, and the sign *Ascending*. Good pressure but *not homogeneous*. She does not appear to be mired in emotional torment or self absorption, but engaged in liberating activity. She typed herself as a Four, but more writing samples would be needed to gain certainty of her type.

In my twilight vision, however, I only vaguely distinguish what these sudden glass panes on the surface of things let show from

Sample 20

Sample 20 Female age 36 - Type Four. She is not sure if she is a Sexual subtype (in my opinion with a Three wing). The handwriting shows a good degree of *Methodically Irregular*, and a balanced *Triple Width*. Energy seems well channeled. The HW shows sensibility and creativity but in a context of organization and mastery over self. The Three wing here has a pretty strong influence.

For graphological definitions and interpretations I used the following texts:

PALAFERRI N., *L'indagine grafologica e il metodo morettiano*, Istituto Grafologico Moretti, Urbino, 1986.
PALAFERRI N., *Dizionario Grafologico*, Libreria "G. Moretti, Urbino, 1993.
PALAFERRI N., *Tipologia umana, caratterologia e grafologia*, Libreria "G. Moretti, Urbino, 1999.
TORBIDONI-ZANIN, *Grafologia* (testo teorico pratico), IV ed., Editrice La Scuola, Brescia, 1986.

HANDWRITING AND ENNEATYPE FIVE

I would like to give the type Five, who is inclined to disappear or disincarnate, a body. And to invade respectfully, through graphic images, the privacy Fives are so desirous to protect and detest having disrupted.

Isolation

If we were to give a symbolic face to the Five's personality, it would be immediately clear that, were it a psychic play between full and empty, it would be empty that prevails. Graphologically that translates into a writing where the blank surface of the paper dominates over areas that have ink.

In this case we are mainly concerned with the defense mechanism protecting isolation. Naranjo comments that it is not the reaction formation against the super ego but rather isolation that defines the Five's character.

By "isolation" we don't mean merely feeling alone or distant from others; it is rather a mechanism of lack of connection in the inner world, between thoughts, impulses and feelings. Each is experienced as separate from the other, as if between each impulse, strong emotion and the context in which they occur, there was a "mental void." In the end only the intellectual contents remains while the feeling part loses most of its initial impact. What remains is something aseptic the Five can look at with detachment as if it had happened to someone else.

All types share some of this defense mechanism that kicks in to protect us from the full exposure and the raw intensity of the power of impulses.

However, according to Naranjo: "Isolation is a core of type V character in that the characteristic detachment not only from people but more generally from the world (including one's own body) depends on the inactivation of feelings and also corresponds to an avoidance of the situation in which feelings normally arise: an interruption of the life process in the service of feeling-avoidance" (pp.90-91).

Sample 1, with its disproportionate white spaces is a good example of this defense mechanism.

"Paths" between the words indicate a trend to separate thoughts from feelings, as if unable to communicate. The handwriting (HW) maintains a good structure, is organized, has a good rhythm and original shapes. And yet, within the HW, there are "holes" that appear to be empty—the mechanism of isolation.

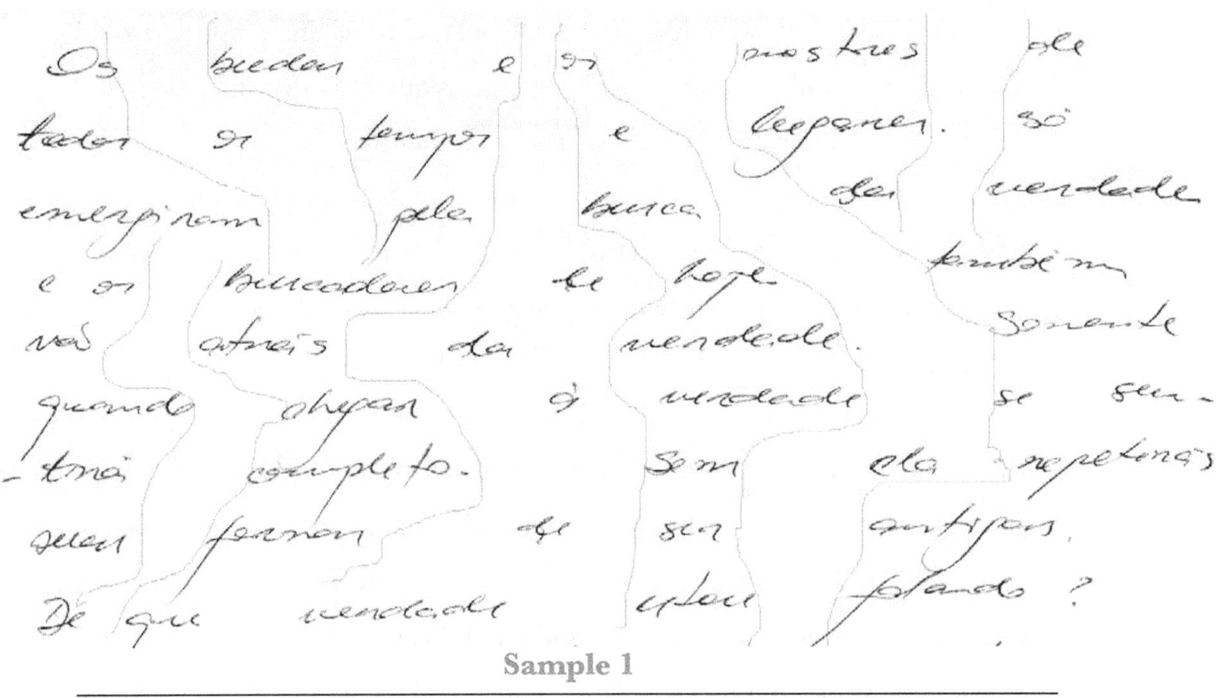

Sample 1 Male - Type Five, Sexual. HW with defense mechanism of isolation.

Intelligence that is sharp and deep

Fives are often truly intelligent. Their intellectual process is typically very observant, reflective, methodical and focused on the essence of a problem.

It is by containing instinctual impulses, spontaneous feelings and imagination that reason is favored. Even when gifted with intuition, Fives apply it to practical understanding of reality.

Creative Fives use their gift in the field of practical reality and social applications rather than in the realm of sentiments or art. They pioneer new areas of knowledge, proceeding always with order, method, system, continuity, tenacity and daring.

Logical, critical and constructive, Fives can think independently, with tenacity, firmness and rigor. Their motivation is finding ways to fulfill life's needs. They seek for perfection and practical applications, for universal principles rarely personal ones, through experimentation.

Wenn es mir schon vor Empfang
Ihres Briefes leid that, dass ich
mich durch eine kleinliche Regung
jene Äusserung über Priorität in der
bewussten Sache diktieren liess,
zeigte mir Ihr ausführlicher Brief
erst recht, dass meine Empfindlich-
keit übel angebracht war. Die

Sample 2

Sample 2 Albert Einstein. The HW is very small, letter shapes are simple and essential, and yet, as a whole the HW is original. The graphic rhythm is vivid but contained. Thomas Chou (see *EM* June 1997) suggested that Einstein might be a type Nine with an Eight wing. Indeed, his HW does not show the typical "detachment" of a Five that a disproportionate blank space vs. ink coverage would point to, but many other indicators confirm type Five. It would be hard to imagine a type Nine, even with an Eight wing with such pronounced mental sharpness, power of observation, personalization of concepts and the systematic organization of the theory.

Angularity in the HW prevails over curved lines, something that makes it diametrically opposed to the likelihood of being a Nine. The HW does not convey an impression of an estranged man feeling alone in the universe; it is rather the image of a very simple person that is extremely curious about life's phenomena. There are no traces of Nine's laziness or sensuousness of the Eight. There is as if a hungering pursuit of experiences which then will be translated and organized into theories. An Eight would probably stop to linger at the experiences themselves instead of making abstract theories. But, there is always room for doubt when trying to assess someone else's type.

do snr. eng. Alvaro de Campos, mando-lhe o poema que escrevi entre as estações de Casa Branca e Barreiro A; terminando a inspiração, entretanto, na Moita.

Sample 3

Sample 3 HW of Fernando Pessoa, the Portuguese poet.

Fernando Pessoa

Fernando Pessoa's HW is extremely bare bones and contained; small, very angular (technically called *Sharp*). Inner space of the letters and the space between them is narrow while the spaces between words are wide—the sign is called *Dry*—letters resemble skeletons, with sharp corners, tightly bunched together and small.

It's the main indicator of "Avarice" which can manifest in a variety of ways, but principally as "I have nothing to give." It is the schizoid that tends towards isolation, distancing from feelings because the mind is focused on it's own contents. There is also skepticism towards life being good.

5

Pessoa's personality is closed and insecure, hypersensitive, introverted and vulnerable, and yet, capable to perceive infinite nuances. However, he is weary of the external world and his relationship with it is strained and formal.

His energy is totally used to relate to his own inner world which is extremely rich. His intelligence is sharp, deep and intuitive; able to speculate and to do research, highly mnemonic and gifted with lively and original thought.

Isolated by a lack of involvement with the outer world and unable to emotionally connect or express in a vital way, his impulse towards the other remains active but cannot unblock in an affective relationship. This leaves a sense of need that is impossible to quench.

The inability to give, because of skepticism about having something of himself to offer, creates a permanent sense of hunger. To counteract this hunger, he transforms himself into an antenna that assimilates, gathers, receives and appropriates; first with the senses, and then mentally, everything, every situation and every persona that touches him. This is his food.

All this occurs internally. Any person or emotions that he just touched is immediately ingurgitated avidly, microscopically analyzed in depth to the point of exasperation with a perfectionism that detests the obvious - each person gets fragmented and decomposed in little pieces.

Pessoa's HW has a feeling of the sea, where all the data that he collected are uneasily awaiting a response. But this is a sea that remains contained in it's restlessness without being oxygenated or calmed by the encounter with other waters.

Students of Enneagram personality may think that Pessoa had to be a Four, what with being an artist and all, but that would be stereotyping. Graphologically, types Four and Five often get mixed up, but there is an underlying difference in the HW that makes the distinction easier.

Both types' HW is generally small, airy and agile, but the Five's is more angular an pointy, more "held back," dry, with more space between words and

5

less within letters; all signs of holding back emotions and have thought dominate. This fits also the schizoid attitude of isolation, of feeling separate from others unable to connect with the rest of humanity.

Fours, even being introverted, are in the Heart center and as such softer, sinuous and more flexible than the Head centered Five. Fours are also more emphatic and try to express their feelings, while the Five withdraws into his or her self.

In essence, the Five is more indifferent towards others while the Four is susceptible to the pain of others. Fives are equally delicate and sensitive as Fours, but they manage to not get involved in other's feelings and instead of allowing themselves to be invaded, they file feelings at a distance in broader impersonal concepts avoiding emotions "personalizing" and thereby expending time and energy. Not so the Four who has a hard time finding the proper distance and takes things way too personal.

One of Pessoa's poems (1918) that renders the personality of a Five well:

Whether we write or speak or do but look
We are ever unapparent. What we are
Cannot be transfused into word or book,
Our soul from us is infinitely far.
However much we give our thoughts the will
To be our soul and gesture it abroad,
Our hearts are incommunicable still.
In what we show ourselves we are ignored.
The abyss from soul to soul cannot be bridged
By any skill of thought or trick or seeming.
Unto our very selves we are abridged
When we would utter to our thought our being.
We are our dreams of ourselves souls by gleams,
And each to each other dreams of others' dreams.

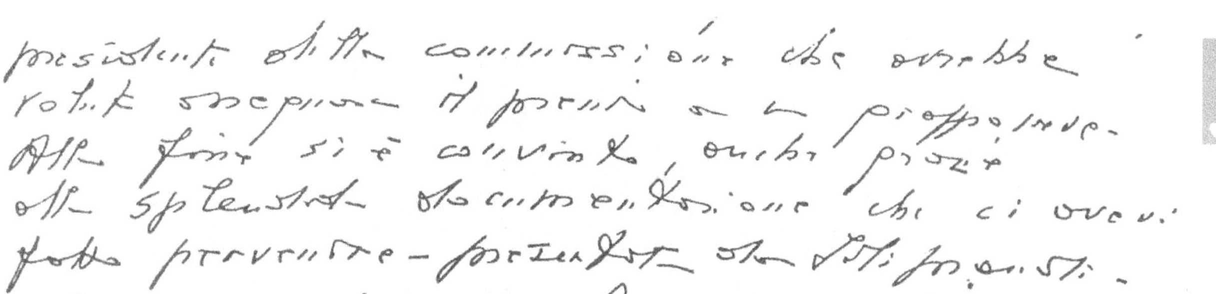

Sample 4

Sample 4 HW of Rita Levi Montalcini when she was 80.

Rita Levi Montalcini taught neurobiology for 30 years in several universities in the USA. She was awarded the Nobel Laureate for medicine in 1986 for her discovery in bodily substances that stimulate and influence the growth of nerve cells (Nerve-Growth Factor, NGF). The justification for awarding her the prize read: "the discovery of Montalcini is a fascinating example of how an acutely aware observer can recognize valuable hypothesis from an apparent chaos."

Aside from a pronounced originality and geniality of this HW (personal re-elaboration of the scholastic model with a high degree of *Methodically Irregular*), which may be even obvious to an eye untrained in graphology, the most striking aspect is *Disconnected* to a very high degree.

Disconnected is when letters within words are not linked and stand as if independent. In this sample, we see such disconnect even within the individual letter itself, for example the "m" or "n" bars. This sign is the main indicator of analysis, reflection, the ability to think in abstract forms and an inclination to research.

Montalcini never married and always wanted to dedicate her life completely to research. Her personality shows a high level of perfectionism, pride in her work, attention to detail and hyper-criticalness. The sign *Disconnected* also indicates a certain level of rigidity and mistrust. She most certainly was extremely demanding in her personal relationships.

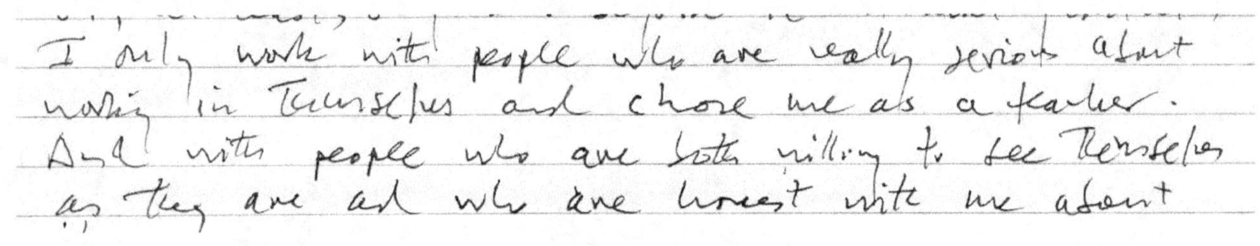
I only work with people who are really serious about
working in themselves and chose me as a teacher.
And with people who are both willing to see themselves
as they are and who are honest with me about

Sample 5

Sample 5 Male - Type Five, Student and researcher of the Enneagram, the sign *Sharp* at a very high degree.

Sharp is when the angles of the upper and lower extremities of the letters (especially the ovals) are very pointy. Consequently we will find also the signs *Narrow Letter Breadth*, and a medium degree of *Space between Letters*.

In this context it is an indication of an aggressive intellect with a distinct taste for going against the flow (also we find here a high degree of *Methodically Irregular*, which denotes a certain genius of combining intuitive personalizing ability that is manifestly non-conformist).

Sharp is a complex graphological sign containing several elements. Basically it shows an irrational craving of the ego to "have" a distinct personality with one's own points of view, taking strong positions (*Sharp Angles*), while all along distancing from all that is collective and not self (*Narrow Letter Breadth*).

Sharp indicates someone very demanding and insisting on unconditional respect. Gifted with an aggressive intellect (let's remember that in this department, the Five is not the least bit passive), opponents are put in their place with biting irony, cutting sarcasm or pointed ridicule.

The intelligence of *Sharp* is refined and capable of depths unknown to most; able to cut through to the core of a question and put the answer into the right words to make the point. There is pride in having one's own ideas prevail (which is often the case) because they were thoroughly thought through with obstinate tenacity by a quick mind. There is also a strong sense of individuality, of craving for adulation and being revered, along with an attitude of mistrust, competitiveness, and elitism.

Type One may also show *Sharp* but Fives, even if honest and incorruptible, will seek to affirm their own position, but their concept of justice may be very subjective indeed. Ones on the other hand are always seeking affirmation of what is right and their aggressiveness, in the HW is more prone to manifest by *Straight Extensions*, while the Five's will be *Sharp*.

It is almost impossible to see the pure *Sharp* in the HW of Twos, Threes, Nines or Sixes; but yes in Sevens as well as disintegrating Eights (when going respectively to One and Five), or in angry Fours.

Sharp is the sign that conveys the ability to confront obstacles and challenges especially the intellectual kind; a highly advantageous quality in the pursuit of research or presentation of data. In this sense a Five could be removed from life while assuming a dominant position at the same time.

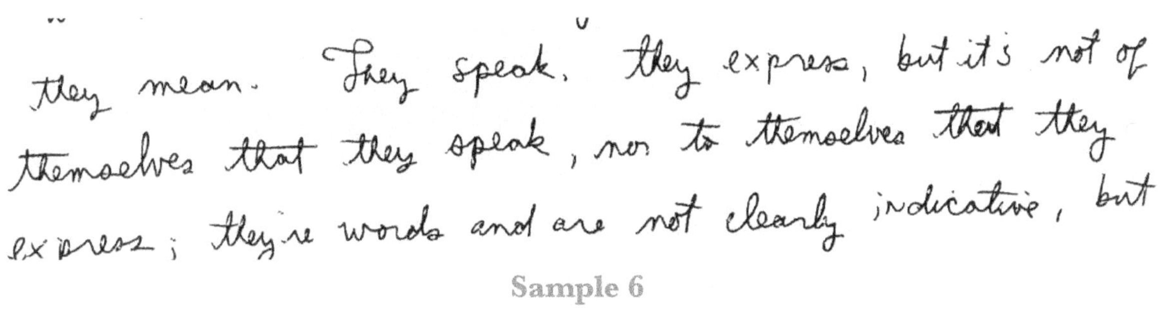

Sample 6 Male age 49 – Type 5w4, Sexual. An American writer and intellectual.

In Sample 6 the HW is *Small* with simplified forms that are sober, essential but original. *Space between Words* is more prevalent than that *between Letters*, including that *within the Letters* themselves, and the end-strokes are contained. His mind is lucid and loves solving riddles—serene, always oriented towards knowledge and curious of the nature of things, passion for theories and going deep with a strong capacity to be selective and aware of conceptual nuances. Emotions that are not repressed (influence of the Four wing) are channeled and expressed soberly. His tendency is to be reflective and introverted; assured intellectual position because well thought through; and upright person but not without pride in self, he disdains superficiality and has a hard time opening up in intimate communication. The dominant sign is *Sober* and the components are:

1. Graphic sense = visually plain, simple in form, orderly and proportioned.
2. Initial and final strokes essential as is every accessorial element of the writing.
3. Small letters.

Essentiality and Concentration

The ability to concentrate and to observe allows the Five to get down to the essentials of a problem. This essentiality finds also expression in the style of communication which is very synthetic and often rushed. When the Five finds time to listen, it is often without appropriate patience and empathy; actually, more attention is given to their own intellectual speculations with which they arrange the feelings of others in a web of a larger impersonal construct so that they need not be affected personally as much. Fives generally do not give high priority to appearance, although they want to appear dignified they pay little attention to image.

The HW reflects these traits faithfully. Letter shapes are fast and essential, without additional frills or embellishments; not contrived, seductive or in other ways designed to attract attention. The writer is focused on the thought process (about which they feel proudly superior). Actually the letter shapes are so bare, sober and dry that they become almost illegible. The communication is laconic, and they tend to say little about themselves. It is hard to guess what the writer is feeling because it is not expressed openly. Intellectually, Fives can go far professionally, in their study and in research.

Fives often are gifted with a refined sense of humor because the finer human incongruities do not escape them. From a spiritual perspective, they risk of overvaluing the role of intellect and consequently may be plagued by excessive skepticism.

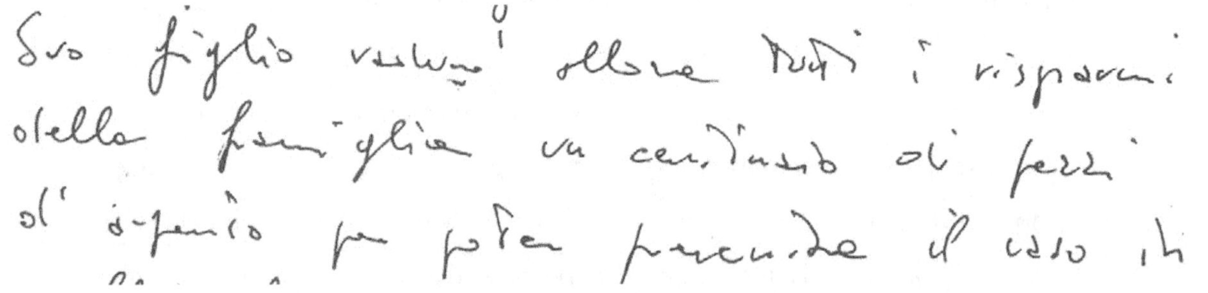

Sample 7

Sample 7 Male age 53 – Type 5w4.

"Non ho tempo, non ho tempo" è la
frase più volte scarabocchiata sui bordi
del manoscritto che avrebbe impegnato
generazioni di matematici per centinaia

Sample 8

Sample 8 Male age 27 – Type 5w4.

I supermercati devono rifornirsi all'estero. I
prezzi sono aumentati con effetti negativi sull'inflazione
Ma il governo impegna i parlamentari a discutere una
questione come l'abolizione dello sport della caccia alla

Sample 9

Sample 9 Male age 48 – Type 5.

Poche scoperte che la capacità di disegnare può
essere acquisita da persone normali da una vista
buona e da una discreta coordinazione.

Sample 10

Sample 10 Male age 54 – Type 5.

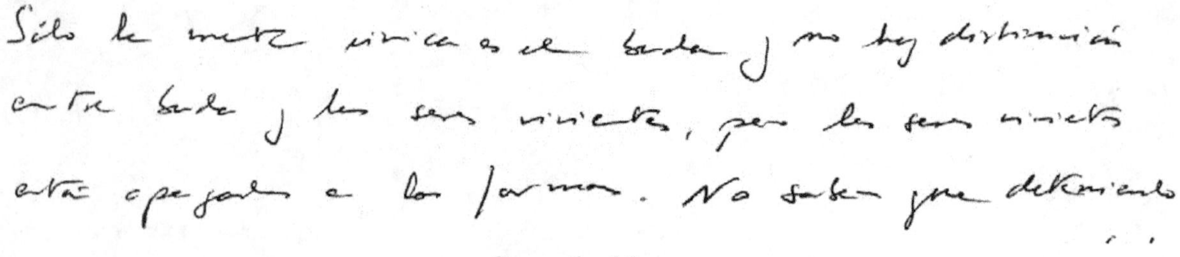

Sample 11

Sample 11 Male – Type 5, Sexual.

Introversion

Type Five is probably the most introverted of all Enneagram types. Looking at handwriting (HW) samples 12 and 13 could you possibly imagine they belong to a type Two or Three with their need to attract attention? or a Seven, who is always moving between various interests? or an Eight who mainly wants to be in charge? or a Nine who does not like to be disturbed, yet feels a need to stay involved for a sense of belonging? or a Six who's fear will not permit withdrawing completely and always provides a push to go out in search of security and protection? or a perfectionistic One who can't sit still and feels a need to make others respect the given order as well?; could it belong to a Four who may feel isolated and special and after a while will need some strong emotions and eventually will do something, even if it is only becoming innerly desperate? Answer is no.

Both HWs can only belong to Fives. The dominant sign is *Small Size*.

The underlying meaning of *Small Size* is power of concentration, above all due to containment of the emotional influence on intellective process; intuition, thinking and inquisitive research become "honed like chiseled" according to Moretti; we see the same tendency in action.

Life is lived internally, introverted and reduced to essentials, yet the mind is able to single out particulars within the greater scheme of things. When *Triple Width* is also present, it's a sign indicating intellectual depth.

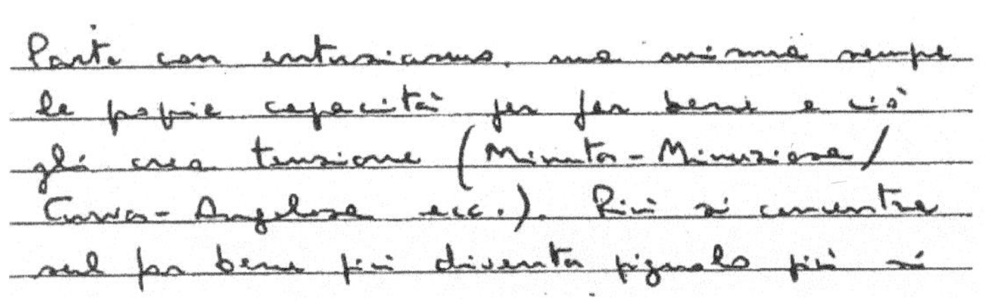

Sample 12

Sample 12 Male age 35 Type 5 a professor of philosophy.

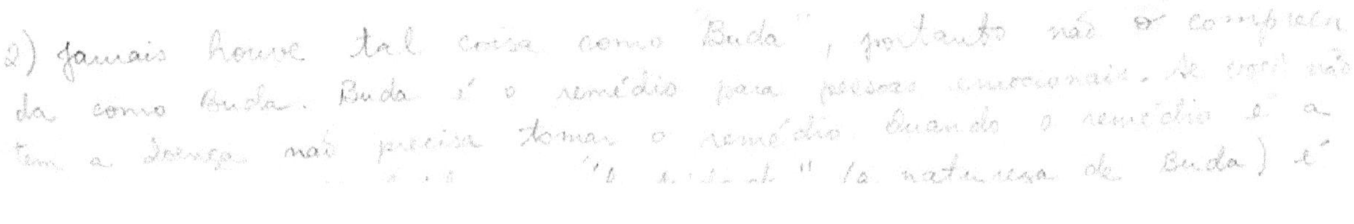

Sample 13

Sample 13 Female – Type 5, Self-Preservation. Written with a pencil

Delicacy of feeling and love for privacy

Surely these traits of a Five are self explanatory, but let's see how they are expressed in HW. Samples 14, 15, 16 are Fives with (almost certainly) Four wings whose dominant traits are precisely sensitiveness, tact and discretion. The context of these HWs always contains *Small Size*, with *Space between Words* that stands out compared to the *Letters Breadth* and the *Space between Letters*. At first sight, these HWs appear to be mainly curvilinear, but looking closer it is angularity that is dominant.

The leading sign is Fine, when a HW contains:

1. Light pressure
2. Graphic accuracy without artificialness
3. A fluid rhythm, but not too fast.

These are signs of sensitiveness pointing at high levels of nervous receptivity.

Fine indicates a refined sense of awareness that touches feelings as well as the thinking; a gift for observation that shuns superficiality and takes refuge in mental order; loyalty and transparency; mental, moral and physical hygiene; appropriateness in communication with focus on what is essential without prying; self-control in expressions of affection; repulsion at vulgarity and overly instinctive reactions; a sense of irony and humor.

A negative side of *Fine* is perfectionism that can degenerate into phobias of contact, and hardship in relating to people that are not of a similar predilection; difficulties in achieving satisfaction in affective matters, because hypersensitivity will cause irrelevant nothings to cause major dramas making cohabitation difficult; underlying sense of superiority; sensibility that avoids impact with reality; touchiness when criticized about performance.

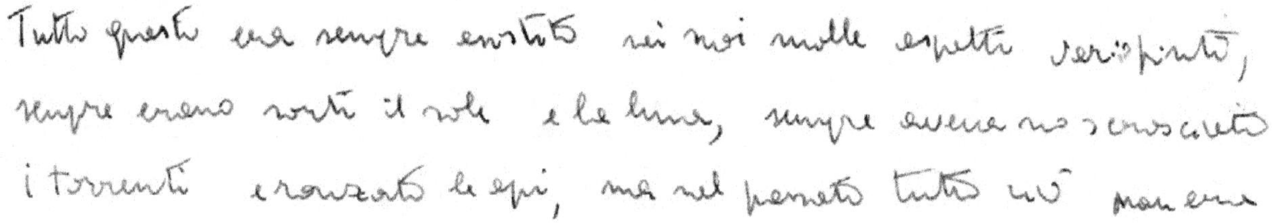

Sample 14

Sample 14 Male age 50 – Type 5.

A pair of Fives. Both writers, in intimate relationship for 30 years, living in separate houses located near each other. They are not yet certain that they are suitable to share the same living space. Both spend a lot of time meditating.

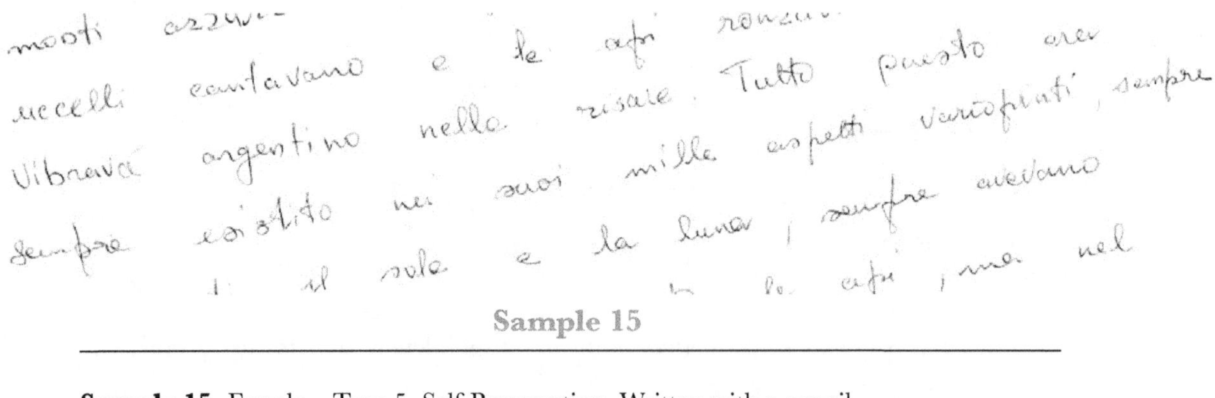

Sample 15

Sample 15 Female – Type 5, Self-Preservation. Written with a pencil

Sample 16 is by a very close friend of this couple who knows how to respect their need for privacy. In this HW we can see many similarities with the scripts of the couple.

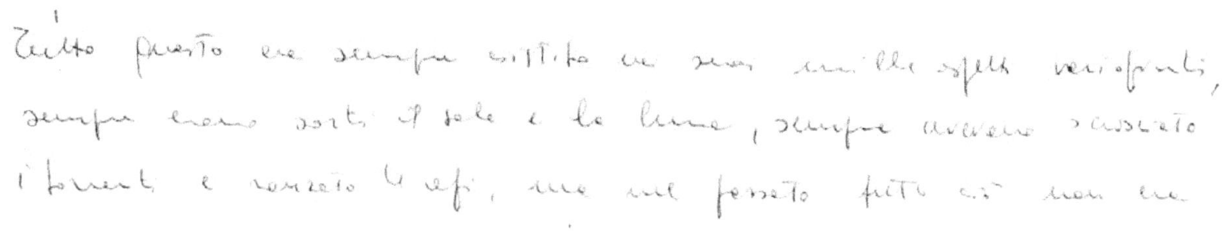

Sample 16

Sample 16 Female age 47 – Type 5.

Two types of Fives

It seems to be a given that the Jungian Introverted-Thinking function is prevalent in Fives, but Naranjo is of the opinion that, "it is definitely in the introverted sensation type that we find the best match for our character". Quoting Jung he says that this type, "May be conspicuous for his calmness and passivity, or for his rational self-control. This peculiarity, which often leads a superficial judgment astray, is really due to his unrelatedness to objects" (*Character and Neurosis*, p. 79)

This is a major distinction and, analyzing handwritings, we find two types of Fives — the Introverted Thinking and the Introverted Sensing— each with its distinct temperament that in characterology are respectively defined as Phlegmatic and Apathetic types.

Externally both types are similar, because both are contained and holding back, but the differences are deeper:
1. The Phlegmatic/Introverted-Thinking (PIT) Five can be mistyped for a type One;
2. the Apathetic/Introverted-Sensing (AIS) Five resembles a type Nine.

The PIT Five is tireless, dutiful, methodical, sober, has dignity, parsimonious rather than avaricious; greed tends to be about autonomy in work and research. Thoughtful, coherent to espoused principles, tolerant but not weak; of even temper, moderate in all things, with rationality ruling passions and instincts. Reserved, but not timid; calm and courteous in a detached way, lacking warmth, appearing indifferent to external events, are some traits that come across as insensitivity.

5

This type is nevertheless active and not castled up in an ivory tower far away from life. Certainly there is some coldness here of feeling and a preference for silence over verbal communication, and then talking rather about things than people; attachment to own ideas to the point of stubbornness; perceives the suffering of others more with reason than with feeling and thus is not exactly a shining example of effusive cordiality.

Introverted Thinking Fives are able to think independently, have good intellectual abilities and love the abstract and theories; passionate about knowledge and method, analysis and scientific research. Even though this type is reserved, they have a rich sense of humor and an inclination to spirituality but live faith as an abstract norm rather than an intimate inner life; their formalism can become skepticism.

It is rare that this type will show impatience, instability, become ostentatious, lose coherence between thought and action, show overt enthusiasm, pliability, warmth, impulsiveness in decisions, or seek public recognition or situations if it involves a scene.

The HW will not:

- contain signs of impatience and spurts due to excitement;
- show sign of being constricted, but rather of sobriety;
- have signs of obvious non-homogeneity
- show exuberance or high speed.

The HW will instead:

- be calm and continuous;
- appear organized and disciplined in the Movement of *Spontaneous Handwriting*;
- use simple and easily legible forms;
- have narrow spaces between letters, but larger spaces between words and lines (an indication of foresight).

Three graphological signs are specifically present: *Minute, Sober, Deliberate*.

We have talked about *Sober* previously, *Minute* was described in association with type One given the similarity of certain traits with type Five. I would like to remind that Minute stands for: "small writing with a high score for *Letter Breadth*, and a flowing movement.

Deliberate is a graphological sign where both *Letter Breadth* and *Spacing between Words* are equally proportioned, while *Spacing between Letters* remains stable around a medium degree. It shows a tendency to reflect, a well-structured mental organization, and strong critical faculties.

(Type Three sometimes is gifted with a good *Triple Width*, that might be mistaken for *Deliberate* in a Five. But *Deliberate* requires a high degree of stability of the signs characteristics, while *Triple Width* can have variations in the proportions of its three components. Side from that, the Three usually also has signs that indicate a desire to be noticed, something completely absent in the Five's HW).

Di recente ho letto una bellissima interpretazione della teoria della relatività, un tentativo di spiegare perché nel nostro mondo si verificano allungamenti e accorciamenti di tempo. Ho scoperto che quello

Sample 17

Sample 17 Male age 32 – Type 5.

Da quando il caldo necessario e la prima leggerezza della pioggia è cresciuta fino a farsi sentire, nell'aria è rimasta una quiete che l'aria del caldo non aveva, una nuova pace a cui l'acqua dava una sua brezza

Sample 18

Sample 18 Male age 46 – Type 5.

In my twilight vision, however, I only
vaguely distinguish what these sudden glass
panes on the surfaces of things let show from

Sample 19

Sample 19 Female age 72 – Type 5, Self-Preservation. Psychologist.

In my twilight vision, however, I only
vaguely distinguish what these sudden
glass panes on the surfaces of things

Sample 20

Sample 20 Female age 72 – Type Five, Self-Preservation. Retired Educator.

Breathing very slowly, and speaking to an another in
a whisper, we pushed open the storeroom door and were
rather astonished and somewhat puzzled to find such a

Sample 21

Sample 21 Male age 25 – Type 5.

my life & managing the stress. I plan to
work past retirement to help with my finances.
I want to deepen my relationship with God
+ allow God time to guide & strengthen

Sample 22

Sample 22 Female age 63 – Type Five.

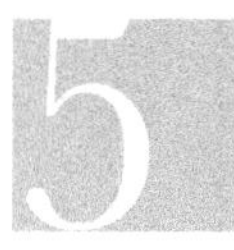

A couple: He a Five w6, she Six w5

La ragazza vive in modo indipendente da diversi anni e nel corso degli ultimi 5 o 6 ha vissuto per periodi abbastanza lunghi in altre città, ogni volta per coltivare interessi nuovi che potessero darle sbocco

Sample 23

Sample 23 Male age 30 – Type 5w6.

Amo il tuo modo di essere scorbutico, orgoglioso, scostante, distaccato, perché mi fa apprezzare mille volte di più i momenti in cui sei dolce, umile, attento e

Sample 24

Sample 24 Female age 26 – Type 6w5.

Samples 23-24 are from a young couple with good affinity. They meet in an intermediate zone between types Five and Six. There are many similarities between the HWs. The *Small Size*, *Moderate Rhythm*, as well as proportions among the various types of width. They obviously could have a profound connection at several levels, both emotionally and intellectually. His handwriting is more stable and decisive. Hers more insecure (this is typical of type Six and we can see it in the inclination of the letters, sign *Wavering*, a script in which groups of letters or entire words show a discordant slant = it means difficulty in making up one's mind, lack of determination, inclined to lean on others. Both HWs show enough intelligence to find common ground needed to remain in harmony.

The Five with the dominant Introverted Sensing function, has the thinking function as auxiliary. Largely static and blocked in the feeling area, but does not appear to suffer from this condition; frequently there is a sense of void and a desire for quietness; difficulty in bringing plans to completion; this Five is often mistaken for a type Nine; gathers data from the senses and bases the thinking activity on that; lacking in imagination; routine bound and taciturn; very preoccupied with safety and security; will break off social relationships over seemingly irrelevant details; social relationships are characterized by awkwardness, timidity, coldness and a tendency to hold back; mistrusts life and fellow man; miserly because thinks never has enough to feel secure.

Intellectually may have a few spikes, but does not feel a need to research, to go deeper, or to theorize; highly reliable for discretion, loyalty and honesty; tends not become a nuisance by holding in all personal problems and disappointments. On the outside this Five truly resembles a Nine, but the difference is that the Nine will seeks contact and relate to others, while the Five will remain detached and shows no concern for the issues of others.

The HW reflects these point;

- First of all there will be a low degree of *Methodically Irregular* (if you observe samples 25 & 26 you will note that the middle zone letters are often of equal height).
- Lack of personality in the graphic expression, simple forms, resembling grammar school writing, impersonal, with precisely placed punctuation.
- Slowness
- Contained and controlled in form and movement
- Feeling of monotony and lack of expansion
- Lack of decisiveness and agility of movement

Apathetic Fives

Originalmente você não reconheceu que o seu conhecimento
inato e sua consciência são seu próprio Buda
e portanto correu a outras partes em busca de Buda.
Portanto você precisou de um Mestre que falasse a

Sample 25

Sample 25 Male – Type 5, Social.

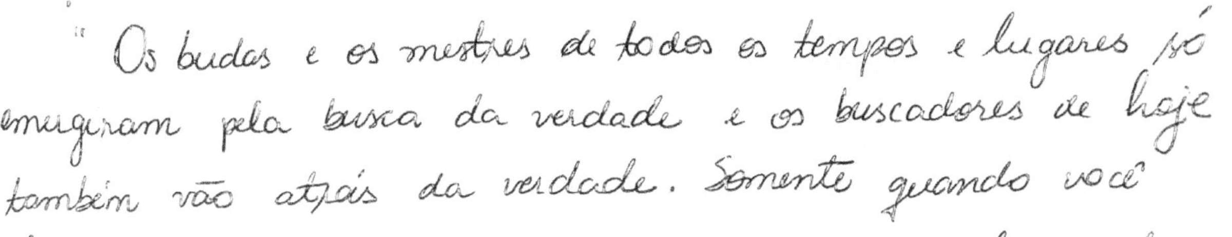

Sample 26

Sample 26 Female – Type 5, Social.

Disintegrated Five

When a Five becomes too much absorbed in their own world, they tend to close off and schizoid tendencies emerge; tortured, obsessive and communicating minimally with the external world; sign *Introverted Mythomania* (this is the technical graphological name for a condition, but graphologists are not be permitted to engage in diagnosis; the term is not indicating a specific pathology). What stand out the most here are the extreme levels of introversion. We can see elements thereof in:

1. Tightness between lines which sometimes may entangle.
2. *Sharp Angles* in the ovals, *Narrow Letter Breadth*, *Narrow Space between Letters* and *Narrow Space between Words.*
3. *Thickened type II.*
4. Generally either *Rightward Slant or Leftward Slant.*

These signs indicate a lack of integration of the various dimensions of the personality; sense of isolation is at the maximum.

The sign *Introverted Mythomania* indicates a compulsive action of internalizing everything in a tortuous ruminating way, with a consequent closing off of the self.

There is confusion between: Security-insecurity, initiative-doubt, aggression-guilt, activity-passivity due to feelings of inferiority, identity or confusion in the sense of "I", opening towards intimacy or shut down, generosity-egocentrism.

There is an extreme psychic and affective contraction, escape from reality and a twisted perception thereof, imaginative fixations, tortuous thinking, mental inability to make distinctions, acute resentment towards life, persecution mania, schizoid tendencies, contradiction between feelings and thoughts and obsessive anxiety.

Samples from 27 to 35 show these tendencies to varying degrees along with a general sense of untidiness in the handwriting.

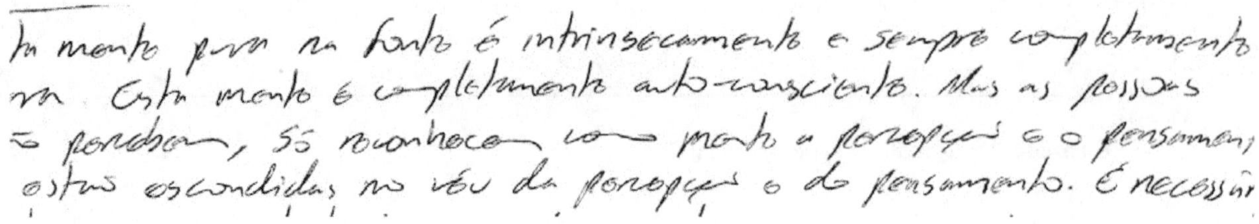

Sample 27

Sample 27 Male – Type 5, Self-Preservation.

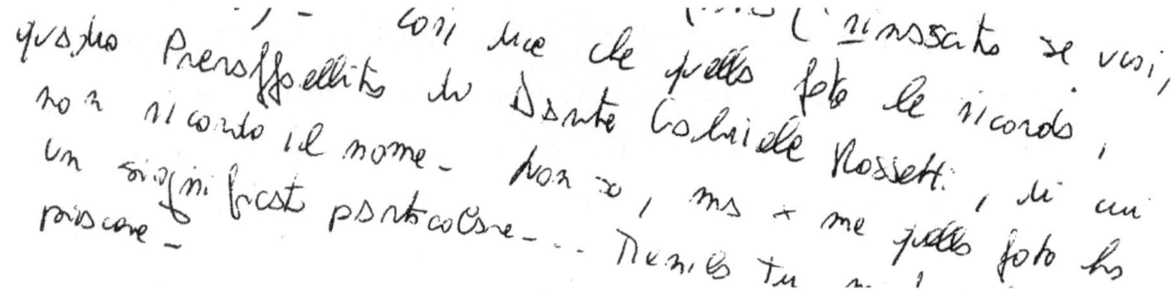

Sample 28

Sample 28 Female age 40 – Type 5.

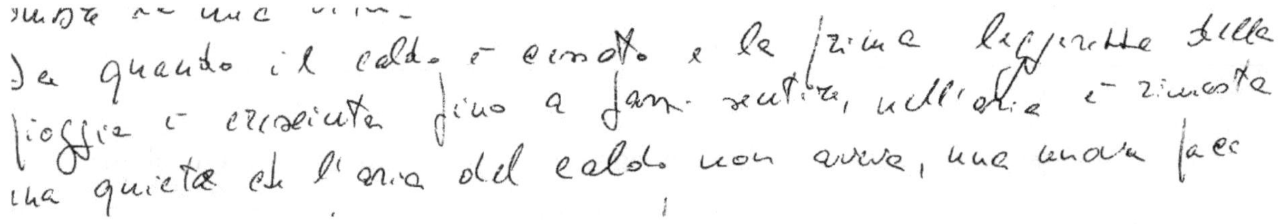

Sample 29

Sample 29 Male age 41 – Type 5, Sexual.

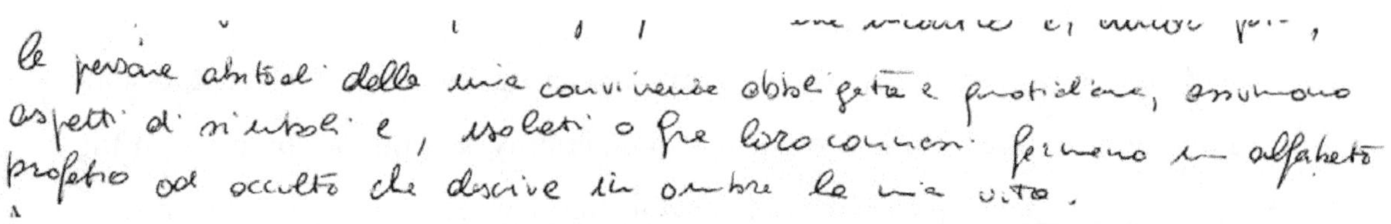

Sample 30

Sample 30 Male age 20 – Type 5w6.

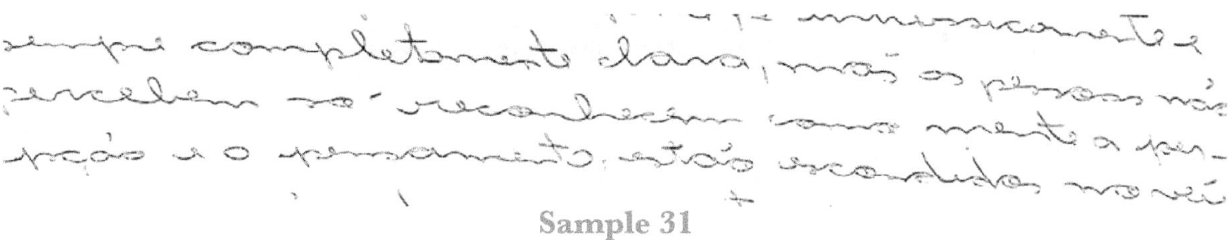

Sample 31

Sample 31 Female – Type 5, Sexual.

Sample 32

Sample 32 Female age 40 – Type 5.

Sample 33

Sample 33 Female age 65 – Type 5.

Sample 34

Sample 34 Male age 36 – Type 5.

Sample 35

Sample 35 Male age 23 – Type 5.

5

A couple of two obsessive personalities, he a Five, she a One

"bombardamento di esami" che la med. ufficiale non risponde per così. È giusto che io debba soffrire, magari compromettendo il lavoro fisico effettuato finora? A settembre,

Sample 36

Sample 36 Male age 50 – Type 5.

Anziché aiutarmi a reagire mi complica la vita. Non voglio un bambino-marito, ma un "vero uomo". Forse non sono ancora diventata una "vera donna".

Sample 37

Sample 37 Female age 45 – Type 1.

Samples 36 & 37 are of a couple, who, unlike the example of the previous couple, have severe conflicts in their relationship. They have been married for several years, and she accuses him of closing himself off in his own world, not giving her enough attention, spending a lot of time in his studio reading and studying even during their free time. He accuses her of being not soft and flexible and to nag him continuously. The conflict has come to a head and the couple is in therapy. From the perspective of the Enneagram we can see that this is an encounter of two different forms of rigidity: that of a One and of a Five. They have difficulty meeting at a level of empathy that is mutually nurturing. Each obsessively defends their own position, unable to change their mental schemas and attitudes. Even though they have deep affection for each other, their dissatisfaction is intense. It is difficult for them to communicate at a level of feeling and tenderness.

The wings of Five

Samples 38 & 39 are examples of American HWs of a Five with a Six wing and a Five with a Four wing. In sample 38 the influence of the Six wing is clear. The basic characteristics are still those of a Five, as for example small middle zone of the letters, angularity of the ovals and a reduced expansion horizontally, i.e. in some endings of words the letters appear crunched together - (the horizontal expansion symbolize the degree of reaching out toward others). Otherwise, the writing is not at all restrained because there are many elongations in the upper and in the lower zones. These elongations are disproportionately large compared to the other letters. We have here a higher level of pride in one's own intellect and a streak of exhibitionism that wants respect from others. Fives generally have a very neutral imagination, whereas here we see a tendency towards projection typical of the Six (projections which are based on fear are largely imagined). Without a doubt the intellectual ability is elevated while emotions are less held back and hence the writing is not as objectively detached compared to a pure Five.

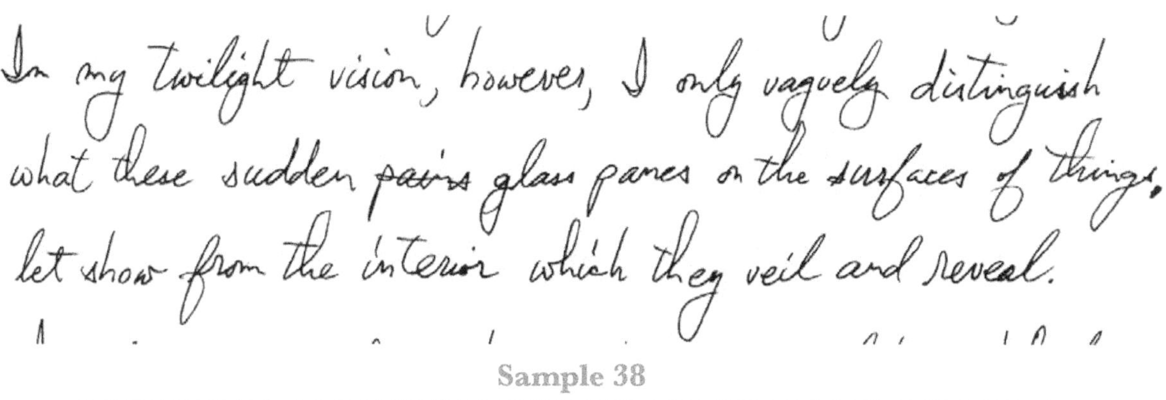

Sample 38 Male age 51 – Type 5w6, Sexual (Counterphobic).

It is always difficult to analyzing printing style handwritings which are quite common in the USA. Sample 39. The writer is certainly a Five with a Four wing; a long time scholar of the Enneagram and without a doubt certain of his type.

Observing this handwriting it would appear that some typical traits of the Five are absent: for example, the large *Spaces Between Words*, as well as the size of the writing is not characteristically small. Detachment and confinement are expressed by the choice of printing over cursive and by the sign *Detached*.

It is difficult to say that this is an *Introverted Thinking* type, and he is more likely *Introverse Sensing*. We see that from the pressure of the writing which is fairly rich, the tight space between words, the average size of the HW and the low level of the sign *Methodically Irregular*. In fact a careful measure of the size of the midrange letters shows that they are often of the same height.

This HW is certainly of an introverted person, but not one that is cold and detached from others. At the same time, this is not a person who will share personal confidentialities easily, but one who will maintain their privacy. We can deduce the influence of the Four wing and the sexual subtype given that, even though using all-caps, the HW is neither stable nor homogenous. Feelings, although contained in their expression, are very influential in the writer's life. Note the waviness of the baseline. Finally, the writing is more curvilinear than angular. And it is Anima rather than Animus in this personality that makes him more open, warm, available and involved than would be a pure type Five.

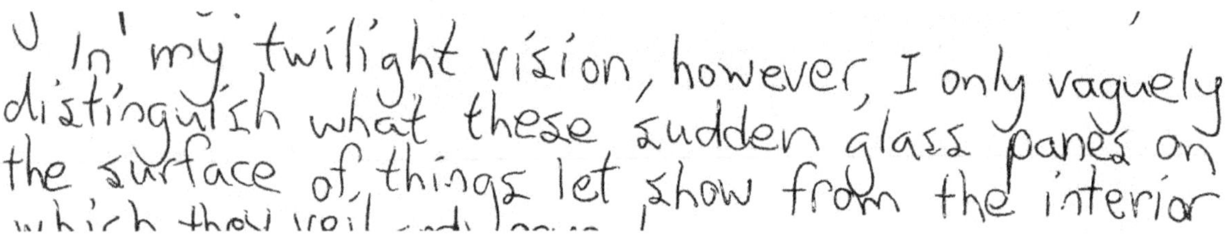
In my twilight vision, however, I only vaguely
distinguish what these sudden glass panes on
the surface of things let show from the interior

Sample 39

Sample 39 Male age 48 – Type 5w4, Sexual – Left-handed, an Enneagram scholar

For graphological definitions and interpretations I used the following texts:

PALAFERRI N., *L'indagine grafologica e il metodo morettiano*, Istituto Grafologico Moretti, Urbino, 1986.

PALAFERRI N., *Dizionario Grafologico*, Libreria "G. Moretti, Urbino, 1993.

PALAFERRI N., *Tipologia umana, caratterologia e grafologia*, Libreria "G. Moretti, Urbino, 1999.

TORBIDONI-ZANIN, *Grafologia* (testo teorico pratico), IV ed., Editrice La Scuola, Brescia, 1986.

HANDWRITING AND ENNEATYPE SIX

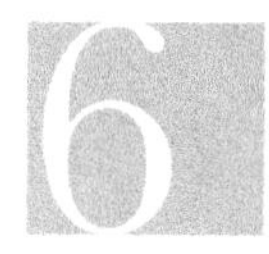

To analyze someone's handwriting (HW) requires applying a rational scientific process that calls for measuring and classifying signs as well as placing yourself into an intuitive, empathetic rapport with the writing itself. This makes graphology a discipline that is on the edge between science and art.

It is not easy to explain what is meant by an empathetic relationship to a person's handwriting. In essence, it involves entering into a relationship with the synthesis of all the graphic elements on the page and the expression of the totality of the personality of the human being. To understand a handwriting deeply it is necessary to perceive the movement underlying it—in other words, the expression of the brain that did the writing—of which the hand was only an instrument.

Anxiety and Identity

If you were tracing the graphic movement of a type Six—you can try that by imitating the gestures that the writers hand had performed on the piece of paper—you may start noticing an intense feeling of anxiety. Generally speaking, the HW of the Six is the one containing the greatest contradictions and the most obvious "non-homogeneity" of all nine types.

Such contradictions are shown by several graphic elements that we can find in the HW of the same person:

- Non-homogeneity of inclination: the extensions are leaning to the right, left, or remain straight.
- Non-homogeneity in the size of letters and spaces between words.
- Non-homogeneity of form: the same letter in one part of the writing is formed differently than in another part. This conveys a visible impression of internal agitation.
- Non-homogeneity of the connections between the letters.
- Non-homogeneity in the relationships of the two basic dimensions of handwriting, the curvilinear and the angular: in some parts of the same page one might be prevalent, in another part the other.
- Non-homogeneity of pressure: sometimes light, sometimes pronounced (always

on the same page); we rarely find the sign *Pure* (clear, well-defined strokes without congestion).

- Non-homogeneity of speed: on the same page, the rhythm of movement keeps changing in an unpredictable pattern.
- Non-homogeneity of concavity of the extensions: concaved towards the right (sign of surrender) or concaved to the left (sign of rebellion), straight (sign of resistance).

This group of characteristics should not be considered negatively: the HW is simply reflecting the inner nature of the writer. The writing of the Six is characterized by ambivalence, doubt in self and others, dependency and a struggle for independence, suspicion and/or fanatical credulity, and oscillation between excessive accommodation and aggressiveness.

Inevitably present is the sense of anxiety and restlessness that pervades all expressions of the type Six—this impedes the best use of the most important qualities of the Six: intuition and imagination.

Anxiety is connected to difficulty in maintaining a stable identity and an autonomous self-image due to all sorts of exaggerated evaluations of external authority. It is well known that type Six employs a variety of strategies when reacting towards those in power: seeking protection and warmth, rigidly following rules, or rebelling in a counter-phobic way.

I have chosen non-homogeneity as the most striking characteristic of the Six. Ironically, in some variations of type Six, probably as a reaction to the multitude of contradictions and in a process of compensation, the writer may become very rigid and authoritarian. In these cases, the HW will present a higher degree of order, in the sense of being more formal and inhibited, and can be easily mistaken for the HW of a type One. Such a HW may contain many obsessive traits.

As the HW of the Six is characterized by non-homogeneity/rigidity, it highlights also traits that are lacking in the Six, namely *tranquil flexibility*— a trait that cannot be identified with a "warm dependence on authority," and that would give a Six the possibility of a stable sense of identity. Instead, very often we can witness a process of self-invalidation that Naranjo describes in *Character and Neurosis*. It is as if the type Six does not give himself the possibility, probably out of fear, to stop and see who he is and then act accordingly. Anxiety trumps most existential manifestations. It would be precisely overcoming this deep restlessness that would allow the Six to be transformed.

Ambivalence and Identity

Entering into the handwriting and looking at the most general characteristics in a Six we find the sign *Wavering*, a "script in which groups of letters or entire words show a discordant slant." It is the main sign indicating ambivalence and doubt when facing the need to make a decision.

It is as if the nervous system of those with the sign *Wavering* acts on conflicting information transmitted to the muscles of the hand, causing confusion as to which neuro-muscular group shall be used to form the words. Ambivalence already manifests at the level of the brain. As a matter of fact, different parts of the brain and different groups of muscles are engaged when the hand is ordered to slant the writing to the right, left or keep it upright. When the brain signals shift around, the information transmitted changes the writing on the same page presenting an image of indecisiveness and hesitation.

At the level of personality, thinking, feeling and will are not line up in the same direction in a unified way. This causes an accumulation of tension, blaming others for one's own inability to be resolute and spontaneous - the writer is simply too preoccupied and busy doubting self and others.

Samples 1-5 show a high degree of *Wavering*.

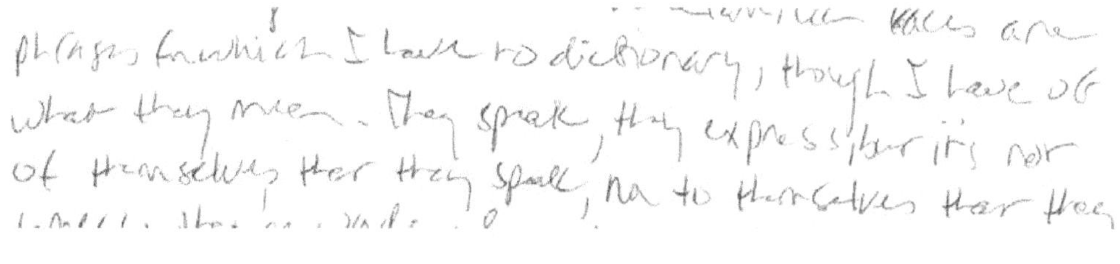

Sample 1

Sample 1 Female age 51 – Type Six, Self-Preservation – Left-handed

Sample 2

Sample 2 **Female age 36 – Type Six**

Sample 3

Sample 3 Male – Type Six, Sexual

Sample 4

Sample 4 Female age 35 – Type Six, Sexual

Sample 5

Sample 5 Male – Type Six, Self-Preservation. This HW has a combination of the sign *Wavering* with a high degree of *Twisted* (extensions of the letters that bend abruptly). *Wavering* indicates doubt, while *Twisted* points at an inclination to be obsessively suspicious.

The positive aspect of *Wavering* lies in mental and emotional mobility. Although somewhat disorganized, it can form the basis for a good intuitive ability that at times borders on premonition. *Wavering* also means thoughtfulness (always with a dose of anxiety) and making choices only after a long period of weighing all the pros and cons making the decisions taken cautious, prudent, and responsible.

Wavering is found often in the HW of those who are well disposed to listening to advice. This is a quality valued in professional or executive positions and is a refreshing divergence from those who do not listen and stubbornly follow their own inclination.

Since *Wavering* is a sign of an apprehensive and anxious character, it is accompanied by feelings of apprehension about some vague sense of danger and concern for one's own safety. It is an indicator of the internal contrast between feelings, desires, impulses and thoughts—in short, a lack of simplicity. That's why many students of the Enneagram consider the Six to be the most complex of all the Enneagram types.

There are other signs in a HW that indicate ambivalence. In sample 6 we can see the left margin drifting visibly to the right. If we could see the entire page, it occasionally moves back to the left only to resume drifting to the right again. This is a form of anxiety, indecision, an urge to flight. The writer does not stop to face what is "behind," the past, the family history, etc. (represented in the left margin) and in order not to face past events she is fleeing into the future. Her difficulty is in remaining calmly focused in the present.

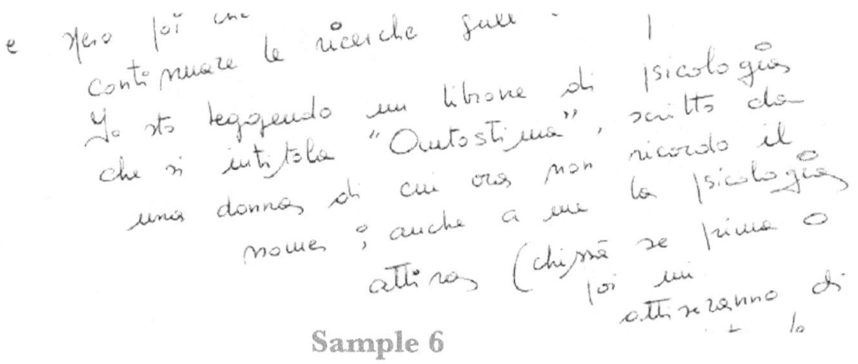

Sample 6

Sample 6 Female age 39, Type Six

Sample 7a is the HW of a counter-phobic Six. We know that this type loves to show force and strength, but also has a propensity for beauty. Looking only at the text of this HW we would assume that it belongs to a personality that is fairly self-contained, sober, profound, intuitive, and restless, but on the whole, balanced. However, sample 7b, the signature, is dramatically different from the handwriting—it is amplified, with huge vertical strokes resembling a wall separating first and last names. This shows a leaning towards aggressiveness along with an imagination and tendency to projection that leave little room for an authentic relationship with others. It may be difficult to reason with this person. Without a doubt he has an interesting personality including a good dose of aspects of type Three, such as vanity. The ambivalence here consists in the sharp contradiction between social behavior, which is mild and thoughtful (as expressed in the body of the writing), and a grandiose megalomaniacal view of self (signature).

estan apegados a las formas. No saben que deteniendo su pensamiento conceptual y olvidando su angustia el Buda se les

Sample 7a

Sample 7a Male, Type Six, Sexual

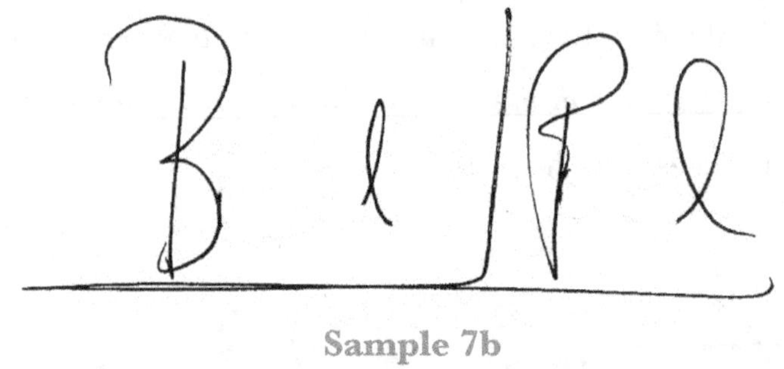

Sample 7b

Sample 7b partial signature (to protect identity) of HW 7a

Sample 8 has all sorts of non-homogeneity. This person is extremely generous and accommodating and has a strong tendency towards dependency. The result is ambivalence and a need for a strong protective external figure as a point of reference. At the same time the writer is aware of being strongly influenced and constantly struggles to maintain autonomy.

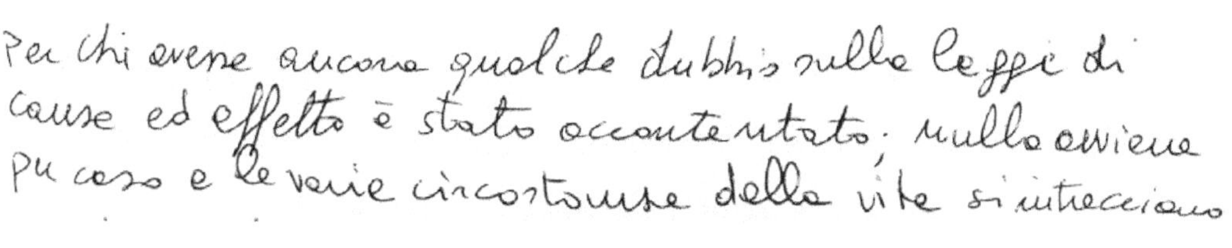

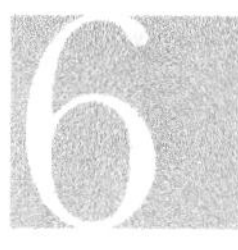

Sample 8

Sample 8 Male age 33, Type Six, Self-Preservation

Another form of ambivalence is seen in the ever-changing shapes of the letters. Sample 9 is an Italian HW using a printing style. In spite of that, the writing is not easily legible. Here too we have the sign *Wavering* and non-homogeneity of pressure.

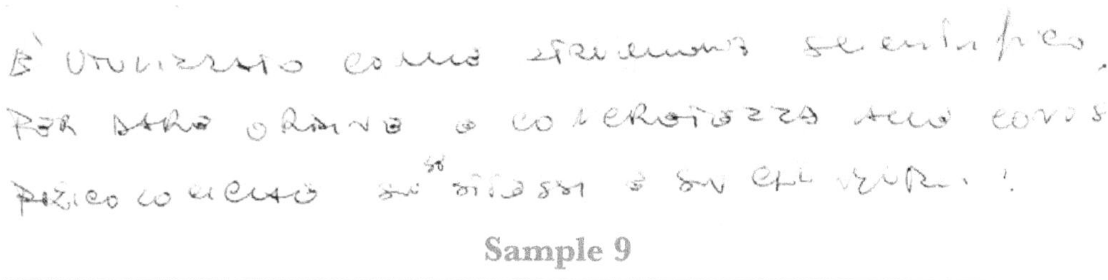

Sample 9

Sample 9 Male age 36, Type Six

Imagination and Identity

In the HW of the self-preservation type Six, who tends to be more endomorphic, warm, and generous in behavior, we can see the underlying presence of anxiety. It is expressed by the sign *Wavering* and several signs of non-homogeneity. We can also see different strategies used in an attempt to overcome contradictions and fear. Fear of what? Knowing yourself. One such strategy includes adopting an attitude of openness without aggression toward others, similar to that of a type Two—or a compensation by amplifying the imagined self-worth and especially by having an inflated view of one's own instinctual drives (for example, when small signals of inner or outer aggressiveness are interpreted as real aggression, or sexual urges are imagined as real acting out).

The imaginary inflation at the level of thinking, feeling, or instincts is not the same as outward expansion (which is more typical of type Two). Indeed, amplification is an internal process that exaggerates one's inner sensations, such as, being very afraid of something insignificant or suspicious of others over nothing;

but also having a distorted view of your own needs, including that for protection. In any case, amplification will distort an accurate evaluation of any situation. Naranjo calls it a "combination of uncertainty mixed with over-valuation of self."

This inner process is expressed by the signs: *Inflated, Large Size, Narrow Space between Words, Curved, Flexuous*.

The sign ***Inflated*** is when letters or some part of a letter are bulging horizontally or vertically. As mentioned in previous articles, the shapes of letters give us a hint of how the writers feel and think about themselves. Obviously this sign indicates a form of over-compensation of the identity of the "I." It is the imagination that plays a dominant part here: as if the writer feels a need to puff up in order to appear bigger. *Inflated* is the exact opposite sign as *Sober*, which is typical for the type Five. On one hand it indicates liveliness, vitality, and warmth because it contains the signs *Curved, Flexuous*, and *Large Size* making this person appear friendly and accommodating, but underneath is a fear of lack of self-worth, of not being properly heard. Were it not so, there would not have been a need to inflate in the first place. An overly vivid imagination can be a resource and contribute to creativity, but of a different kind than for example a type Four who tends to be more focused inward compared to the Six who directs intuition and imagination outward, scanning for danger and for hidden agendas. In brief, amplification of letters is an energy suspended in the realm of idealization and its contents do not bleed over directly into relationships.

Often with Sixes and particularly the self-preservation variety, we find *Inflated* along with *Narrow Space between Words*. In type Five we have seen the typically large space between words, whereas the Six has often a "densification" of the graphic mass. This is interpreted as a lack in rhythm, where fullness and emptiness are not harmoniously alternating; at the level of personality it creates the impression of a lack of psychological breathing room, i.e., anxiety. *Narrow Space between Words* is responsible for an impression of airlessness in the HW, and, when accompanied by *Inflated*, is one of the main graphological sign for projection. Together they denote an anxiety in the writer that does not permit a quiet examination of a situation, as it reduces critical analysis in favor of imaginary flights. In the same way, depth of feelings also is influenced. It is important for people with this sign to develop patience and to accurately examine situations so they can avoid projection and amplification.

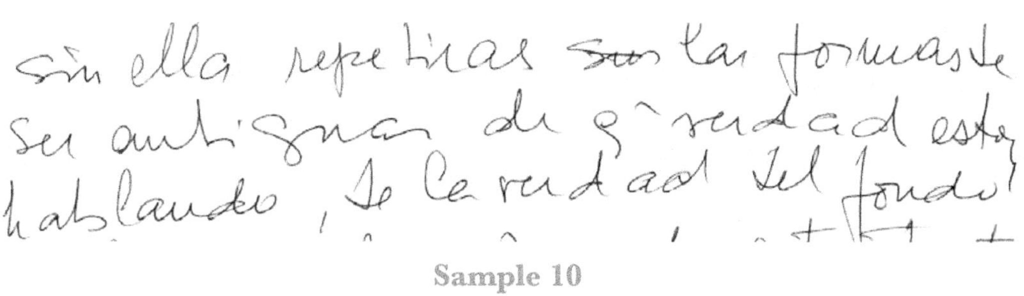

Sample 10

Sample 10 Female – Type Six, Self-Preservation. The HW shows the signs: *Curved, Flexuous, Large Size, Narrow between Words, Inflated, Wavering.*

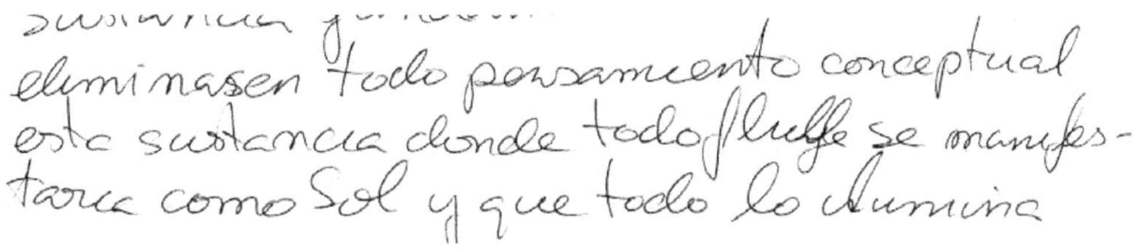

Sample 11

Sample 11 Female – Type Six, Self-Preservation. The HW shows the signs: *Curved, Flexuous, Large Size, Narrow between Words, Inflated, Wavering.*

Sample 12

Sample 12 Female age 44 – Type Six, Self-Preservation. The HW shows the signs: *Curved, Flexuous, Large Size, Not Homogeneous in the Space between Words, Inflated, Wavering, Rising.*

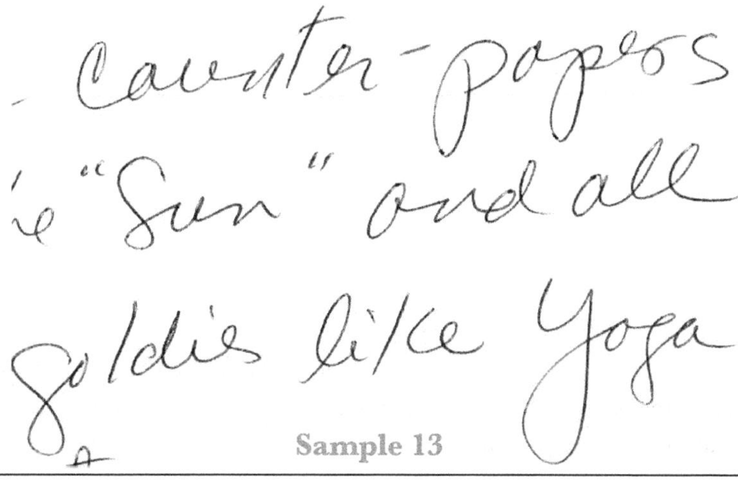

Sample 13

Sample 13 Female, Type Six, Sexual. The HW shows the signs: *Curved, Flexuous, Large Size, Not Homogeneous in the space between Words, Inflated, Rising.*

In my twilight vision, however, I only vaguely distinguish what these glass panes on the surfaces of things let show from the interior which they veil and reveal.

Sample 14

Sample 14 Female age 50 – Type Six, Social. HW showing Narrow between *Words, Narrow between Letters, Inflated* (see arrows), *Entangled.*

There are days when everyone I meet appears as symbol, and individually or together they form a prophetic or occult writing that describes my life in

Sample 15

Sample 15 Female age 49 – Type Six. HW showing *Narrow between Words, Narrow between Letters, Inflated, Entangled.*

oli infuocate forsfor
è un'abitudine il tem
? Volti grigi in processi

Sample 16

Sample 16 Male age 30 – Type Six, Social. A "strange" HW, stretching upwards towards fantasy and imagination (the writer is something of an inventor), but seems to lose touch with reality and with others (lack of horizontal expansion, few connections between letters). The extensions are disproportionately long (sign *Inflated*) compared to the mid-range letters and occasionally entangled/overlapping.

The "Hard" Six

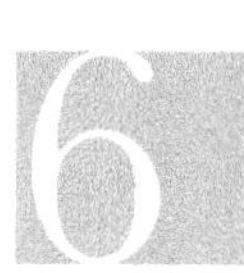

The type Six with a mesomorphic physique tends to be more aggressive and they can have obsessive-paranoid tendencies. Any trace of ambivalence seems to be dissolved in favor of a fanaticism that leaves no room for doubt. This can lead to imagining enemies where none exist, or to have grossly overestimated expectations—fear of, or faith in—the power of an external authority or group.

In this case the HW loses all softness and becomes rigid—resembling the HW of a type One—with high pressure throughout, regardless if it's the ascending or descending strokes, a symptom of continuous tension and vigilance. If we were to give a name to the feeling tone of such HW it would be "wooden."

The HW is more angular than with the self-preservation or social types, the writing looks "breathless," due to a tightening of spaces between words. There is no effort to make the HW aesthetically pleasing or rhythmic—too much worry about authority—the writer is of a hierarchical mindset, not asking too many questions, either following a higher authority blindly, or if in a power position, demanding that underlings follow without questioning.

The characteristics associated with the sign *Wavering* are gone, replaced by the hardness of the sign ***Parallel*** where the "script shows rigidity of the upper and lower extensions, which present identical slants." This is a sign of cold personality, strict, suspicious and a stickler for rules and principles; organized, more inclined to act than to ask why. Will trumps personal feelings, which are relegated to the background, ignoring one's own intuition (which might be totally opposed to the rules followed), as well as expressing creativity.

Projection and flights of imagination are truly a stumbling block to reason. In case of *Leftward Slant*, suspiciousness is at a maximum and repression of spontaneity even more thorough—with an obsessive inability to trust oneself. We need to keep in mind that at the base of this rigidity and aggressiveness there is always anxiety and fear of being punished.

Samples 17-18-19-20 indicate distinct obsessive-paranoid tendencies. The HW is dark and heavy, very angular, with *Straight Extensions*, very little *Space between Words*, rigid, *Right Slant*, with several *Strokes of Mythomania* (explained below), *Inflated* (sample 20), graphic movement lacking breathing room.

Sample 17

Sample 17 Female age 65 – Type Six

Sample 18

Sample 18 Male – Type Six, Self-Preservation

Sample 19

Sample 19 Male age 50 – Type Six, Sexual

Sample 20

Sample 20 Male – Type Six, Sexual

Sample 21

Sample 21 Type Six, Sexual. HW with *Leftward Slant, Narrow between Words*, not *Fluent* and *Non-Homogeneous Pressure.*

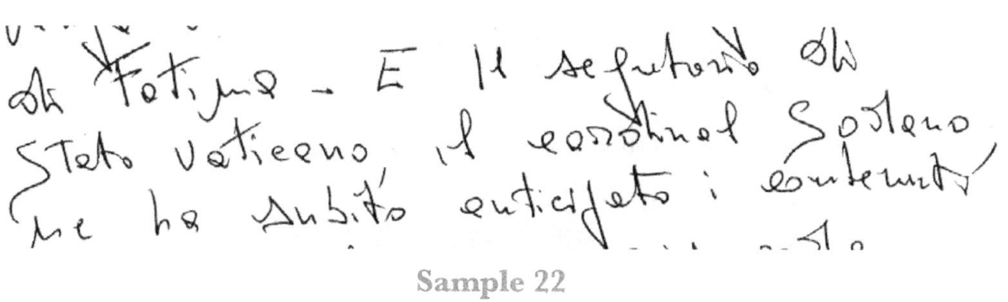

Sample 22

Sample 22 Male – Type Six, Sexual. A woody HW, un-coordinated, *Disconnected, Entangled,* with *Strokes of Mythomania.*

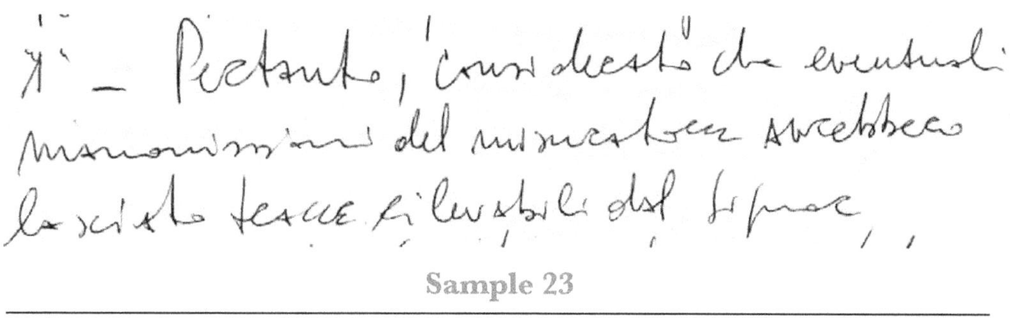

Sample 23

Sample 23 Male age 45 – Type Six, Sexual. HW dark, high pressure, hard to read, *Angular*, little *Space between Letters*, non-homogeneous. May appear at first as dynamic, but actually indicates anxiety, suspiciousness, and authoritarianism.

The Paranoid Six

If we follow this inclination to even more pathological levels we come to projection that is highly accusatory of others. Here the fixation of the type Six is quite consolidated. The sign indicating this is *Strokes of Mythomania*:

- Final strokes at the end of words go to the upper right, higher than the last letter.
- The T-bars are diagonal pointing upwards to the right.
- Alternatively, the final strokes at the end of words sink below the base line that loop backwards and could extend as far as under the next word.
- Or, final stokes of the words or letters extend downwards, perpendicular to the baseline, straight and pronounced.

The psychological meaning is: being fixated on an idea and giving a lot of mental space to imaginary facts. There is no space here to give adequate explanation of the complex symbolism behind this type of stroke, nor the motivations and their

meaning. It is enough to understand that in the West writing proceeds from left to right and that the relationship between letters and words symbolizes the way in which the writer relates to others. If the writing does not flow normally from left to right, with end strokes that continue to the right, i.e., towards the other, and instead, the stroke go either upwards, downwards or is strangled off, it means that the attention goes towards an idea or something imaginary instead of objectively being focused on the present situation—hence mythomania.

Samples 24, 25, 26, 27, aside from being somewhat rigid and exercising heavy pressure, show several strokes of mythomania (see arrows).

Sample 24

Sample 24 Female – Type Six

Sample 25

Sample 25 Female age 38 – Type Six, Sexual

Sample 26

Sample 26 Male age 50 – Type Six, Self-Preservation

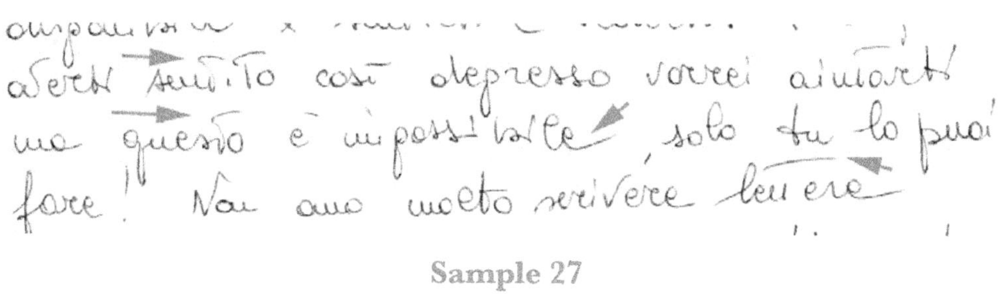

Sample 27 Female age 34 – Type Six, Self-Preservation

To this rather hard and rigid type Six two other "varieties of Six" are a counterpoint: one is timid and indecisive or hesitant, the other is more adaptive. The adaptive Six is conforming, respecting traditions and institutions, looking to them for protection, and is devotedly dedicated.

The Timid Six

The timid Six is constitutionally and temperamentally more ectomorphic with a tendency towards dependency and may look like a Nine (for the way they tend to keep a low profile) or resemble a Four (for their sensitivity and delicateness). The passion of fear is more visible here and the demand for protection more evident; however there is no mechanism of over-compensation. In fact, the size of the writing is somewhat smaller and the distribution of the graphic mass is more spacious. Thoughtfulness and anxiety are manifested as an inner disturbance, without the need for rebellion or strict adherence to institutional norms.

The dominant sign in this case is ***Hesitant***:

- The graphic rhythm is somewhat insecure and a little contracted.
- The letters tend to curl back upon themselves (lack of tension and a fear of acting).
- The lines undulate.
- The final strokes of the words barely poke out, as if they are afraid to expand towards space.

Hesitant is the sign of insecurity, doubt, and scruples indicating low vital energy. The dynamic impulse towards expansion is quite low and the consequence is indecision in action. Such hesitation to act is conducive to reflection but of the

doubting and speculating kind. There is also timidity, a difficulty in taking initiative and an inclination towards submissiveness. Here too the basis of the problems is an uncertain sense of self-worth and identity.

On the positive side, this personality is not aggressive, docile, reserved, prudent, and shows understanding towards others - a modest person who avoids exhibitionism. On the negative side, a lack of self-confidence stands out along with excessive self-criticism and guilt, a lack of autonomy and initiative, timidity, doubtfulness, and pessimism.

Samples 28, 29, 30, 31 show the sign *Hesitant*.

È utilizzato come strumento scientifico, per dare ordine e concretezza alle conoscenze psicologiche su se stessi e sugli altri: un filo di Arianna nel labirinto del carattere

Sample 28

Sample 28 Male age 42 – Type Six, Self-Preservation

Da quando il caldo è cessato e la prima leggerezza della pioggia è cresciuta fino a farsi sentire, nell'aria è rimasta una quiete che l'aria del caldo non aveva, una

Sample 29

Sample 29 Male age 40 – Type Six, Self-Preservation

Da quando il caldo è cessato e la prima leggerezza della pioggia è cresciuta fino a farsi sentire, nell'aria è rimasta una quieta che l'aria del caldo non aveva, una nuova

Sample 30

Sample 30 Male age 48 – Type six, Self-Preservation

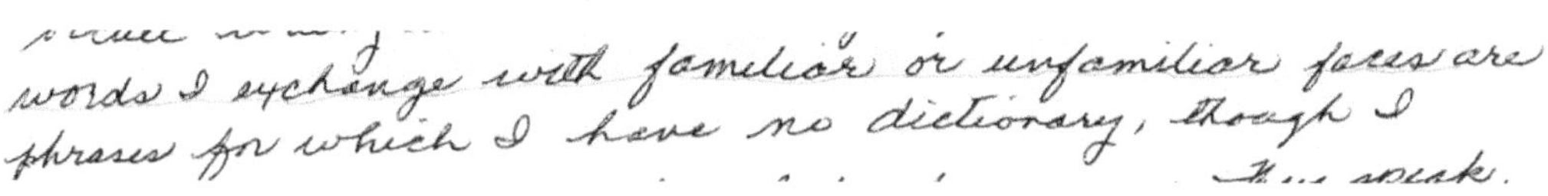

Sample 31

Sample 31 Female age 61 – Type Six, Self-Preservation. Uncertain and hesitant progression on the baseline.

The Adaptive Six

The most dominant traits of the adaptive Six are a sense of duty and dedication. In this case the HW does not show excessive signs of *Wavering*, a particular compensating rigidity, or hesitation out of timidity. A sense of belonging, especially to family, is very pronounced. It is difficult for this type to consider their own autonomy outside of an institution. These people are characteristically highly reliable and loyal, and perform their duties with dedication, responsibility, and generosity. They act like glue in a well-functioning society. Their HW tends to follow scholastic style (respectful of tradition and avoiding any form of deviation from it). It does not have particularly creative graphic movement, and the energy is focused on the performance of everyday duties. The HW would therefore be ordinary and of regular size. See samples 32, 33, and 34.

This type is at risk of uncritically identifying too much with the values of the group. The challenge here is not to lose sight of personal and intimate goals and not to renounce them with an excuse such as "thinking about the family."

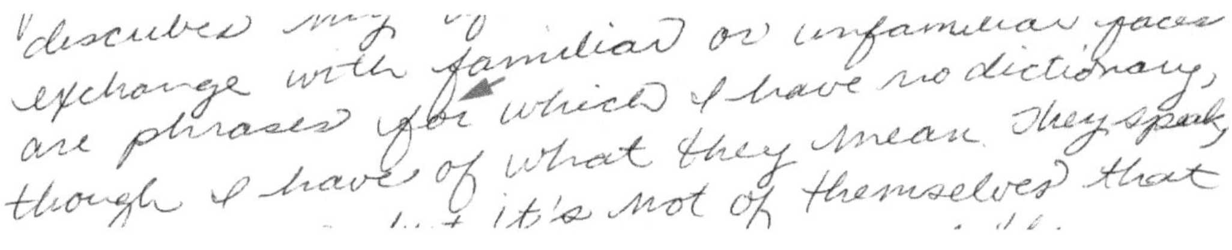

Sample 32

Sample 32 Female age 41 – Type Six, Self-Preservation

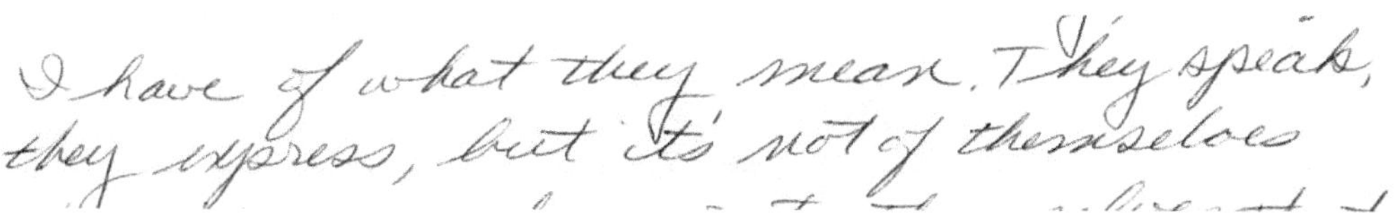

Sample 33

Sample 33 Female age 62 – Type Six, Social

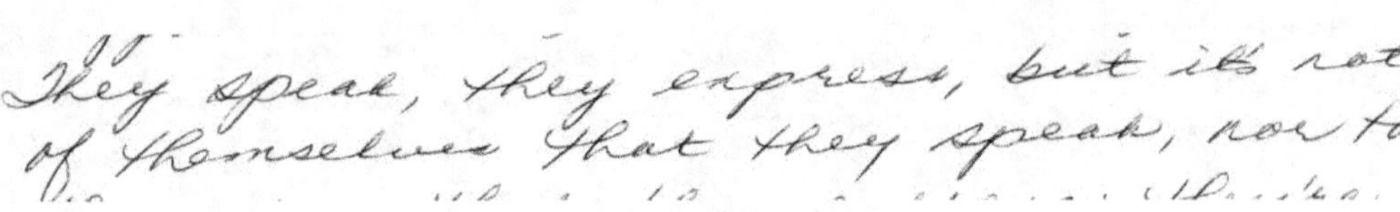

Sample 34

Sample 34 Female age 69 – Type Six, Social

Samples 35 and 36 look very different but share the sign *Wavering* which is typical of the Six, indicating underlying indecisiveness. But here we can see the different influence of the wings. Sample 35 with a Five wing writes in a rather literal and essential way with ample space between words and small. He seems to inclined towards analysis, introversion and intellectualism with a hint of suspiciousness.

Sample 36 type Six w7, has forms that are more amplified and rounded; there is more vitality, expansion, and pizzazz. However, the imagination (*Inflated*) would influence rational thinking. This person is obviously more extroverted than sample 35, the type Six w5.

Sample 35

Sample 35 Male – Type Six w5, Self-Preservation

Sample 36

Sample 36 Male age 60 – Type Six w7, Social

Six in couples relationship

Samples 37 and 38 are remarkably similar. Both writings are dominated by non-homogeneity, typical of type Six. In spite of their emotional variability, this couple may reach a good level of mutual understanding. It would however be difficult for them to form a united front communicating a sense of stability, for example, when dealing with their children. These two seek safety and protection from their insecurities by seeking closeness, which shuts them off in a world of their own. The outer world is seen as a threatening entity that needs to be defended against by sealing themselves off in a familial cocoon.

Husband and wife, with two children:

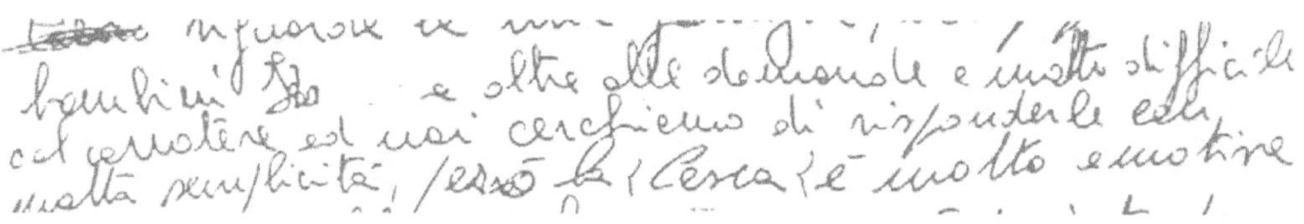

Sample 37

Sample 37 Male age 43 – Type Six; and

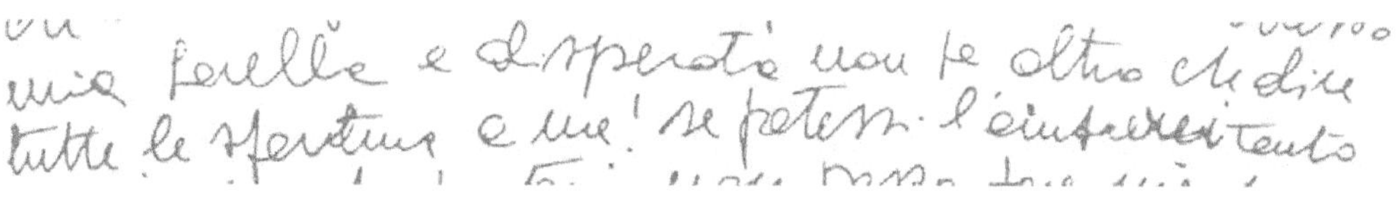

Sample 38

Sample 38 Female age 39 – Type Six

Samples 39 and 40; she a type Eight, an important career woman, finds in the sweetness and passivity of her Six partner a space where she needs not fight and be competitive. He shows a high level of docility, rather effeminate, with a tendency to be dependent, while her aggressiveness is more masculine. As this compensation seems to be working and lasting, it appears to be compatible. He needs to develop more autonomy and lean less on his partner while she needs to develop more openness and to show her vulnerabilities, even if it means exposing herself to the risk of confrontation with a more autonomous and self-assured man without worrying about competition.

Couple, engaged to be married

In questi anni mi accorgo che a frequente tendo a ritornare indietro ed ad apporre delle correzioni alle lettere precedenti

Sample 39

Sample 39 Male age 41 – Type Eight; and

Eppure, a chi si vuole bene, e' bello a volte svelare come eravamo.

Sample 40

Sample 40 Male age 38 – Type Six

Sample 41 and 42 both are very reliable and can count on the loyalty and trust they have developed over time. He is more rigid and determined (sign *Parallel*) and finds her softness soothing. She is a little more insecure (*Wavering*) and finds in him stability. Both know that they can deeply trust the other. Neither of them uses emotional manipulation because there is a respect for the rules and a good level of seriousness.

Married couple

è trascorso un bel po' di tempo da quando ho iniziato tuo tema di uscita, ma è stato assolutamente necessari

Sample 41

Sample 41 Male age 54 – Type One; and

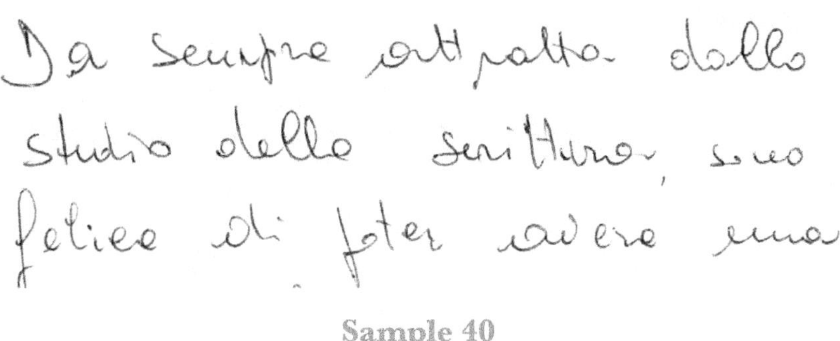

Sample 40 Male age 38 – Type Six

Final Notes

A close look at the handwriting samples in this article reveals that for the most part they show more Curvilinearity than Angularity. For a graphologist this means that the Six gives more importance to social belonging than to the affirmation of their own personality. This may have originated from insecurity, but it makes the Six extraordinarily vigilant and perceptive of the motivations of others. And not only perceptive of others, but often warm and sensitive towards them—and very sweet. Fear is a passion that makes it unlikely to be indifferent towards others and it can make the Six psychologically solicitous and present.

Every (sixish) quality has its counterpoint: fear - courage; doubtfulness - fanaticism; insecurity - loyalty; uncertainty - reliability. Aside from that, each quality, good or bad, can have a low and a high side. For example, fear can be incapacitating or lead to caution then prudence and finally to far-reaching premonitions. Doubtfulness can go from paralysis, to caution, or turn into an antidote to arrogant self-assured cockiness; loyalty can range from slavish dependency, to a solid source of stability, to becoming a custodian of high principles.

It seems ironic, but historically, most extraordinary doctors have suffered diseases in their youth or had weak constitutions. It gave them an incentive to develop their skills. In the same way, most psychologists or psychiatrists entered their profession to gain clarity over their own mental confusion. This makes the Six act like a canary in a mine, an early warning system, able to detect danger

long before others do.

The ever vigilant Six is light-footed in its leporine nature; alert and spooked in an instant, darting between one possibility and another in a way that would surely exhaust other types rapidly. This cannot be sustained indefinitely. Hence the Six almost needs some diametrical opposite: rigid fanaticism.

In most samples of the HW we can see these two extremes alternating. Just as cement will flow into the gaps between bricks, first malleable and fluid, then hardening, Sixes tend to be the glue that holds groups and society together.

Integrated Sixes will eventually gain "peace of mind," but like a good watchdog, will sleep with one eye open and one ear cocked.

HANDWRITING AND ENNEATYPE SEVEN

7

Before investigating the graphological characteristics of type Seven, I need to point out that I have not known very many Sevens intimately. Maybe as a Four, I assumed that Sevens live in a different universe as far as personality is concerned, and initially my assessments were a tad distorted or idealistic.

After getting deeper into the handwriting (HW) of Sevens, the veils began to lift.

An Aggressive Butterfly

I had always known that Sevens are brimming with vital energy, but what had escaped me was their aggressiveness—it jumped out in their HW loud and clear.

Aggression is a natural component in the human psyche and as such should not be seen as necessarily a problematic aspect of personality. Each Enneagram type will manifest aggression in a different way.

Type Eight is considered the most aggressive of all nine types, but from the graphological perspective, type Seven is equally aggressive. I had underestimated the significance of the proximity of the Seven to the combative Eight. Whereas it is true that Sevens are often considered to be "light" like a butterfly, at times they have a set of pretty heavy wings.

The Eight's aggressiveness is generally oriented towards maintaining control and power over the environment. The Seven manifests aggression when in rebellion and above all as a constant "wanting more." Lack of discipline and insatiability emerge in the HW as the most telltale signs along with all their psychological spin-offs.

But Sevens are part of the fear triad, which expresses itself in anxiousness. Rebellion and anxiousness together translate in real life into an urge to elude. If we were to define the HW of a Seven by a single word it would be: escape. The Seven flees limits, pain, excessive depth, boredom, routine, conformity, and often (if avoiding working on oneself) feelings.

Two more characteristics stand out in the HW—intensity and speed that stem from impulsiveness. Sevens are very mobile and react rapidly to stimulation. They are often extroverted with a need for movement and risk getting sucked

7

into vertiginous hyperactivity. Sevens are the opposite of an ascetic, of someone inhibited and/or rigidly controlled. They are at risk of being dispersive and prone to flights of imagination.

The HW of Sevens contains:

- Strength
- Speed
- Impulsiveness
- Rebelliousness
- Dispersiveness

Strength, speed, and impulsiveness are also typical of the Eight, who is less dispersive and less inclined to give space to imagination and flights of fancy.

These characteristics are also found in Ones who react by controlling and inhibiting their impulses.

Type Three also has these characteristics even though we can't say rebelliousness is one of them, given that they tend to be preoccupied with projecting the right image outward.

The Six, especially the counter-phobic variety, can also have strength and speed; but ambivalence and constant reference to authority tend to sabotage and reduce the efficiency and impact of their actions.

Impulsiviness is certainly a characteristic typical of Twos who, however, are less likely to be dispersive or to flee situations.

Strength, speed and impulsiveness together are unlikely to occur in:

Type Nine, who tend to be slow and lazy;

Type Five, who lack the capacity to engage in rapid and intense action and are very reflective as well.

Type Four, whose vital energy is mainly directed inwards and its intensity used up by self-absorption.

In short, Sevens are highly spontaneous, full of initiative, mobile, big-hearted, cheerful, and facile with words. They tend to come across as pleasant because of their extroversion and optimistic enthusiasm. It is easy for them to be social, expansive, and cordial. They are ready to forgive, because feelings don't linger very long. Sevens have good practical and commercial abilities and value improvised actions even when the direction taken is risky and uncertain. They can easily become hyperactive, impatient, and impulsive, even to the point of violence, especially when reacting to restraint or limitation. The inconsistency of Sevens comes from the rush to finish what they are doing so they can move on the next thing. They tend to remain with a situation, a thing, or a person as long as it is stimulating. It takes maturity for Sevens to maintain commitments; this they do by reclaiming ground they had previously ceded to their senses in an excessive pursuit of satisfaction.

A common sign encountered in their HW is *Flung Out*—the strokes appear jotted down spontaneously and without care. There are several styles of *Flung Out*. In some, the HW maintains order, in others, it looks dispersive and disorganized. Essentially, it is the result of thoughtless spontaneity in response to any type of stimulation. We could call it the "opposite" of the sign *Careful* (control and inhibition in the expression of impulses).

The positive side of *Flung Out* is intelligence that is intuitive, creative, and full of initiative. We see this sign in people who are very active, fast, and quick to recharge but who are also prone to impulsively disperse energy. This is also the mark of a very lively imagination. Moretti considered this sign as part of being a genius.

Sample 1 Male age 36 – Type Seven. Handwriting showing the sign *Flung out*

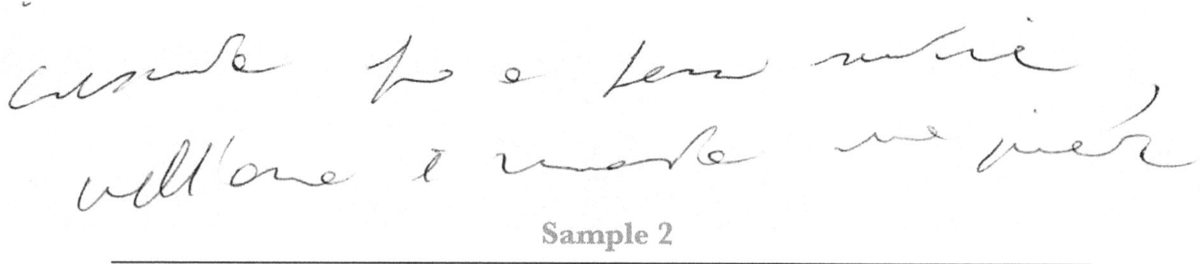

Sample 2 Male age 42 – Type Seven. HW showing the sign *Flung out*

Sample 3

Sample 3 Female - HW showing the signs Flung out and hints of *Confused*

Sample 4

Sample 4 Female age 57 – Type Seven, Sexual – HW showing the signs *Flung out*, *Thrusting* and *Springing*. Nevertheless it maintains order

Another common sign found in Sevens' HW is *Springing*, when letters within the word jump up and down on the baseline; such up-and-down motion can be either rhythmic or disorganized.

Springing is a sign of being excitable, psychologically jumpy, impulsive, and/or frazzled. According to Moretti *Springing* indicates being able to do many things well but also doing many things badly. The type of HW contains a sense of anticipation, a readiness to sprint and a quick reaction time—passion, rage, verbosity, mental flights, all happening at the same time before control is imposed by conscience or will.

Sample 5

Sample 5 Male age 36 - Type Seven, Sexual. HW showing the signs Springing (look at the words "familiar" and "unfamiliar"), *Flung Out, Impatient, Disconnected.*

aquello que ve, escucho, siento y sabe, no perciben el sello espiritual de la sustancia fundamental. Si solo eliminasen todo pensa-

Sample 6

Sample 6 Male - Type Seven, Sexual. HW showing the signs *Springing*, *Impatient*, and *Disconnected*.

Thrusting is composed of:

- Vivacity and intensity of graphic movement.
- Horizontal stretching out of some of the letters (m, n, u, i, and r)
- Final strokes of words as well as T-bars, accents, commas, and dots are launched in space but in an orderly, non-random way.

Thrusting indicates an explosive temperament with a low level of containment regarding ego expansion. The energy is directed outwards rather than inwards. Moretti states that: "Optimistic enthusiasts often have *Thrusting* in their writing. When they fail at something, it fazes them only for a brief period and they try again. If they fail again, they simply go back to it until they succeed." This sign is often found in Sevens' HW and is also inherently aggressive. Such a person is generally rebellious, not likely to be a follower, someone who listens to their own tune and follows their own intuition. Often this goes hand-in-hand with an excessive amount of self-assurance and actions that can be pursued vigorously but without much reflection. This personality is uninhibited and adventurous; they avoid routine, boring jobs requiring patience. The intelligence here is very intuitive and if properly trained, can muster a huge amount of talent for such things as medical diagnosis.

I exchange with familiar or unfamiliar faces are phrases for which I have no dictionary, though I have a sense of what they

Sample 7

Sample 7 Male age 60 – Type Seven, Social. HW showing the signs *Thrusting* and *Impulsive*.

Generosity

The sign ***Profuse*** shows:

1. Wide spaces between letters
2. Large size

Profuse is the sign of generosity and the Seven is generous. But the flip side of generosity is dissipation of vital energy. The attention is most often focused outwards towards the general at the expense of inwardness; feelings are expressed with plenty of intensity but, alas, with less durability.

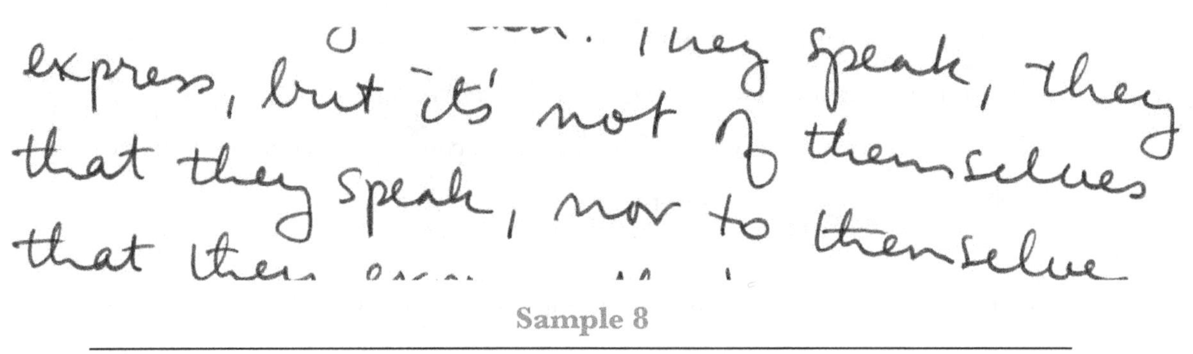

Sample 8

Sample 8 Female age 57 – Type Seven, Self-Preservation – HW showing very well the sign *Profuse*. Left-handed.

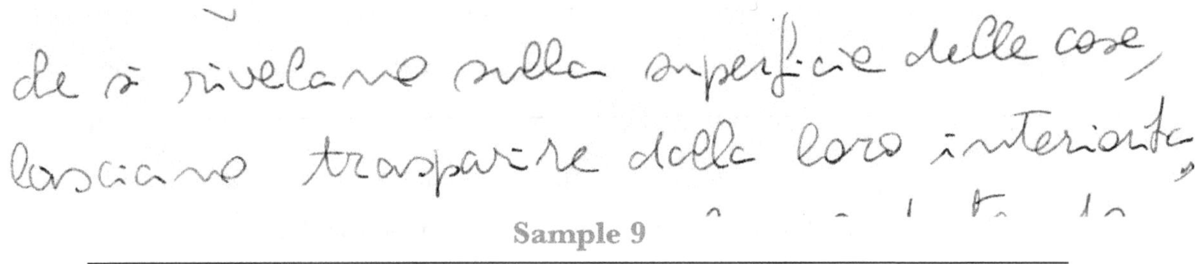

Sample 9

Sample 9 Female age 54 – Type Seven. HW showing the signs *Profuse* and *Springing*.

Impulsivity and Impatience

The sign ***Impulsive*** in a HW gives the appearance of being taken by excitement and moved by an out-of-control impulse; we see this in the contractions, convulsions, launches, and sudden interruptions. In essence this sign indicates that the first impulse becomes the course of action. It also hints at the underlying fear, because in difficult situations the writing shows an impulse to react by attacking or panicking.

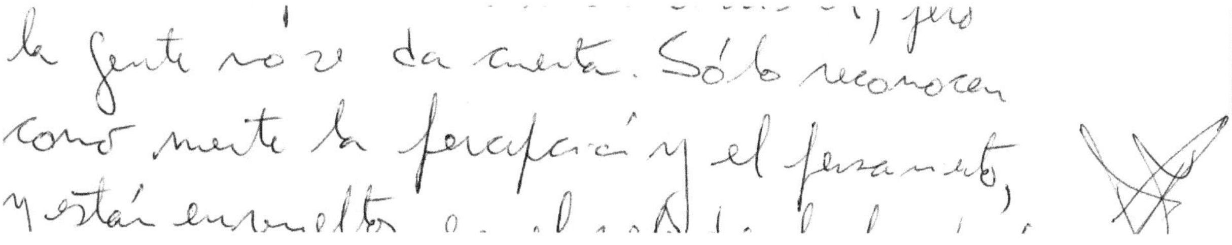

Sample 10

Sample 10 Type Seven, Social. HW showing the sign *Impulsive.*

We often see also the sign *Impatient*, i.e. a HW with ill-defined and incomplete letters with omission of T-bars, dots, or accents. The underlying feeling of the HW is rapid, restless and excited. This is a nervous HW characterized by a need to hurry, often without due attention to important particulars. The attention here is bundled and restricted—as when driving a car at high speed one has difficulty noticing the landscape.

Obscure indicates that individual letters are not clearly legible. This has two main meanings: intellectual activity that is continuous, very intuitive, and able to synthesize multiple sources of information; and also a lack of consideration for others—even though handwriting is a way of communicating, the writer does not seem concerned whether others will be able to decipher it or not.

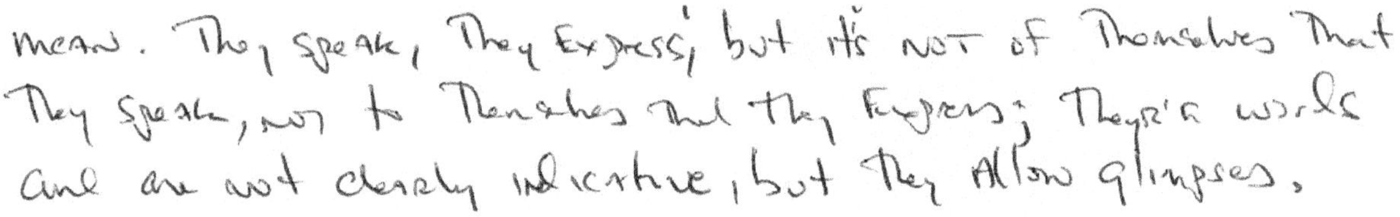

Sample 11

Sample 11 Male age 44 – Type Seven, Social. HW showing the signs *Impulsive, Obscure, Springing.*

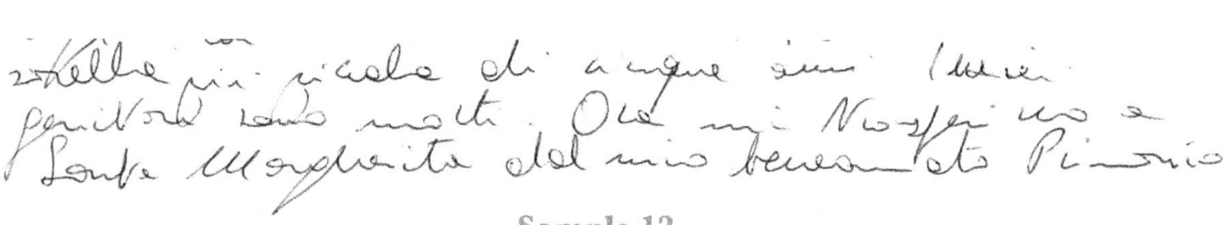

Sample 12

Sample 12 Female age 36. Type Seven, Sexual. HW showing the signs *Impatient, Springing, Thrusting, Obscure.*

7

In summary, the main signs of the Seven's HW are:

- *Flung out*
- *Springing*
- *Thrusting*
- *Profuse*
- *Impulsive*
- *Impatient*
- *Obscure*

They all share a common characteristic of speed, spontaneity, response to stimuli without reflection, an intuitive grasp of a situation, extroversion, intuition, and forceful impact when encountering an obstacle. But these signs also include a mixed bag of traits: dissipation of energy, lack of stability and constancy, difficulty in slowing down for details or savoring deeper meanings, impulsiveness ruling over will-power, generosity, vivid intelligence and imagination, quick wit, rebelliousness, lack of calm, emotional perceptiveness (oriented, however, towards the collective rather than individual deep feelings), aggressiveness (stemming from impulsiveness rather than destructiveness), optimism, enthusiasm, a certain superficiality (from moving rapidly), impatience and lack of attention towards feelings, and a constant need for stimulation.

These signs taken together show that in Sevens the ability to go towards life and take what is needed coexists with weakness when faced with their own impulsive drives.

Taken together, these signs are completely incompatible with the characteristics of types Five or Nine and fairly remote from the characteristics of type Four. These types lack the ability to project their vital energy outwards.

Ones certainly show impatience in the HW, but it is controlled and shows inhibition of impulse—we can see that in the rigidity of the HW with its many straight extensions.

Threes are optimistic and energetic like Sevens but preoccupied with the opinions of others and hence unable to be spontaneous. We can't call Threes non-conformists either, since their HW is generally *Careful*.

Twos are as impulsive as Sevens but allow more space for feeling—for say, being preoccupied with the needs of others. Thus the HW of Twos is much softer than that of Sevens, more rounded, and more legible.

Sixes are too preoccupied with their own fears and doubts to express themselves like a Seven. We saw how the principle sign of the Six was *Wavering*: the indicator of intellectual and emotional ambivalence. And ambivalence is something we rarely find in Sevens who throw themselves into situations without too much caution.

Eights share some of the graphological signs with Sevens. Whenever we look at neighboring types it is often difficult to draw a distinct line—for example between a Two and a Three or a Four and a Five. Similarly Sevens show an impulsive launch in the writing that at times seems to ignore objective reality, while Eights are not able to give as much room to the unconscious (or to playfulness). This makes the HW of Eights heavier, less generous (i.e., smaller size), with more straight extensions and angularity. Unlike Sevens, Eights have difficulty losing control.

Reason and Instinct, and Feelings?

As a counterpoint to the list of traits we discussed, and much to my surprise as a graphologist, I found a very high incidence of the sign *Disconnected* in the HW of Sevens. *Disconnected* seems to be the shadow side of the Seven—not to be mistaken for another kind of disconnectedness (quite common with Fives, but originating from a completely different context, that is, by walling off different part of themselves).

Disconnected means the letters within a word are unconnected as if they were independent. Please note, this is a graphological term and not a description of inner psychological lack of connection to this that or other.

Most signs mentioned in Sevens are a product of an impulsive, hard-to-control temperament, quite unlike the diametrically opposed qualities of *Disconnected* that signify having the ability and also the urge to analyze. How can a genuinely fast handwriting that contains all the elements of launch also have such a halting element—an element, that suggests driving with one foot on the gas and the other foot on the brake?

If we were exclusively looking at signs such as *Flung Out* and *Springing* as the "product" of Sevens, it would be a conceptual stretch to call the Seven a mental type, as opposed to a gut type. It is true these signs show how little space Sevens give to deep feelings, but this is mainly due to their dynamic speed that leaves insufficient time to stop, listen, and be present. At the same time, as a graphologist, I ask myself what are the signs that indicate that all this is happening at the mental level?

The key for me was that *Disconnected* is more than just the shadow of the Seven. It is the balancing element neutralizing too much impulsivity and, at the same time, it is a sort of contradiction in the inner personality of the Seven, as if underneath the apparent hyper-spontaneity would lie a vigilant and attentive calculation. From this perspective *Disconnected* can be said to indicate anxiety.

It is by multi-tasking at high speed that Sevens reflect and analyze. They can juggle several projects simultaneously which results in networking. *Disconnected* can enhance the Sevens' ability to intellectually synthesize (which requires a good dose of detachment and coldness).

The connection between individual letters in a word is also symbolic of how "I relate to you." For example, it is almost impossible to find a high degree of *Disconnected* in the HW of a Nine or a Two, and it is not by coincidence that these two types are among the warmest and most engaging of Enneagram types.

Moreover, the sign *Disconnected*, in this graphic context, says that Sevens are able to pursue wildly different kinds of activities and relationships, keeping each hidden from the others, and insulating themselves emotionally from the consequences of merging them together. Sevens, after all, can be very secretive—not in the sense of being buttoned up, but more like flooding you with information, including something revealing about themselves, but it is up to you then to find the needle in a haystack.

Disconnected is certainly a major factor of balance in the personality of Sevens that acts as a bulwark against the impulsive temperament, so that the intellect does not fall prey to the urges of the senses. *Disconnected* allows the mind to be in control of the senses and not get lost in the deep waters of the unconscious.

But another way of looking at it is that, by disconnecting, Sevens can indulge in sensory stimulation to their heart's content, because in the next moment they have the power to flip the switch and become practical, rational, or cold without experiencing the emotional consequences - to self or others—of the sensory bath.

At the same time, this means that Sevens have two dominant dimensions, instinct and reason. The question remains the same, so beautifully stated by James Empereur in his *Enneagram and Spiritual Direction,* that the growth of the Seven occurs via authentic and profound contact with their feelings. When this happens, the HW changes in appearance and becomes softer, rounder, less jerky and obscure; these changes are evidence of a genuine attention to and participation with others.

Samples # 13, 14, 15, and 16 show the sign *Disconnected* to a high degree. In a previous article we have stated that this sign is typical of the Five. Nevertheless the Five's graphic context is not so impatient and impulsive as in these samples.

Sample 13

Sample 13 Female – Type 7w8, Self-preservation. Besides the sign *Disconnected*, we have some hints of *Confused*. The graphic pressure is very intense.

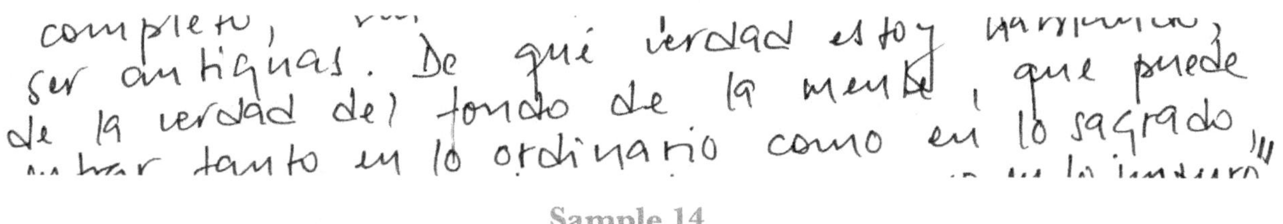

Sample 14

Sample 14 Female – Type 7w8, Social – Besides the sign *Disconnected,* again, we have strong graphic pressure.

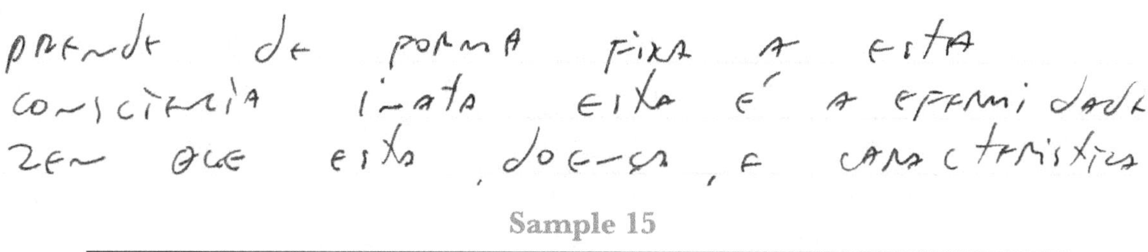

Sample 15

Sample 15 Male – Type Seven, Social. HW shoving the signs *Disconnected, Impatient, Thrusting.*

las formas. No saben que deteniendo su pensamiento conceptual y olvidado su angustia el Buda les

Sample 16

Sample 16 Female – Type Seven, Sexual. These few lines don't allow us to see all the impulsiveness in this handwriting.

Tombé sur quelqu'un qui m'a dit de vous laisser les messages ô

Sample 17

Sample 17 (French HW) Female age 70 – Type 7, Sexual. A well-developed Seven. Underlying are the signs *Thrusting, Profuse, Springing,* and fairly *Obscure*; yet the HW is very elegant, with a harmonious rhythm, without disorder and confusion. The high degree of *Disconnected* in this sample shows a high level of integration towards the sobriety of type Five.

Inexhaustible Energy

The main graphological signs of Sevens are characterized by great vital force. Addressing this, Naranjo states that "…in Sheldonian terms Enneatype Sevens tend to be predominantly ectomorphic with endomorphia as a secondary component, yet as a whole seem to be the most balanced in the distribution of the three components. This matches the personality in which intellectual and spiritual interests exists side by side with social extroversion and active or even restless disposition." (*Character and Neurosis*, p. 169).

From a graphological perspective this balance of strength of temperament is reflected in a rather pronounced pressure—we rarely see the sign *Light*—and in writing with a *Large Size*, because that person is expansive and full of vitality. Finally, we are more likely to see the HW lines rising (the sign *Rising* indicates enthusiasm and optimism). It is also difficult to find signs of excessive containment, inhibition, or restriction in the HW of Sevens.

7

they mean. They speak, they express, but it's not of themselves that they speak, nor to themselves that they express; they're words

Sample 18

Sample 18 Male age 58 – Type 7w8 Social – Besides the signs *Thrusting, Profuse, Springing* we find a strong degree of *Thickened* I (strong pressure = lot of energy) and many sharp strokes. In this personality a deep generosity and availability coexist with an intense aggressiveness.

connessi; formano un alfabeto profetico di seguito che divenire un ombra la mia vita. Da quando il calcio è cessato e

Sample 19

Sample 19 Male age 47 – Type 7w6. HW with a strong pressure, *Thrusting, Springing, Disconnected*, some hints of *Confused*. Moreover we can see the influence of the Six wing as expressed by some traces of *Wavering*.

Always Wanting More

Very often the sign *Rightward Slant* is found in the HW of Sevens. It would be complicated to explain the neurophysiological symbolism of this sign, but we can say that on a psychological level this indicates that the writer has a need to always feel connected to others. There is a need for "tasting" the influence from contact—in other words, an egocentric need for others.

Depth of feeling in graphology is expressed by curves, whereas *Rightward Slant* is a way of "leaning" towards enjoying the tenderness and sensuality that emanates from others. This is true only up to the point of satisfaction having achieved possession rather than following an urge for sharing and connecting.

Incidentally, another graphological indicator for emotional independence (among other signs) is *Upright Slant*, but one that is soft and modulated, not rigid—meaning, approaching the other with sensitivity rather than from an exaggerated need for emotional reassurance.

The level of narcissism of this need, indicated by *Rightward Slant*, is seen in the degree of inclination of the vertical extensions towards the right. The sharper the angle of the inclination respect to the baseline, i.e., less than 45°, the more intense is the need of the Seven to "want more." If the angle of the extensions is more upright, say about 800, it is simply a sign of a more extroverted attitude and greater social ease.

Samples 20-21-22 have a strong influence of the Eight wing. Here the border between the two types is very thin.

Sample 20

Sample 20 Female age 60 – Type 7w8, Sexual – Handwriting showing the signs *Rightward Slant, Strong Graphic Pressure, Rising, Springing, Sharp Strokes, Angles, Straight Extensions.*

Sample 21

Sample 21 Male – Type 7w8, Sexual. High degree of *Rightward Slant*, in a context of impulsiveness.

Sample 22

Sample 22 Male age 47 – Type 7w8, Self Preservation. A very sharp handwriting, with a high degree of *Rightward Slant*. Here impulsiveness and rigidity coexist. Besides the influence of the Eight wing, we can infer the hypercriticality and anger of point One. We can't define this HW as belonging to a "joyful Seven."

Imagination and Confusion

Two signs seen in the HW of less healthy Sevens are *Pompous* and *Confused.*

Pompous is exaggerated vertical and horizontal extensions of letters. It is generally interpreted as an inferiority complex compensated by a superiority complex born of fear. The positive aspect is confidence in one's own resources, imaginative exuberance and optimism (often unfounded); the negative aspect is intellectual and emotional superficiality, hype and boasting. *Pompous* often means the writer talks too much, blames others for their failures, and is unable to be self-critical.

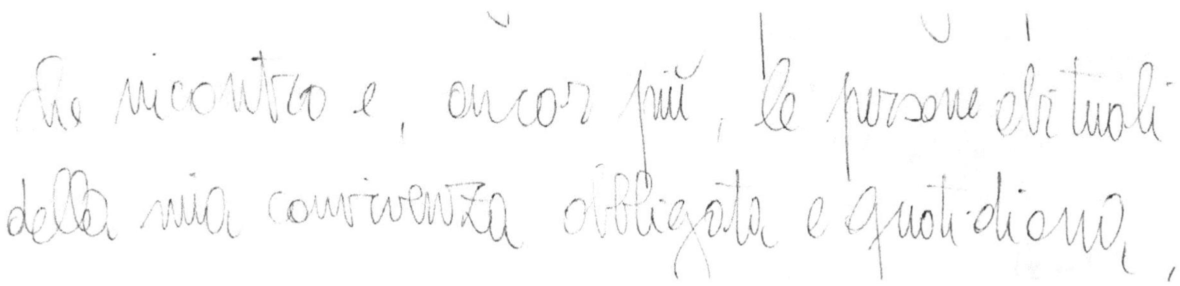
che incontro e, ancor più, le persone abituali
della mia convivenza obbligata e quotidiana,

Sample 23

Sample 23 Male – Type Seven. HW showing the sign *Pompous*.

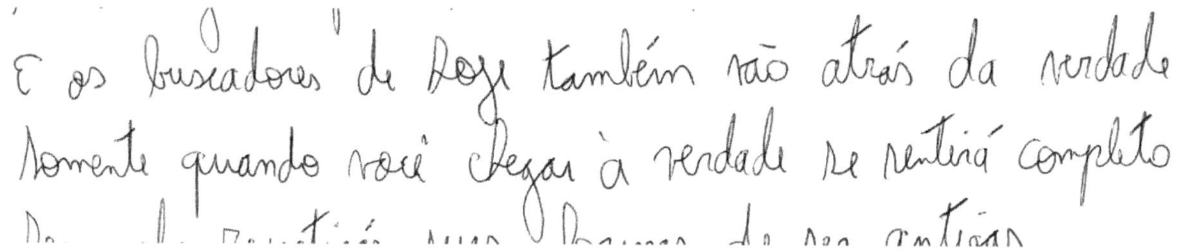
E os buscadores de Deus também vão atrás da verdade
Somente quando você chegar à verdade se sentirá completo

Sample 24

Sample 24 Male – Type Seven, Sexual – HW showing the sign *Pompous*.

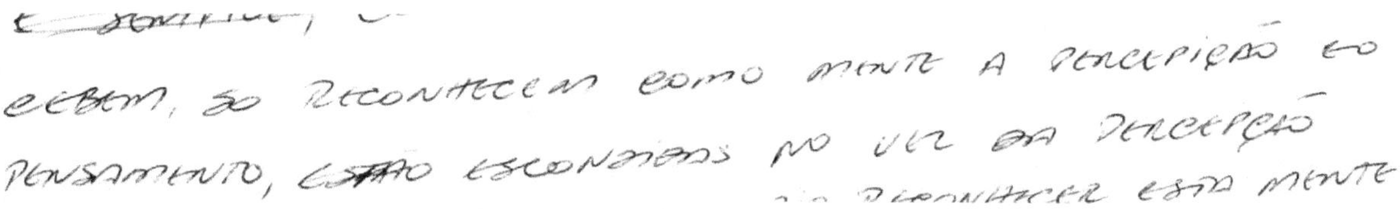

Sample 25a

Sample 25a Male – Type Seven, Sexual

Sample 25b

Sample 25b Signature pertaining to sample 25a (partially concealed for privacy). Note the tendency of boasting (grandiose letters) and how different it is from the regular HW.

In the sign *Confused* the strokes of individual letters invade and touch other letters or the lines touch creating the impression of confusion and lack of clarity.

According to Jacoby-Bosquet the sign *Confused* is found in HW of people who mix the instinctive, the emotional, the intellectual, and the spiritual. For example, in Sevens this may manifest in flights of fantasy affecting all parts of the personality.

He sends to me. Its good for me to have struggles
because I realize I can't do everything by
myself. God is safe to be with. I can trust

Sample 26

Sample 26 Male age 58 – Type Seven – Showing the sign *Confused* (but with a laudable effort to maintain mental clarity; indeed, the letters often touch but do not tangle with each other. In this context it means effort and difficulty in controlling impulses).

Vitality and Joi de Vivre

Samples 27 and 28 express the joy for life so typical of Sevens. The HW is fairly original, expanding into graphic space with letters that are exuberant with firm pressure. The graphic rhythm is good without being disorganized or dispersive.

Sample 27 has a well-proportioned *Triple Width* (that is, a good combination of *Letter Breadth*, *Space between Letters*, and *Space between Words*) indicating a substantially balanced personality (with only slight exaggerations in the lower extensions—a hint of being inflated coming from the Six wing).

Sample 28 is a musician with distinct signs of narcissism. Among the other signs are also *Flexuous* and *Narrow between Letters*, pointing at the ability to elicit admiration. The behavior of these Sevens (27 and 28) could be easily confused with that of type Two.

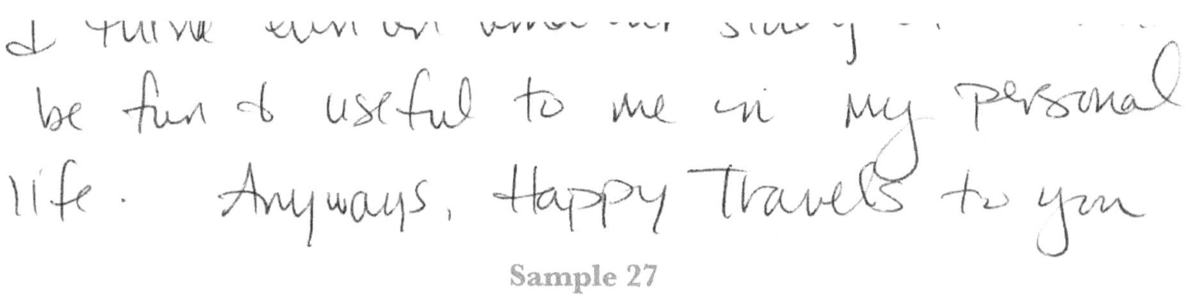

Sample 27 Female age 26 – Type 7w6, Sexual.

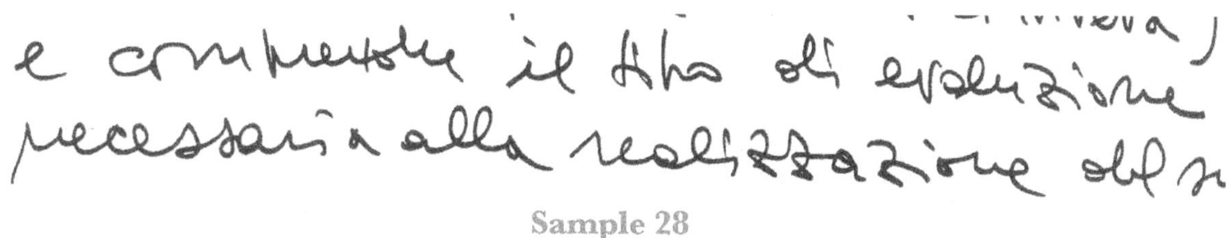

Sample 28 Male age 50. Type 7w8. Musician.

Seven with a Six Wing

Sevens with Six wings maintain the basic characteristics (signs: *Flung Out, Impatient, Disorderly, Thrusting*) but with a notable lessening of vital energy. The pressure is lighter and there is less expansion in the graphic space. More important, we see a strong influence of the sign *Wavering*, so typical of the Six. Sevens with Six wings appear more insecure and have difficulty organizing their lives. Their spontaneity is hampered by the doubts of the Six wing.

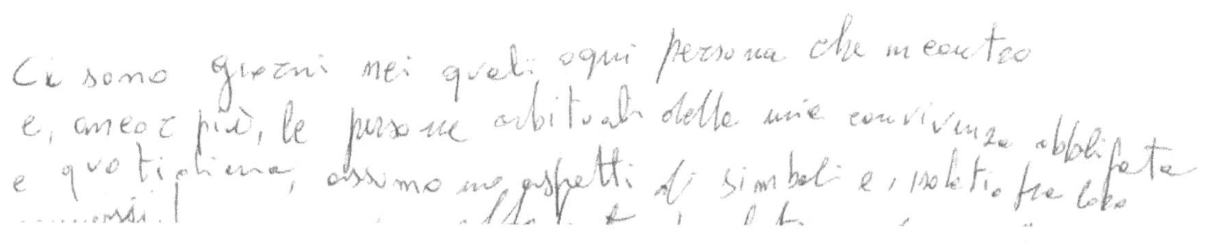

Sample 29 Male age 22 – Type 7w6

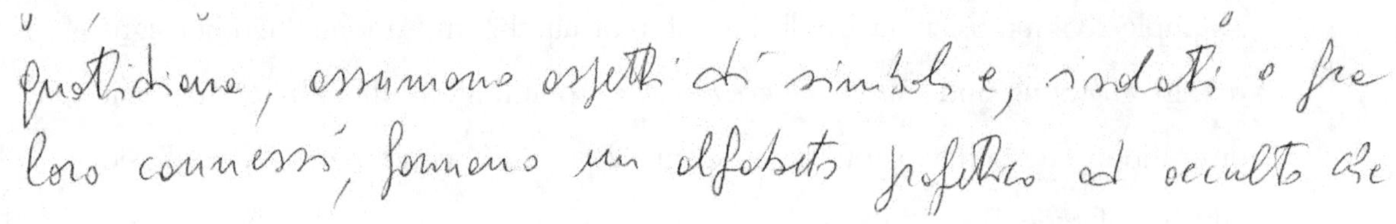

Sample 30

Sample 30 Male age 50 - Type 7w6

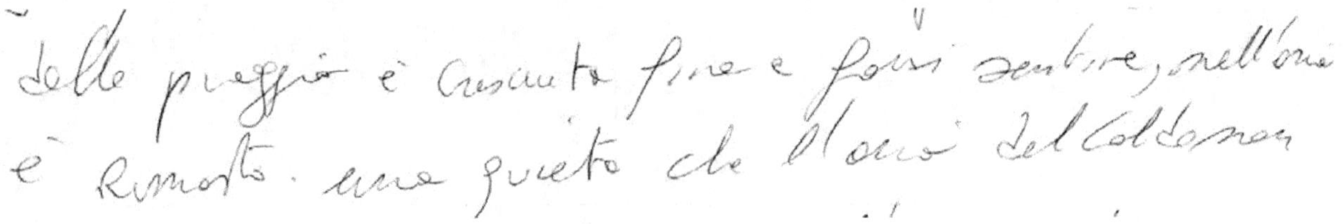

Sample 31

Sample 31 Male age 38 - Type 7w6

Seven with an Eight Wing

Sevens with an Eight wing, among all the types, appear probably the most aggressive outwardly. In a certain way the characteristics of Sevens with a Six wing cancel each other out, while the characteristics of Sevens with an Eight wing enhance each other—they almost always obtain what they want, they are not held back by the ambivalence of the Six, but are strengthened by the Eight. Still impulsive, the HW is better organized, more angular, and with regular spacing. The HW has many sharp strokes. The Eight wing brings stability and tenacity.

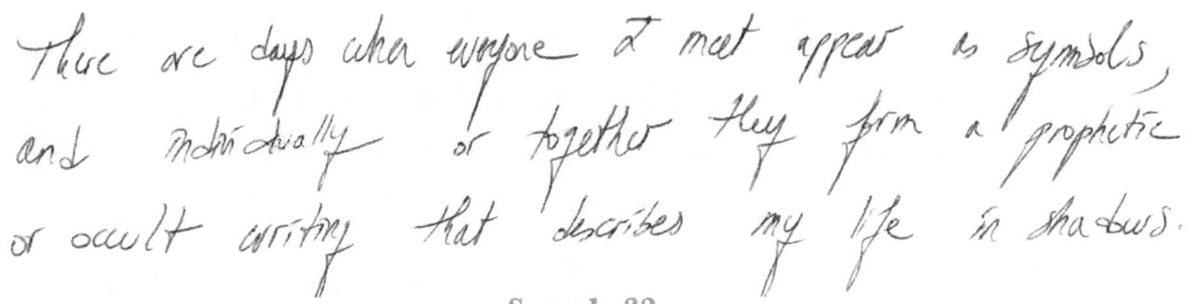

Sample 32

Sample 32 Female age 25 – Type 7w8, Sexual. HW very *Angular*, and showing the signs *Springing, Impatient, Strong Graphic Pressure, Obscure, Disconnected, Sharp Strokes, Amplified* and *Straight Extensions, Rightward Slant, Good Organization of Space and Widths*. A lot of space is given in this sample to mental and instinctual energy; feelings are secondary, or rather, hidden behind a façade of aggressiveness.

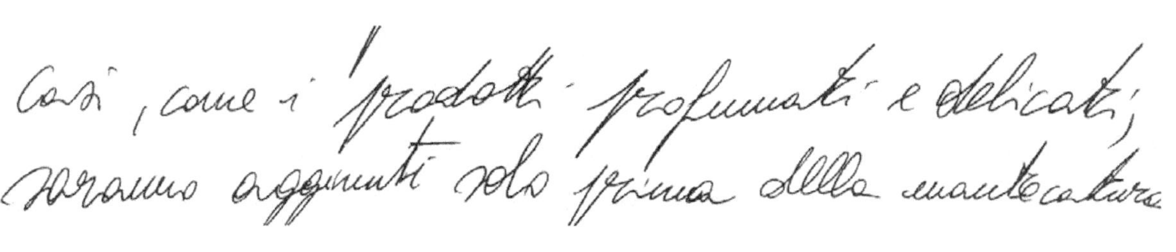

Sample 33

Sample 33 Male age 42 – Type 7w8. HW with the signs *Profuse, Thrusting, Large Size, Strong pressure, Rightward slant, Amplified extensions*. This person is as if constantly on the attack and does not rest until the desired result is achieved.

Couples (these examples are real couples)

Che ti può essere utile di scrivere l'inizio
di questa lettera anche in stampatello.

Sample 34

Sample 34 Male age 48 – Type Seven, Sexual.

trati e che, probabilmente, anche questo
scritto porterà qualcosa in più alla nostra
vita, pur nella superficialità di quanto

Sample 35

Sample 35 Female age 42 – Type Two, Sexual.

The writers of Samples 34 and 35 have been married for 20 years and have two children. He is an important entrepreneur, and both share interests in social life and sports. He is brilliant and dynamic, needs freedom and to be in movement (signs: *Flung Out, Thrusting, Springing, Profuse*); she is a rather typical Two, more stable, and cultivates an attractive femininity based on capriciousness and privilege (signs: *Curved*, combined with *Straight Extensions, Loops, Warm Graphic*

Pressure, Narrow Space between Letters and Words). Tension might arise caused by his need for freedom and her urge to possess; however, both partners stimulate each other. This happens not so much intellectually as by maintaining energy, vital exuberance, and a pleasant playfulness in life.

Sample 36

Sample 36 Female age 25 – Type Nine – Ex-wife of sample 37. HW with a high degree of *Curved* (lack of angles) and *Slow Rhythm* (we will analyze that in the article on Nines).

Sample 37

Sample 37 Male age 35 – Type Seven, Sexual

Sample 38

Sample 38 Female age 33 – Type Six counter-phobic (see article about the Six). Currently partnered up with Sample 37.

As in the previous example, in this couple the Seven male (Sample 37) is very restless and is moving constantly in search of new experiences (*Thrusting, Springing, Impatient, Flung Out*). He has difficulty finding a stable professional identity. He has a need for continuous, unimpeded movement while also needing some points of stability.

His ex-wife (Sample 36) is a type Nine, a quiet and very stable person. Initially the attraction was very intense and he probably felt that he had found a quiet harbor where he could rest while she probably found in him a source of vital stimulation.

A few months into the relationship they got married and had a child, but the marriage lasted only a few years due to irreconcilable differences. He would feel suffocated and she did not feel she could count on his emotional support.

Their ability to communicate became difficult. She'd shut down into long and stubborn periods of silence and he'd react by escaping and withdrawing more and more until they finally divorced.

As so often happens, the motives that attracted them to each other did not become integrated with their respective personalities and they grew apart.

Presently, he is in relationship with a counter-phobic Six (Sample 38). In a different form, the same problems are arising with his new partner who happens to be more active and also more aggressive. She sees his excessive need for freedom as threatening, just as did his type Nine wife.

Stai tranquilla che scrivo!!
Sono pericolosissimo! Perché

Sample 39

Sample 39 Male age 60 – Type Seven. Ex-partner of Sample 40.

ipotesi ma ho la sensazione,
legata al mio progresso di sofferenza, di perplessità
sulla durata e sulla capacità di amore non

Sample 40

Sample 40 Female age 52 – Type One (see article about the One).

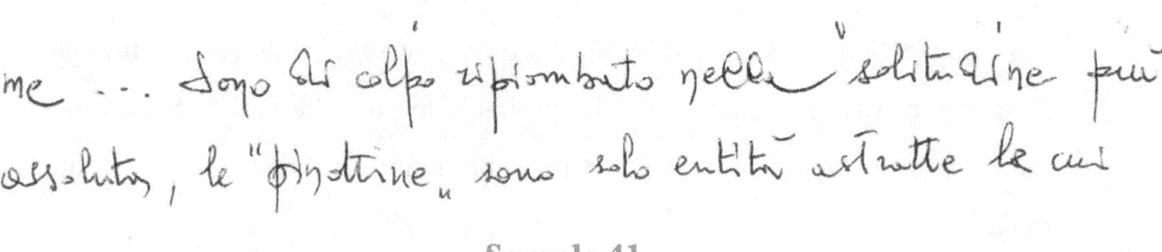

Sample 41

Sample 41 Male age 53 – Type Three. Current partner of Sample 40.

Our last couple, a type One woman (Sample 40), had been married for a long time before she met the type Seven man (Sample 39). Their past experiences are very different. She is very traditional and family oriented and has never been able to outgrow the influence of her severe father. Her writing is rigid, controlled, and fairly accurate (we can see strong influences of the superego and of perfectionism). She is not the kind of person who would easily engage in lighthearted fun or give up being austere. Nevertheless, she thought to have found a playmate in him.

He (sample 39) had lived a life of travel, was tired of it, and now craved some of the stability he saw in her. He liked her solidity and felt appreciated and honored by her seriousness. His HW expands a lot in the graphic space and contains *Impulsivity*, *Disorder*, and not much sign of sensitivity. He probably misread her rigidity and her seriousness.

This couple stayed together two years fairly trouble free but with some underlying doubts on her part regarding his long-term reliability (she was afraid of failing yet another marriage). She then decided that in spite of the good parts they shared, he was not giving her enough security and left the relationship.

She then met the type Three (sample 41) who is very formal; his HW is accurate and has little spontaneity. Note the *Strokes of Affectedness* at the ends and also within words. She is enticed by his elegant manners but is a bit disappointed in his emotional lack of openness (note how both writers have a rigid slant but hers is *Rightward* and his is *Upright*). However, she does find him more trustworthy than her Seven.

Conclusion

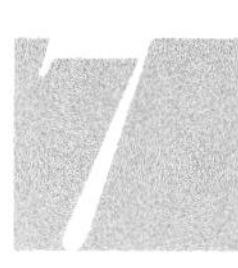

Recapping the most salient characteristics of the Seven's handwriting:

- Elevated vital intensity = strong pressure with intense ink-flow and tonic strokes.
- Impulse to expand = ampleness in the graphic movement.
- Vivid vital rhythm = speed and dynamic rhythm in the graphic strokes.
- Impulsivity = *Springing, Obscure, Launched Strokes.*
- Low level of control of reactivity and emotionality = variations that are non-homogeneous in size, form and rhythm.
- Personalization of the HW = rarely a precise and careful writing.
- Spontaneity = *Thrusting, Profuse, Springing, Impulsive, Impatient.*
- And the shadow side of the Seven: *Disconnected* = the implication is that the mental level dominates and together with the other signs indicates a powerful instinctualness. Feelings get less space. Lacking are elements of calm, patience, softness, and the ability to listen quietly. These qualities would be more evident in those whose HW showed more curves, moderate graphic rhythm, slight inclination of the extensions, medium to small size, and light pressure.

It goes without saying that in this series of articles highlighting graphological connections to Enneagram types, the purpose is not to do exhaustive studies of types, but rather to single out particulars in handwritings that can help determine type.

Graphology is a system that can be mined for information and is a wonderful tool for cross-referencing. I tried to keep it simple enough even for an untrained eye to recognize traits in handwritings. Try it out on friends and family whose type you know and see if it works for you.

HANDWRITING AND ENNEATYPE EIGHT

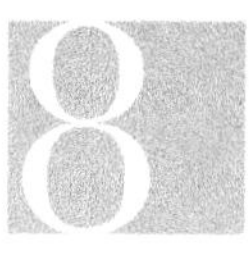

Since we now have explored the handwriting (HW) of most Enneagram types, we can lay out this article recapping and highlighting the most salient characteristics of each type's writing styles, and, through comparison, try to give an identity to the Eight's graphic movement.

Ones are tense and rigid (many *Straight Extensions*); Twos are more outward oriented (overly *Flexuous*); Threes are concerned with image (too *Careful*); Fours are delicate and original (very *Methodically Irregular*); Fives tend to be analytical (*Small Size* and too high a degree of *Space between Words*); Sixes doubt a lot (excess of the sign *Wavering*); Sevens are impulsive (compulsiveness of the sign *Flung Out*); Nines are monotonous and steady (excessively *Slow* and *Curvy*). The excess of Eights consists of being rather callous: their HW shows mainly this armor, expressed through different graphic displays. They will be the focus of our examination.

Aside from being careless, Eights' HW generally shows strong pressure, not so much from a compulsion of excess, but from the strength of their constitution. Eights pay little effort to precision, order or aesthetics; they focus on what they care to communicate, without embellishments. A special intensity gives the HW a three-dimensional quality on the paper. A high level of energy and decisiveness makes the graphic pressure seem to stand out physically on the sheet (if you touch an Eight sample, you can feel the script embossing the paper on the back, while on the front it gives the impression of being in relief, or raised). This characteristic indicates that the Eight has the power to modify reality (symbolically, "the paper"), instead of merely adapting to it. Finally, Eights are often considered socially less than gracious and tend to be inconsiderate of others, especially when pursuing their goal.

And now, comparing Eights with the other types makes them easy to recognize:

First, the perfectionist One. The HW shows no frills, but it is not as sparse as the HW of Fives; the intensity of the graphic movement is partially held back and controlled. We see a high degree of *Straight Extensions*, and a rather formal and precise writing. Ones' HW is predominantly angular rather than curvy, a sign of inner nervous tension and difficulty in adapting to the environment—hence anger.

In my twilight vision, however, I only
vaguely distinguish what these sudden glass
panes on the surface of things let show from

Sample 1

Sample 1 Female age 74 – type One. The main signs are: *Angular Ovals, Straight Extensions, Stable Baseline, Clear Space between Words, Regular Left Margin, Careful*. In this context Careful means the "form" predominates over "movement."

In complete contrast to the One is the exuberant HW of the Two. Expansive in space, with soft letters and curves, the HW shows no particular inhibitions or restrictions in the graphic rhythm. The script emanates from a sense of abundance, of nourishment (the graphic pressure is pasty) and the narrow space between words shows a lack of willingness to welcome self-criticism. Twos are always engaged in some form of relationship and they need attention. Consequently the HW often tends to be large and contains amplifications in certain letters.

In my twilight Vision, however. I only vaguely
distinguish what these sudden glass panes
on the surfaces of things let show from the

Sample 2

Sample 2 Female age 47– type Two, Sexual. The main signs are: *Flexuous, Regularly Alternating Inclination, C Angles, High Middle Zone, Narrow Spacing between Words, Curved.*

Juxtaposed with the warmth of the Two is the colder, self-controlled, and less expansive HW of the Three (strong pressure with less curves, carefulness). Preoccupied with projecting an image, Threes accept a reduction of spontaneity in exchange for obtaining a desired effect on the environment. The HW is accurate, as strong and energetic as that of Ones—but without the underlying feeling of inhibition expressed by Ones.

Threes typically use flashier strokes, for example, at the beginning or end of words, indicating a desire and ability to transmit different feelings outward than they have internally. Generally the HW is *Upright*, indicating self-control; Threes ooze good organization in life as in their HW. We see that in the management of various spaces (*Space between Letters, Space between Words*).

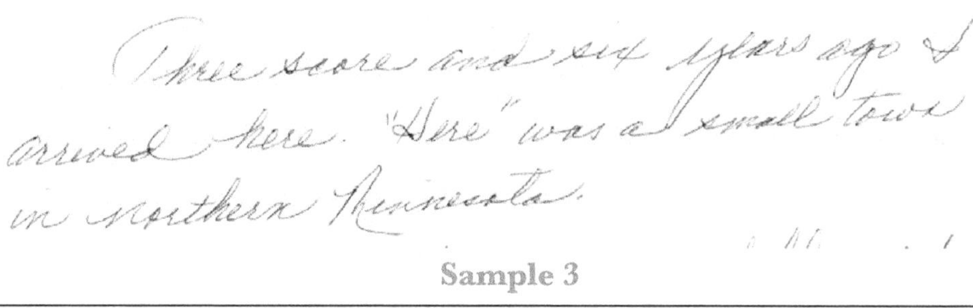

Sample 3 Female – Type Three, Social.

In the HW of type Four, the dilemma of self-image is more obvious. In fact, Fours are constantly searching to understand who they "really" are; the HW is less structured than that of Threes who do not suffer from that question, or at least, find different solutions to satisfy their quest for identity from Fours' penchant towards self-absorption. This makes the Fours' HW more contained, with slightly less pressure, without trying to create an artificial image, more spontaneous, and less careful (*Spontaneously Careful*); the letter shapes do not appear very defined and lack tension and strength of graphic gesture.

Fours are also non-conformist and their HW tends to deviate from the model taught in school; containing many creative strokes and generally *Methodically Irregular* (dimensions of the letters vary in a rhythmic way). Their HW shows sensitivity, vulnerability, and difficulty in defending themselves in ways without using introjection. Fours' HW is breezy, delicate, flexible, generally curvy, but at the same time tormented (seen in congestion of pressure, contortions, and scattered non-homogeneity).

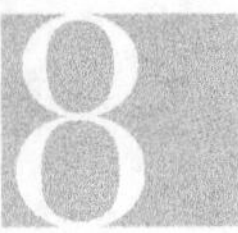

There are days when everyone I meet appear as symbols,
and individually or together they form a prophetic
or occult writing that describes my life in shadows.
The word I exchange with familiar or unfamiliar

Sample 4

Sample 4 Female age 49– Type Four, Social.

Fives have a similarly delicate HW as Fours, but respond to situations differently. In fact, the strategy of Fives to defend their privacy accepts the risk of possible isolation and includes a profound analysis of the situation. From this perspective, Fives differ form the emotional Fours in that they face emotions with detachment. And contrary to Twos, who tend to write big with scanty space between words, Fives have small HW with ample space between words.

Fives' HW is essential and sober, somewhat similar to Ones' but not as excessively restrained; more stable than that of Fours; less exuberant than the HW of Twos; and less accurate and contrived that the HW of Threes.

The sign *Disconnected* is common; rarely will we find strong pressure, but often a certain sharpness (sign: *Pure*) indicating clarity of thought.

they mean. They speak, they express, but it's not of
themselves that they speak, nor to themselves that they
express; they're words and are not clearly indicative, but

Sample 5

Sample 5 Male age 49– Type 5w4, Sexual.

The HW of type Six contains a strong sense of ambivalence and anxiety; we see this mainly in the signs *Wavering* and *Not Homogeneous*.

Sixes have a hard time with maintaining uniformity and stability in their HW, which can express warmth and availability like that of Twos—large-sized letters, with adequate pressure; and also with some of the hardness of type Eight (in the case of the counter-phobic Six). Rarely will we see the calm of Nines or the elegance of Fours.

If the Five wing is dominant, the space between the words will be larger; if the Seven wing is dominant there will be more disorder. When Sixes try to write accurately as would Threes, it comes out a bit stilted and gawky. The HW of Sixes contains many contradictions in graphic movement and in the shape of letters. It might start out rich in intuition and imagination, mobile with amplified forms, and then revert to scholastic forms as if respecting school rules.

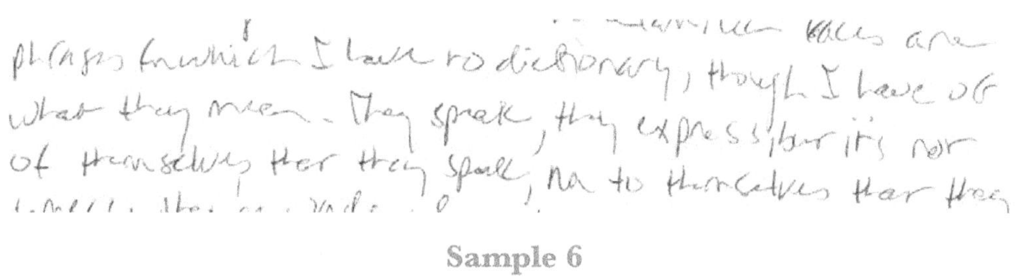

Sample 6

Sample 6 Female age 51 – Type Six, Self-Preservation – Left-handed.

Sevens have a fast and dynamic HW; the letters seem launched in space and bouncing on the baseline (signs: *Flung-out, Springing, Profuse, Thrusting*). Gifted with high energy, similar to Eights, Sevens do not show signs of inhibition or perfectionism like Ones (whose writing is much more controlled). Sevens have the exuberance of Twos, but without their emotional availability (Twos' writing is much curvier). They have the enthusiasm of Threes, but do not have signs of feeling tortured like Fours, mainly because their attention is directed towards external stimulation. Neither do they have the sobriety of Fives: rather, the Sevens' HW is launched and not restrained. Nor do they have the intellectual doubts of Sixes or the reactive slowness of Nines.

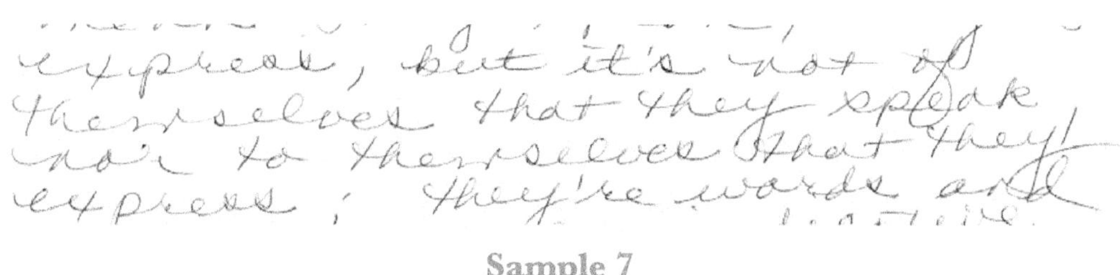

Sample 7

Sample 7 Female – Type Seven.

We will come to type Eight after a look at type Nine. This is just a little advance notice on Nines who will be the subject in the next article.

The main problem for Nines is recognizing and affirming their own individuality. Their HW reflects this characteristic by *curviness*, a sign of availability, but also of extreme ability to adapt; slowness of rhythm, indicating difficulty in moving into action from sloth; a drop in energy (the letters tend to slacken); and "softening up" of letters (sign *Neglected*, marking the inclination towards surrendering or giving up).

Nines' HW resembles that of Twos but is less lively; we could say it has qualities opposite that of Ones, which is tense and rigid; it has neither the organization, care nor will of Threes, and lacks the spirit and introspection of that of Fours. It is more monotonous and regular than the HW of Fives, but without the tendency towards detachment or isolation—in fact it is larger with stronger pressure and smaller spaces between words. It does not contain elements of doubt like the HW of Sixes, even though there seems to be an equal amount of insecurity present; and it lacks the launch of Sevens. Finally, Nines' HW is slower and does not show the aggressive impact of Eights.

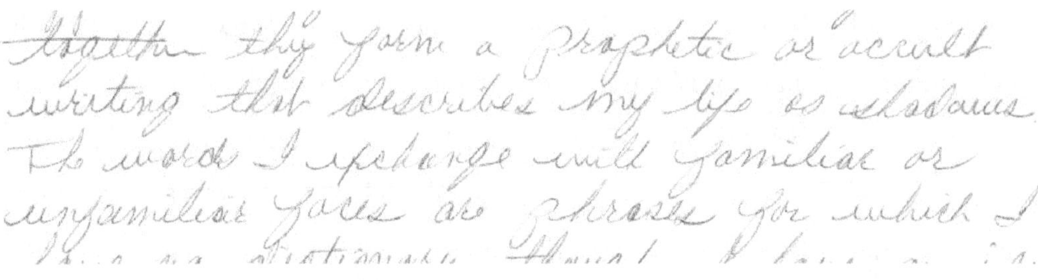

together they form a prophetic or occult
writing that describes my life as shadows
The words I exchange with familiar or
unfamiliar faces are phrases for which I

Sample 8

Sample 8 Male age 57 – Type Nine, Sexual (note how the letter *w* is curvy but slowed down and dilated, i.e. less force and tension).

Returning to Eights, the first thing that jumps out is a sense of self-assuredness. The energy expressed in the graphic space seems to have no worries other than showing its own intensity. We can see that from the intense and continuous pressure flowing without inhibition, almost an animal-like sense of self-assuredness, full of vitality, with **Thickened I** (when the descending strokes are thicker than the ascending ones)—a sign of strength and confidence because it can only be achieved when all the muscles of the hand and nervous system are functioning in a coordinated and firm fashion. *Thickened I* shows the absence of inhibitions of psychological or physical nature, such as insecurities, hyper-emotionality, indecision, torment, and timidity. *Thickened I* means that the graphic movement follows straight from its inception to the execution without dispersion or parasitic interference from thoughts or emotions.

Obviously we need to look at the entirety of the HW to determine if a HW with a high degree of *Thickened I* uses energy constructively and for the common good, or in an ugly and destructive manner. Both personality styles can have natural leadership qualities that will spring either from charisma and self-assuredness or else from sadism and absence of scruples.

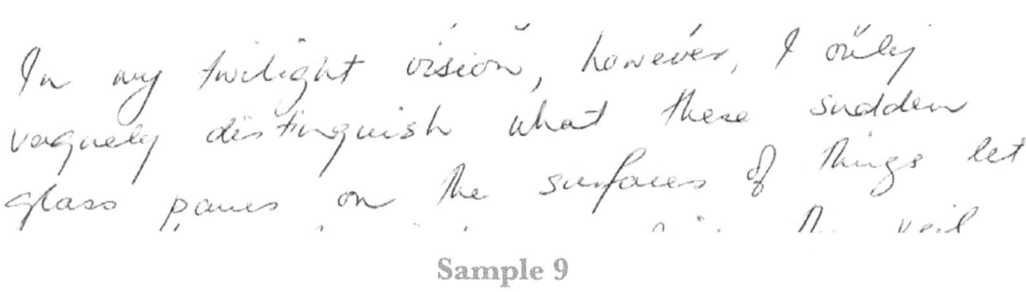

Sample 9

Sample 9 Female Age 60 – Type Eight, Sexual. The graphic movement is very secure and decisive. Technical limitations of reproducing this image permit only a partial glimpse into the raw force that is present in the original where the descending strokes are much more impactful than the ascending ones (sign, *Thickened I*); we also have the sign *Truncated* as in "I" which looks as if it was cut off without follow-through.

All types have to manage their strength but Eights spontaneously organize theirs in a sure and efficient way. In Enneagram theory it is assumed that Eights had to struggle in early childhood and as a result developed the ability to be assertive, but the HW shows us that this is a gift they are born with. For example—some rare exceptions aside—a delicate child, will become a delicate adult, and can only learn to manage delicacy in a more effective way.

Eights develop assertiveness because it is already in their nature to use strength rather than isolation, as would Fives, or self-absorption as would Fours. If you look at the scribbles of children you could realize that. Each Enneagram type has a

tendency, an inclination. Over time, the environment and education will transform this tendency into a compulsion or, on the contrary, if the environment is positive, the inclination will remain just a predisposition.

The HW of Ones also contains a lot of energy and a fair amount of *Thickened I*, but at the same time there are inhibitions of impulses, and nervousness and anger due to perfectionism that create an inner tension reflected in the HW. That makes Ones more controlled than Eights and influenced most strongly by ethics and guilt. If we compare the HW of Ones and Eights side by side, we will see that Ones spend a lot of their energy on the maintenance of order and in search of correct behavior and virtue; while Eights are mainly interested in action for its own sake without dissipating into abstract perfection. Indeed, the HW of Eights is often fairly disorganized.

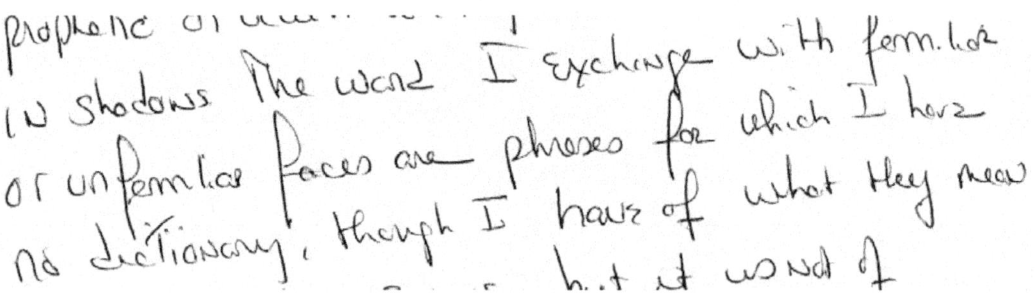
in shadows The word I exchange with familiar
or unfamiliar faces are phrases for which I have
no dictionary, though I have of what they mean

Sample 10

Sample 10 Female age 62 – Type One, Self-Preservation. Script showing the sign *Austere*.

Samples 10 (type One) and 11 (type Eight) both show strong pressure but note how the One's HW looks more rigid and less fluid. It appears that the energy of the One tries to flow outward but remains trapped, creating a sense of tension.

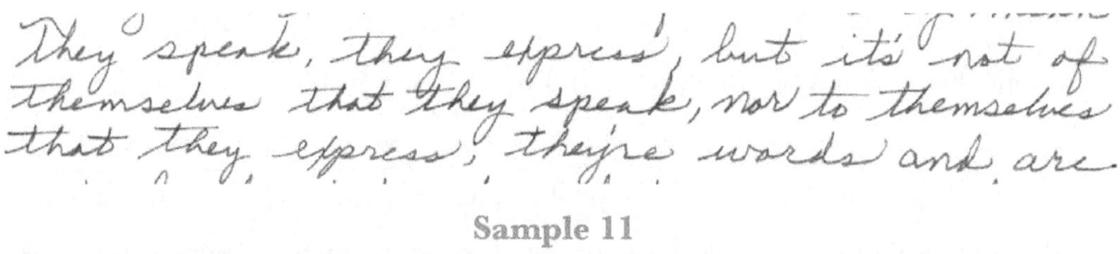
They speak, they express, but it's not of
themselves that they speak, nor to themselves
that they express; they're words and are

Sample 11

Sample 11 Female age 69 – Type Eight, Sexual.

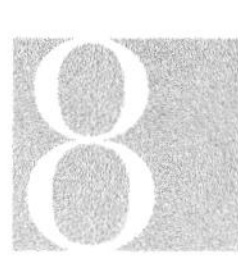

los seres consientes no son mas que la mente
única aparte de la cual no existe nada.
Esta mente que no tiene comienzo es no

Sample 12

Sample 12 Male age 53 – Type One, Self-Preservation

Samples 12 (type One) and 13 (type Eight) both have *Thickened I* to a high degree but in the One's HW it looks like a brake—the writing is more static, while the Eight's HW moves outward.

Esta mente pura que es la fuente
de todo brilla por siempre sobre todas
las cosas con el brillo de su perfección

Sample 13

Sample 13 Male – Type Eight, Self-Preservation

Twos are gifted with a good dose of energy and vital exuberance but their HW, even though it has good pressure, looks more rounded and soft than that of Eights. There is a higher degree of sensitivity and receptivity towards the feelings of others, whereas Eights at times appear indifferent, hard nosed, and without an inkling of guilt. We could call Twos' HW more embracing and maternal and the Eights' hard HW. It is not by chance that these two types are connected by a line indicating the Eight's evolutionary development towards the Two which would include an altruistic inclination to serve others. We can actually see a change in the HW when Eights subdue their armor and allow the mellower and more vulnerable qualities to come to the surface—it softens the graphic movement.

When rejected, Twos have been known to turn hard and vindictive like Eights. In that case, the HW which is normally flexuous and curvy becomes more rigid and aggressive.

Verò ulteriormente una decina di voghe, altrimenti lo occuperei tutto, per farei stare più "discorso" –

Sample 14

Sample 14 Female age 55 – Type Eight. High level of pressure (*Thickened I*). She is willful and knows how to impose if needed. Her forcefulness is balanced by the sense of fairness (curvy, good spacing between letters). The HW is fluid but without a lot of attention to self-image

su pensamiento conceptual y olvidando su angustia el ruido se les aparecerá. Esta mente pura que es la fuente de todo brilla por siempre sobre todo con el

Sample 15

Sample 15 Female age 40, type Two, Sexual. The script is very Flexuous, with *C Angles, Loops, Regularly Alternating Inclination, Narrow spacing between words.* The *Pressure* is mellow and fluent.

Samples 14, 15 & 16 illustrate the difference in energy of the Eight, Two and One. The Eight's HW is essential without frills; the Two's HW is soft and lively; the One's HW is sober and less expansive.

that describes my life in shadows. The words I exchange with familiar or unfamiliar faces are phrases for which I have no dictionary, though I have an idea of what they mean.

Sample 16

Sample 16 Female age 76 – Type One. The main signs are: *Angular Ovals, Straight Extensions, Stable Baseline, Clear, Space between Words, Regular left Margin, Careful.*

Type Three also has a high level of *Thickened I*. Naranjo states that: "…as a whole, the enneatype III population may be the highest in mesomorphia after the type VIII and that of the counter-phobic character" (*Character and Neurosis*, p. 216); and in reference to the Eight: "Constitutionally the ennea-type VIII individual tends to be mesoendomorphic, and on the whole this ego type is the most mesomorphic of all." He adds, "…a corresponding lack of cerebrotonia may be posited as the background of this highly extraversive disposition" (p. 147). On the contrary, Fives are the most cerebrotonic. Naranjo also observed that Ones are more often than not "mesoendomorphs."

Sample 17

Sample 17 Male age 47 – Type Eight. Good level of *Thickened I*, *Angular*, fairly fluid and yet substantive; *Narrow between Letters* in this context points at a certain wish to dominate and to remain guarded towards others.

Sample 18

Sample 18 Female age 46 – Type Three, Self-Preservation. High level of energy, yet the HW is more accurate and better organized.

Sample 19

Sample 19 Female age 57 – Type Eight, Social

Samples 19 & 20, of type Eight and type Three have a high level of energy which allows an efficient organization of graphic movement. The Three's HW however contains *Strokes of Affectedness, i.e.*, the end-strokes and those at the beginning of words are rather ample and curvy. This goes with a need to present a good self-image, a need the Eight does not feel. The Three's HW is more regular in its *Triple Width*, while the Eight's HW has a less regular *Space Between Words* and *Space Between Letters*—here we see the Three's better ability to concentrate.

There are days when everyone I meet appears as
symbols, and individually or together, they form a
prophetic or occult writing that describes my
life in shadows. The words I exchange with

Sample 20

Sample 20 Female age 48 – Type Three, Self-Pres. Balanced Triple Width.

These last samples go to illustrate that regarding temperament, Eights, Threes, Ones, and counter-phobic Sixes have a lot in common. Graphologically, these types will have a robust level of *Thickened I*, but organized slightly differently.

For example, the Three is concerned with self-image and the Eight is not. Therefore, the Three's HW generally contains the sign *Careful*, while the Eight's is more sloppy.

Type Four is located opposite the Eight on the Enneagram symbol. Fours have less vital energy but are endowed with more sensitivity and depth than the Eight. The Four's HW appears less solid, with less pressure, and lacks the "armor" and sense of impermeability that is seen in the Eight's HW. Comparing the two, we could also say the Four is more thin skinned than the Eight.

Fours often seek refuge in aesthetics and beauty as a compensation or consolation for their own dissatisfaction (including their organic tenuousness), areas that seem to matter little to the Eight who prefer to be pragmatic, avoid empty chit-chat, and don't get lost meandering through emotions. The Eight's HW tends to be neglected and crude, where the Four's strives for elegance.

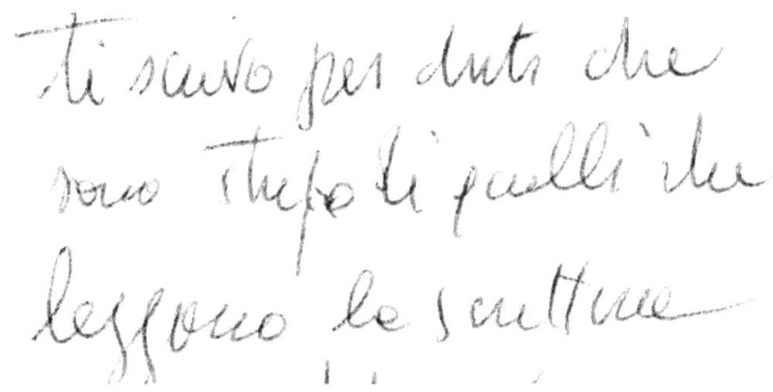

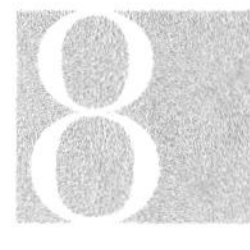

Sample 20

Sample 21 Male age 47 – Type Eight.

Sample 21 & 22 are a comparison between an Eight and a Four. The HW of the Eight shows strong pressure, angularity, and high energy levels—the writer has started many spiritual groups across Europe—yet in the background of the personality we can see a tendency to dominate, strong psychological armor, and also a relatively low level of sensitivity. The HW of the Four is much more delicate, receptive, sensitive, and open towards others (*Curvy, Flexible, Light*).

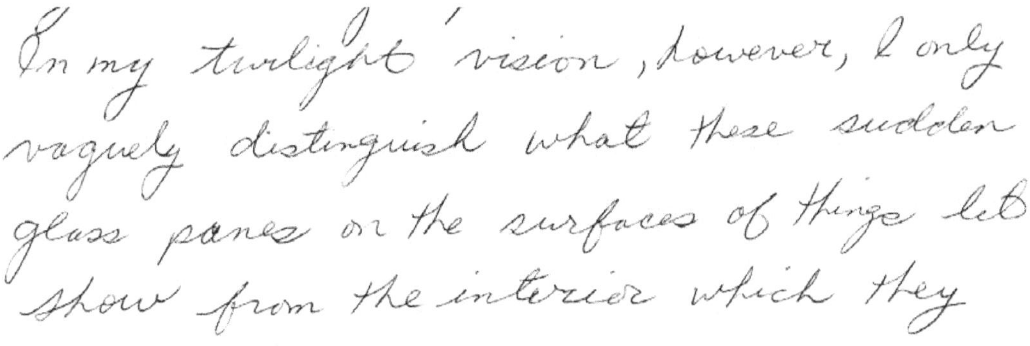

Sample 22

Sample 22 Female age 55 – Type Four. Handwriting showing the sign *Spontaneously Careful.*

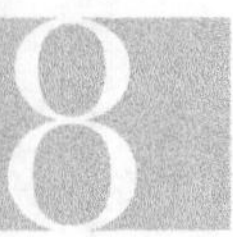

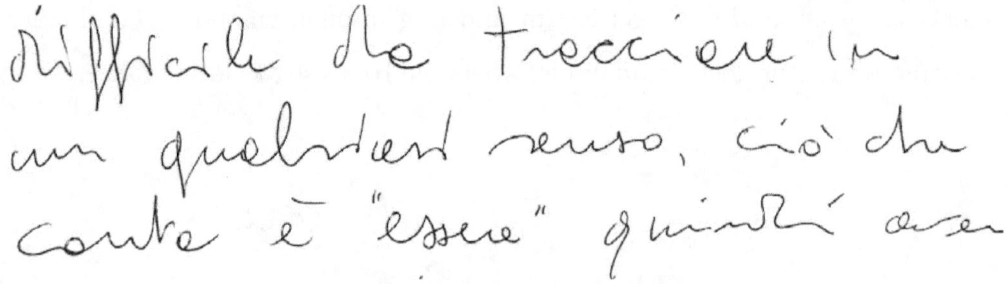

Sample 23

Sample 23 Male age 47 – Type Eight w7.

Samples 23 & 24, type Eight with Seven wing and type Four. Both reveal lively movement, but the rhythm of the Eight is less regular and individual letters are formed with little care—the graphic movement springs from impulsivity and haste. The writing of the Four is a good re-elaboration of the scholastic style adding originality, creativity, and elegance.

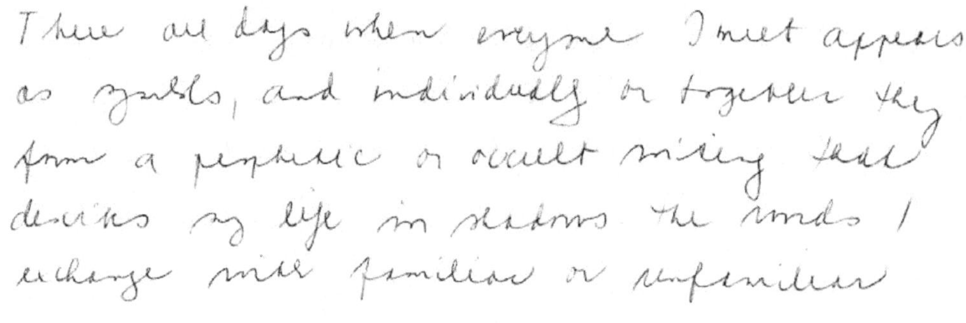

Sample 24

Sample 24 Female age 37 – Type Four, Sexual.

It is impossible to mistake an Eight's writing for that of a Five. They are psychological opposites even though the Five's intellectual aggressiveness is no less than the Eight's will to dominate. The Five's writing is small, airy, contained, and with plenty of space between words, but above all, light in pressure and almost dry. The Eight's HW is dense, occupies the graphic space with confidence without holding back, is impulsive and, as mentioned before, displays strong pressure. When Eights go to Five, their HW shows a higher degree of *Disconnected*.

Breathing very slowly, and speaking to an another in a whisper, we pushed open the storeroom door and were rather astonished and somewhat puzzled to find such a

Sample 25

Sample 25 Male age 25 – Type Five.

Samples 25 & 26, types Five and Eight. Both writings have the sign *Disconnected*, letters that do not have strokes connecting each other. The graphic gesture of the Five is organized, clear, small—signs of thoughtfulness all, but also of emotional isolation. In the writing of the Eight we see a disintegration towards the Five. The writing appears heavy, neglected, aggressive and above all not loose. The writer seems to be very closed and angry towards others. The sign *Disconnected* in this case indicates a tendency to ruminate rather than to analyze or reflect.

a esta consciencia imediata ... isto se chama a doença Zen. Que esta característica de um ... fanatico. E como agua que se torna

Sample 26

Sample 26 Male – Type Eight, Social

It is also easy to distinguish between the HW of a phobic Six and an Eight. The phobic Six's HW compared to that of an Eight appears to be without backbone; it looks timid and doubtful, indicators of internal indecision that corrodes direct action; we see the signs *Wavering* and *Hesitant*, and above all, pressure that is *Not Homogeneous*. The Eight has none of these signs.

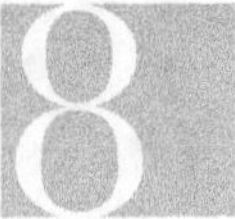

words I exchange with familiar or unfamiliar faces are
phrases for which I have no dictionary, though I

Sample 27

Sample 27 Female age 61 – Type Six, Self-Preservation. Uncertain and hesitant progression on the baseline.

Samples 27 & 28, types Six and Eight. The HW of the Six is indecisive with an underlying impression of doubt (the baseline is hesitant). The Eight's HW is decisive, aggressive, and proceeds to direct action without stopping for remorse (high level of *Thickened I, Angular, Rightward Slant*).

delle mie conoscenze obbligate e quotidiane,
assumono aspetti di simboli e, isolati o
fra loro connessi, formano un alfabeto

Sample 28

Sample 28 Female age 42 – Type Eight, Social

There are several areas of resemblance between the Eight and the counter-phobic Six. Both have an aggressive style with strong pressure and decisive movement. The essential difference is that the counter-phobic Six lives this aggressiveness as a reaction to fear so we find many amplifications of letters (sign *Inflated*) that indicate compensation through imagination (fear is replaced with a sort of courage).

Furthermore, in this compensation the Six tends to overdo, so what would otherwise look like a sign of strength looks instead like rigidity. Both these types have a different relationship to anxiety. The Eight deals with it without difficulty and is actually stimulated by it whereas the counter-phobic Six is burdened and destabilized by it and expresses it in various kinds of non-homogeneousness.

spiagge popolate di palme.
di notte vedevo ordinarsi in cielo le
stelle, e la falce della luna gialla

Sample 29

Sample 29 Male age 50 – Type Six, Sexual.

Samples 29 & 30, counter-phobic Six and Eight, look similar from the perspective of the strength of the graphic movement, but the HW of the Six is much more rigid (the long extensions are parallel) and monotonous (brooding, imaginary fantasies). The Eight's HW is strong, not rigid, and comparatively more elastic.

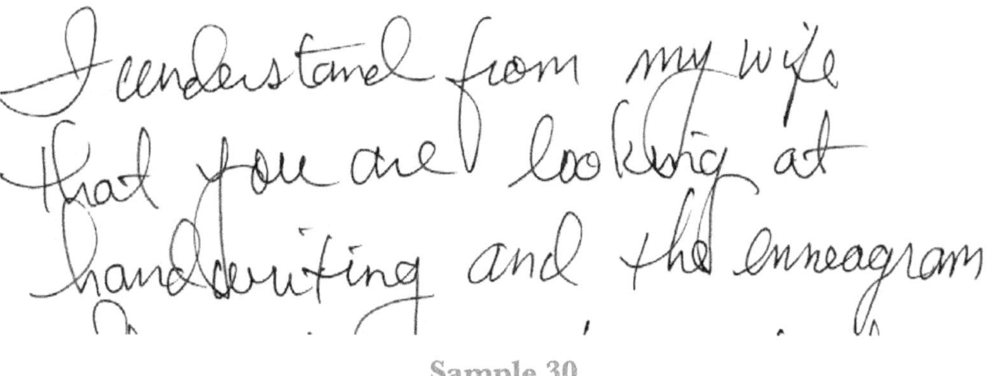

Sample 30

Sample 30 Male age 67 – Type Eight, Self-Preservation.

Sevens' HW has as much energy as that of Eights. Rarely will a Seven's HW have light pressure. We can say that Sevens' aggressiveness co-exists with a lightness of spirit and great mental curiosity, whereas Eights' aggressiveness, especially the less developed ones, tends to be heavy, pushy and dominating. The HW of the Seven would thus be more mobile and fast, nervy and skittish, compared to the Eight's, who, although not really calm, is better able to keep impulses under check. Both types love excess and intensity, so we will not see a small HW with inhibition, restraint, lack of vitality, or a turning in on oneself.

Sample 31

Sample 31 Male age 60 – Type Eight.

Samples 31 & 32, types Eight and Seven. This Eight probably has a strong Seven wing. The writing is heavy with strokes of aggression that resemble a whip. The Seven's writing is looser and more fluid. Both writings, however, show inclinations to excess and a difficulty remaining contained.

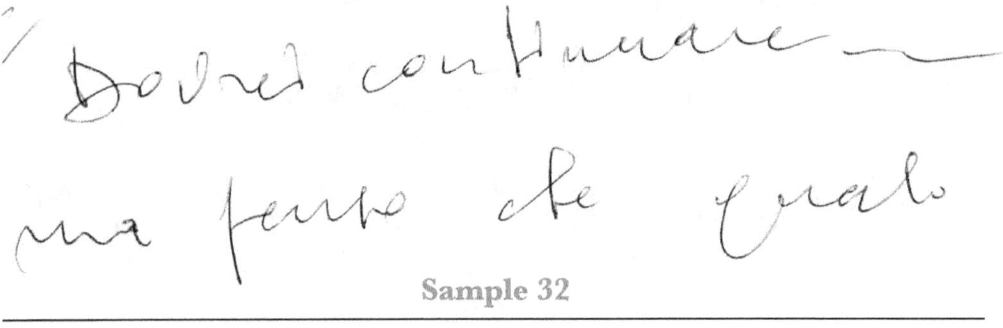

Sample 32 Male age 60 – Type Seven, Social. HW showing the signs *Thrusting and Impulsive*

Samples 33 & 34, types Eight and Nine. The Nine's HW is slow, curvy, with few dynamic movements and a lack of tension. The pressure can be strong but not as differentiated compared to the Eight's. Nines do not often express their aggressiveness; they prefer to compromise. We can see that by the small difference between the rising and the descending strokes—this too is a form of laziness. The Eight's HW is more energetic and appears to cut through the graphic space with assuredness and decisiveness. Both types share an inclination towards sloppiness, *i.e.*, they don't care about their image; the writing reflects this by being disorderly and rough in the case of the Eight, and for the Nine, with awkward dilatations in the shapes of some letters.

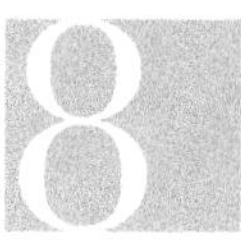

telefonico e ti invio questo foglio,
con i miei dati, chiedendoti di
periziare la mia grafia, sperando

Sample 33

Sample 33 Female age 33 – Type Eight.

Samples 33 & 34, types Eight and Nine. We can intuit the difference: the HW of the Nine is slow, curvy and relaxed, while the Eight's is willful, energetic, with a strong graphic gesture.

Ci sono giorni nei quali ogni persona
che incontro e, ancor più, le persone
abituali della mia convivenza obbligata

Sample 34

Sample 34 Female age 43 – Type Nine.

Comparing different types should have illustrated the ways in which Eights' writing is distinct from others.

In brief, the Eight's HW has strong pressure; it is almost impossible to find an Eight with light pressure; it is fluid, but not very fast and has an aura of heaviness. The Seven's HW is more nervy and fast. The Eight does have a streak of vanity and likes to show off—we see that in some of the upper case letters that tend to be pompous. Eights are pragmatic, realists, don't get lost in theoretical abstractions, so their HW stays fairly close to the scholastic model but to a lesser degree than that of the Nines, whose HW remains simpler because they are more passive. Eights put little effort into trying to be original and elegant, as would Fours; nor do Eights need to maintain an image and be accurate as do Threes. The Eight tends to be a little slovenly, similar to the Nine, and able to adapt to the

environment if necessary, so the HW is fairly regular but less so than that of the controlled One or the reflective Five, and more disciplined than that of the Seven.

Eights do not have the largest HW of all. That privilege to occupy more graphic space belongs to Twos and Sixes. Twos do it out of emotional exuberance pushing outward, Sixes out of amplification as a compensation for their insecurity. Eights can write very small or very large according to the level of energy required to dominate the environment.

Other typical signs are:

Truncated, as seen in a HW that is clipped and decisive, where the final strokes of letters are cut off rather abruptly (sharply). This sign indicates straightforward action, resolute decisions, self-confidence, impatience, sticking to essentials, little mental agility. This sign also indicates strong will-power that can even go so far as despotism that does not allow room for discussion.

Ci sono giorni nei quali le persone che incontro e, ancor più, le persone abituali della mia convivenza obbligata e quotidiana, assumono aspetti di simboli e, isolati o fra loro

Sample 35a

Sample 35a Male age 45 – Type Eight, Sexual. Handwriting showing the sign *Truncated*, in addition to *Thickened I* and *Angular* ; a heavy HW.

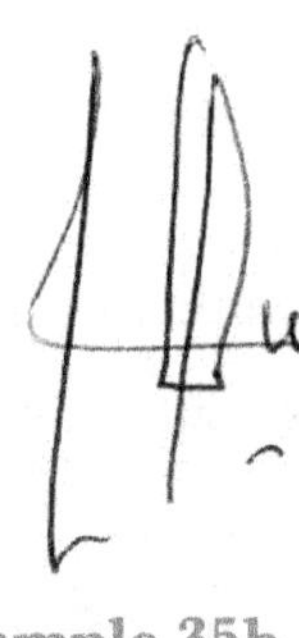

Sample 35b

Sample 35b Fragment of signature (to maintain anonymity) of 35a. Very aggressive strokes, clipped or truncated, totally lacking any sense of aesthetics.

Bold, script which is traced with certainty and power. Showing the ability to have impact, a powerful sense of well-being, full of vitality applied to affirming life.

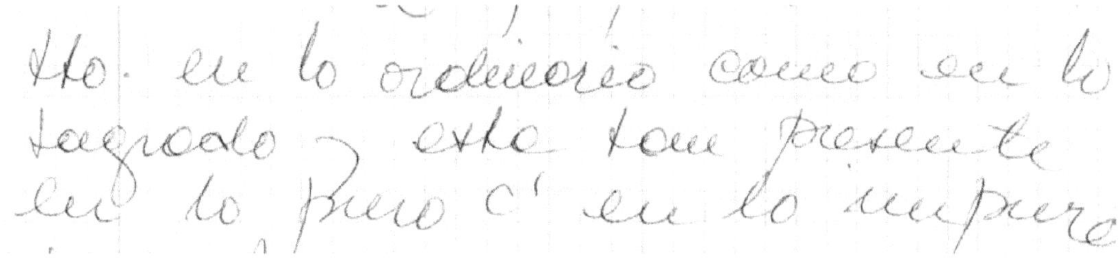

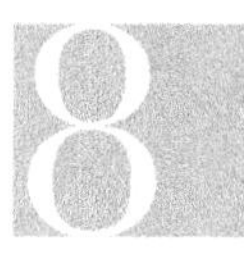

Sample 36

Sample 36 Female – Type Eight, Social. HW showing the sign *Bold*.

Careless and *Disorderly*, appear in writings that make no attempt to be esthetic and contain irregularities that are visually disturbing—a sign of doing things in a rushed manner without stopping for particulars. It also means there is difficulty in concentrating for a long time on a subject.

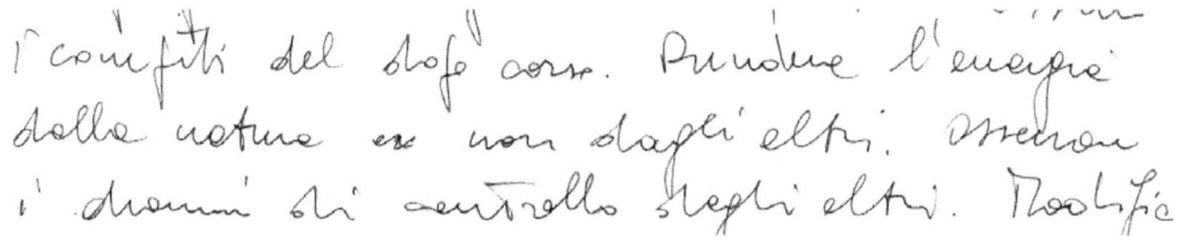

Sample 37

Sample 37 Male age 49 – Type Eight.

Samples 37 & 38 both Eights, with a high degree of *Thickened I*. The graphic movement is fairly fast, disorderly, and not very legible. Psychologically, this indicates a lack of interest in others.

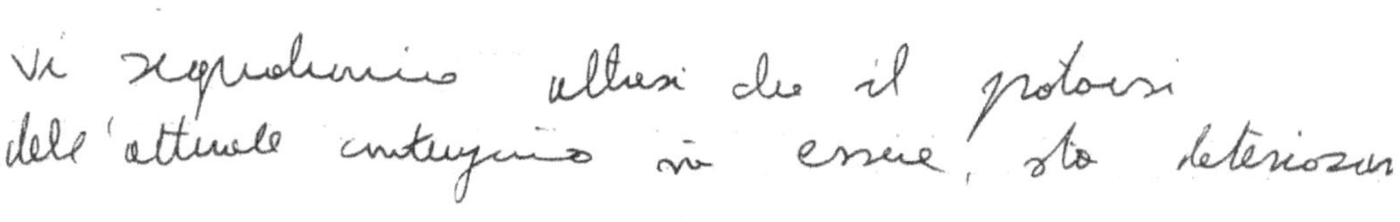

Sample 38

Sample 38 Male age 51 – Type Eight, Sexual.

Gross, writing with heavy strokes, a sign of scanty sensitivity and an inclination towards materialism.

Angular, pointy writing with many sharp angles in the oval letters, suggesting strong self-interest and protectiveness of one's own turf without consideration for others' rights.

Extensions Concave to Left, script where letter extensions (t, d, l, g, f, p) show concavity to the left; denotes inclination to prejudice, suspicion, and repulsion.

Da quando il calcolo necessario e la
prima leggerezza della pioggia è cresciuta
fino a farsi sentire, nell'aria è rimasta

Sample 39

Sample 39 Female age 49 – Type Eight. Handwriting showing the sign *Extensions, Concave to Left* (letter t); psychologically, a move out of repulsion.

Stable Baseline, a script that proceeds on the base-line without rising or descending. This sign along with *Thickened I* and *Angular* show firmness of character and psychological stability.

As usual, we need to keep in mind the sum total of all the graphic signs before deciding on their meaning.

It would be interesting to look at the Eight's HW from the perspective of Jungian functions. Keeping in mind that the Eight is non-emotional would explain why it is hard for them to express tenderness. Claudio Naranjo states: "In Jung we can recognize our ennea-type VIII under the label of the Extraverted Sensation Type, though only in its aspects of realism and lusty orientation and not in that of dominance." Don Riso, on the other hand, describes the Eight as an intuitive extrovert.

Examining the HW would make one think that this type is dominated by extroverted thinking and as an auxiliary function would have extroverted sensing. On the other hand, if we think about the intellectual process, we can see that the Eight has an intelligence that is gifted with clarity of thought, speed, a good practical grasp of situations and people, but without true creativity, precisely because they are non-emotional. Eights have good observational abilities principally oriented towards reality and facts, without excessive subjective interpretations arising from emotions and sentimentality. This makes them realistic and pragmatic.

They love to acquire a lot of experiences in the world, are generally not sparkling with originality and show very little interest in systems and theories—mainly because the dominant function of thinking looks at things objectively, while the auxiliary function of sensing gathers only what is tangible and concrete. Therefore they exhibit much clarity about how to get something done, but little theoretical creativity.

Were the sensate function prevalent, Eights could not express a high level of will-power. Indeed the sensate function is more dominant in Nines who are less strong-willed—their HW shows this enhanced sensate function in its greater receptivity, absorbency, softness, and curviness, compared to the generally impermeable HW of Eights.

Were intuition dominant, we could assume that Eights would be less pragmatic than they actually are. In that case the HW would be lighter and airier, given that intuition needs a high level of inner mobility to express itself. Anyway, these are assumptions that need to be researched and verified.

I would like make a few comments about sexual identity and how we see ourselves in male-female roles.

In Enneagram literature, Eights are considered the most masculine of all types, whereas Twos and the Fours are the most feminine. Depending on the cultural context it could be uncomfortable for women to express their Eightish qualities (the same would apply to males expressing Twoish or Fourish qualities).

Without entering too deeply into the mystery of the feminine or masculine, and without any value judgment other than furthering understanding, let's look at a few differences in the HW.

Male Eights use strong pressure and angularity, whereas female Eights also write with strong pressure but with more curviness; Eight women desire their own independence, rather than controlling others (that is more male); for them it's more a way of claiming equality.

However, intensity of pressure also indicates a difficulty in letting go, expressing tender feelings, or showing vulnerability. It is not uncommon for Eight women to enter into a competitive relationship with their partners; at the same time we can say that the female Eights' ability to be independent makes them able to share life's struggle as an equal partner. At times, Eight women may prefer a weaker male who could play the feminine role in that relationship.

Sample 40 – female, type Eight – is not a hard and rigid HW, but neither is it soft and flexible (as the HW of Twos), nor does it seem to be concerned about esthetic appearance. It's a strong and fluid HW, pragmatic, without wasting time on frills. It belongs to a person with presence, a mother who is respected by and strict with her sons. All consider her strong and reliable. Yet an Eight female can secretly admire the warmth and the ease of a Two female. Similarly, it may happen that male Fours may feel envious of the self-assuredness of the Eight male.

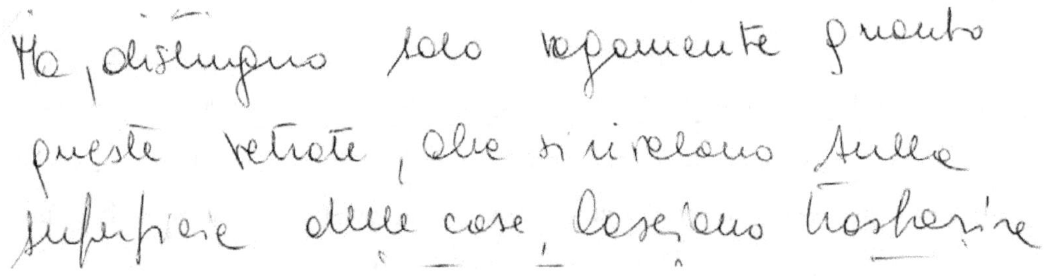

Sample 40

Sample 40 Female age 51 – Type Eight.

Comparing the HW of the female Eight with that of the female One, we can see a higher level of self-control in the One's writing, which lacks spontaneity (*Upright, Straight Extensions*) but is more refined (*Careful*) and shows a dominant dose of perfectionism. Reliable and disciplined with herself and others, the female One may be inclined to self-punishment or, in an attempt to rebel against a strong super-ego, she may appear surprisingly unpredictable.

Comparing this HW with sample 42, a female Two, we can see how the One's HW is more rigid, less curvy and soft, than that of the Two; it is also less impulsive than the HW of the Eight, but more severe and demanding.

Sample 41

Sample 41 Female age 56 – Type One.

It is easy to recognize the Two's HW, with its appearance of abundance expressed in the fullness of curves and the almost complete filling of the graphic space; the pressure is strong and pasty and the long extensions are flexible—this is a very different image from the rigidity of the type One (sample 41), and the Eight (Sample 40). The Two's HW has more movement, but also less space between words, an indicator that she uses emotion to approach situations. The Eight's and One's HW are more spaced out, a sign of using reason more than intuition. The Two's HW is a bit "capricious"—impulsive and seeking admiration. The predominant impression is that of "woman" in the nourishing and "seductress" sense—always with a tinge of emotional manipulation lurking in the background. The fullness of this writing with all the characteristic *Loops* is certainly of a different mold than the rigorous One, or the straight-forward Eight.

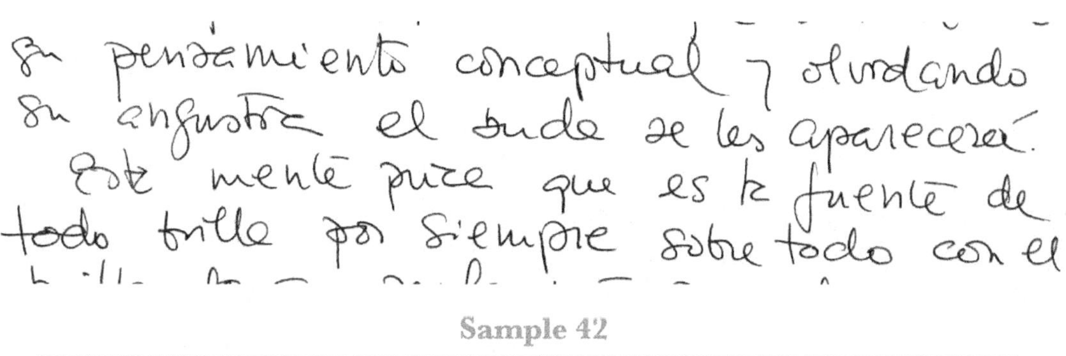

Sample 42 Female age 40, type Two, Sexual (same as Sample 15).

A different kind of femininity is in sample 43, the female Three. Her HW is immediately more precise and organized; absent is the spontaneity of the Two, but neither do we see the austerity of the One nor the native instinctiveness of the Eight. It is an elegant script, but obviously a little contrived from the effort of presenting a desired image to the world—we could even say it is calculated. The balanced spacing between and within words, the proportions of the letters and their sizing shows a high level of balance between thinking and feeling. It is not easy to determine how much this Female Three is in touch with her inner feelings, or if she has entered the role she is playing—the perfect wife, mother or lover… an image that is merely projected outward by a narcissistic motivation.

y todos los seres conscientes no son más
que la mente única a parte de la cual
no existe nada. Esta mente que no tiene

Sample 43

Samples 4 Female, type Three, Self-Preservation.

We end by commenting on a few characteristics of the female Four. The first thing we notice is that her HW does not have the exuberance of the Two or Eight by occupying the graphic space; nor do we see the rigidity of the One or the preoccupation with image of the Three.

The Four's HW is small and contained, with the sign ***Flexible*** that manifests in the soft bending of the extensions towards nearby letters—a sign of psychological intuitiveness and of tuning into the feelings of others, *i.e.*, empathy. This is the strength and the weapon of the female Four, at least from the graphological standpoint. Whereas female Twos and Threes bank on attracting attention and admiration, the female One want to convey reliability and the female Eight uses independence.

The Four's HW shows also a certain anxiety (sign, *Touching Letters*), expressing a need for help in defusing overwhelming situations (something the Eight can take in stride); anxiety is also indicated by congestions (ink accumulations in the graphic pressure)—signs of hyper-emotionality, all pointing at difficulty in

resolving internal conflicts simply and smoothly. This makes the female Four appear introspective, deep and intense. By comparison, the female Eight is emotionally less intricate; the One solves her emotional labyrinth by being decisive; the Two is less inclined to torture herself and the Three doesn't want to make things complicated.

There are days when everyone I meet appear as symbols, and individually or together they form a prophetic or occult writing that describes my life in shadows. The words I exchange with familiar or unfamiliar faces are phrases for which I have no dictionary, though I have of what they mean. They speak, they express, but it's

Sample 44

Sample 44 Female age 42, type Four, Sexual.

HANDWRITING AND ENNEATYPE NINE

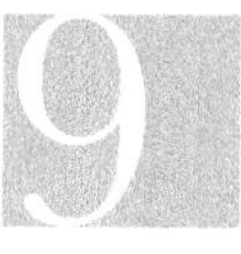

A restful place

We have come to the end in our exploration of the inner meaning of the graphic style of each Enneagram type. We began our journey with the rigid, austere type One—a rough and edgy terrain. With the exuberant Two and the restless Seven it was hard to find a moment of peace. Three, though organized and precise, never revealed what he was thinking, while the creative Four could also complain about everything and behave bizarrely. In the Five's minimalist house there was too much empty space and too many cold drafts, while the ambivalent Six expressed doubts about everything. With the forceful Eight, we always felt a sense of being under pressure.

This brings us to the Nine space—smooth, without too much friction. The words line up with a sense of order but without precision, moving along at a moderate, unruffled pace, restful and relaxed. Life in the presence of a Nine flows without too much movement, quite comfortably, and apparently unaffected by external threats. We are surrounded by warm sweetness, finally able to sink into a deserved rest. Nothing disturbs us; this is the reassuring territory of the Nine.

There are also Nines who appear to be extremely active. In case of well-integrated Nines this may be well-paced and productive activity, but self-forgetting Nines upon closer examination seem to be engaged in lots of activity without importance. They putter around the house tinkering now with this or that and maybe forget an important appointment. Their energy has the same characteristic appearance of being unperturbed as the inactive Nines, even though they may feel frazzled inside.

In the house of Nine everything is simple and soft; nothing is missing. We can talk or be quiet; we can express our needs and know they will be heard. It's a little paradise. But in this comfortable atmosphere of harmony, at times we run into little distractions, deflections, or forget a thing or two, but are not really bothered by it.

In the HW of such an accommodating person, the first shapes that come to

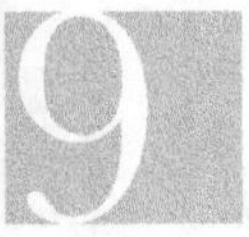

mind are curved, round and soft. It is not conceivable that this type could write with strokes that are rigid, angular, impulsive and unusual. Is it not natural to assume that the graphic movements would be ample, calm, curvy, a bit slow, not particularly elaborated or complicated?

We could sum up the basic characteristics or the Nine's HW as:

- Curvy
- Graphic movement is slow (very rarely fast)
- Not very elaborate or complicated forms.

There are other characteristics as well, but as with the analysis of the HW of the other types, there are no graphic signs that are specifically or exclusively used by a particular type; rather, we have a "general writing style."

If we were to take only these three principal characteristics into consideration; the moderate rhythm, the lack of angularity, and the absence of personalized forms that deviate from the scholastic model, we could immediately see that such a HW can't belong to any of the other eight types.

- Type Seven almost never has a slow graphic movement.
- Type Two, like the Nine has a graphic movement that is *Curved* but is much more exuberant and impulsive.
- Threes present more care and write with less curviness. *Curved* is a trait generally characterizing passive adaptation, and Threes are not reputed to possess much of that, but rather have a necessity to show off, and as such, can't have a rhythm that is too slow.
- Ones are too tense and dynamic to express slowness; besides, the underlying anger produces a handwriting that is rather angular.
- Eight's strong energy will not allow the writing to be slow.
- Sixes do not possess the mental tranquility to have a steady and homogeneous HW like that of the Nine.
- Fours are creative and internally restless which makes their HW more vivid and original.
- Fives show a similar level of apathy as the Nines, but while Nines prefer fusion with the other, Fives generally want to stand alone. Also, Fives analyze

situations, which is something Nines avoid in order to prevent conflict. The graphic mass of the Nine is more compact and dense than that of the Five who tends to have a lot of white space. And finally, the HW of the Five is definitely more angular (intellectual aggression) compared to that of the Nine who always wants to mediate.

Curved at a maximum, which is rare, is a sign of abrogation and lack of care for the rights of the "I," along with inaction, dependence and lack of autonomy. Moretti called it "neurotic blindness," which is experienced by the person as a form of bliss. This label, coined seventy years ago, seems to fit our type Nine very well.

A medium amount of *Curved* indicates a natural tendency toward altruism, willingness to accommodate, and openness of heart and mind. It is a sign of responsiveness and flexibility. Its negative meaning, when the handwriting does not have personal quirks and is slow, indicates a lack of initiative or taste for action and being prone to excessive passive adaptation. On the surface this may seem positive and accommodating but there is little follow-through. Being kind, generous and accommodating without follow-through loses its positive nature. An inability to defend oneself by choosing to rather get along, be comfortable, and take it easy, are things associated with being too soft.

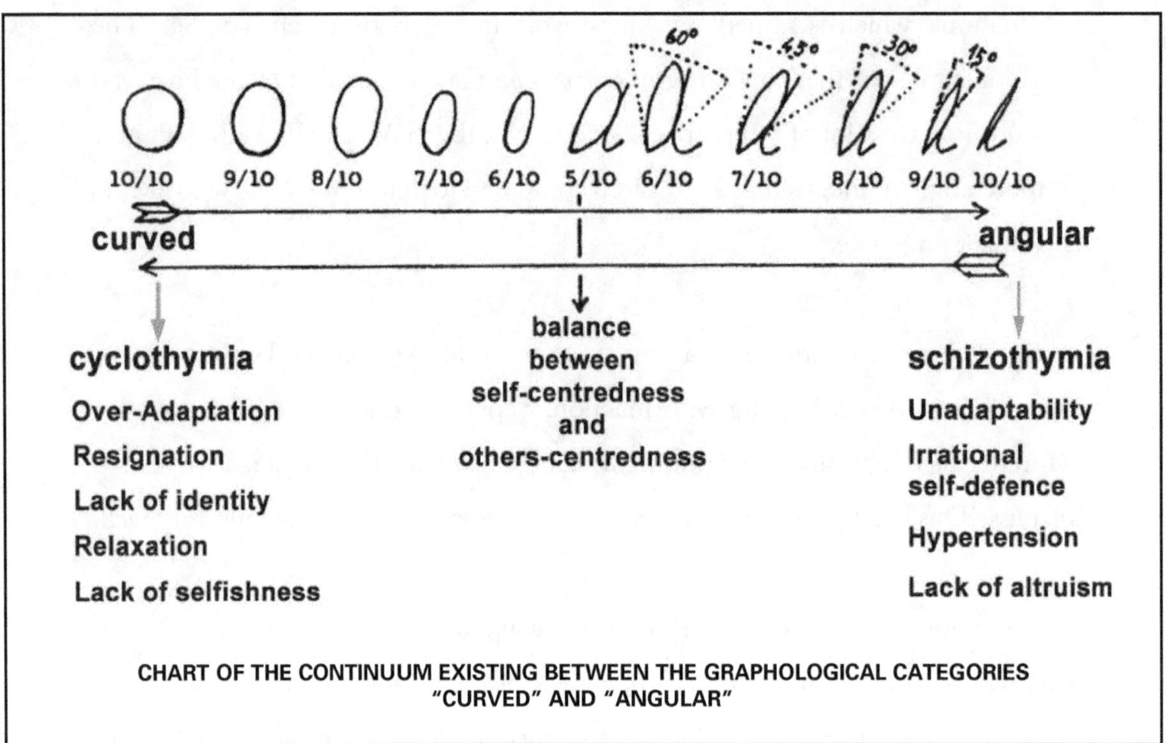

CHART OF THE CONTINUUM EXISTING BETWEEN THE GRAPHOLOGICAL CATEGORIES "CURVED" AND "ANGULAR"

Diagram 1

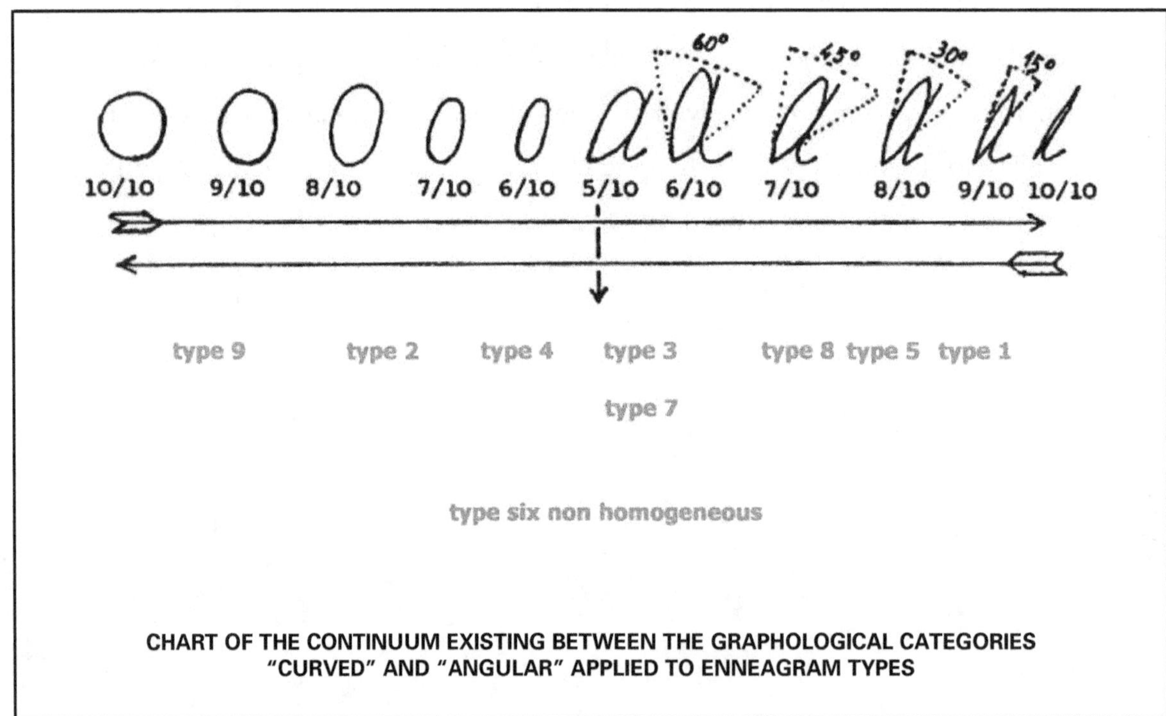

CHART OF THE CONTINUUM EXISTING BETWEEN THE GRAPHOLOGICAL CATEGORIES "CURVED" AND "ANGULAR" APPLIED TO ENNEAGRAM TYPES

Diagram 2

As previously described (see the measuring scale applied by Moretti that goes from 1 to 10), the degree of *Curved* is measured not only in oval letters (for example the Italian handwritings present rounder shapes compared to the American) but in roundness generally and the way it pervades the entire HW—as opposed to

angularity. This is not a value judgment: *Curved* does not mean "generosity," nor does *Angular* imply "selfishness." To determine such specific traits requires looking at and considering the entirety of the HW. An excessive presence of curves as in a HW of type Nine may indicate generosity, but also an undeveloped sense of individuality. Excessive angularity could indicate a high level of activity or it could point to reactivity and tension.

The HW of a Three, for example, could be predominantly angular—not surprisingly—given that the personality is dynamic and purposeful. That makes the person more "self-centered." Yet, their graphic movement is not very spontaneous and we find an excess of carefulness; hence they could be defined as other-centered.

To *Curved* we can often add ***Concave Extensions to the right***. When we see this sign to a high degree, it indicates a tendency to comply and the incapacity to openly oppose unfair demands from the environment. Over time this will translate into depression. On the positive side there is a conciliatory spirit and cooperation. This sign is found rarely in type One, because of too much inner tension, and it is rare in type Eight who has an excessive need to prevail over the environment.

The sign ***Slow*** is when there is a general lack of rhythm and dynamic expression, giving the appearance of monotony. This goes with ***Narrow Space between Words*** which is an indicator of apathy and lack of motivation.

Slow is the opposite of *Truncated*—typical of Eights, who tend to truncate the final strokes as if making a decision or an affirmation. A Nine, on the other hand, will not have this sign because of their preference for continued mediation.

Slow also occurs when scholastic forms are maintained—inner experience has no effect on the original form of the HW. The positive side of *Slow* is stability, absence of impulsivity, and a need for calm and serenity. On the negative side the person can be lazy and have a slow reaction time. A *Slow* HW is characteristic of people who give little room for intuition but favor habits and conventionality. Such people require a lot of stimulation to overcome their resistance to change.

The hyperactive Nines' HW is frenetic rather than *Slow*. However, the lack of engagement manifests in the graphic movement by appearing strewn about on the page and seemingly directionless.

There are days when everyone I meet appear as symbols, and individually or together they form a prophetic or occult writing that describes my life in shadows. The word I exchange with familiar or unfamiliar faces are phrases for which I have no dictionary, though I have a sense of what they mean. They speak, they express, but it's not of themselves that they speak, nor to themselves that they express; they're words and they are not clearly indicative, but they allow glimpses.

Sample 1

Sample 1 Male age 46 - Type 9w1, Sexual

Sample 1 is of a well-integrated Nine. The HW is generally soft, simple, and curvy. There are no excesses or disproportionate shapes. Considerate, generous and open, this individual does not relinquish his own identity when relating with others. We see that in the well-organized *Triple Width* spacing. The rhythm is not very fast and yet the HW moves fluidly. The ampleness of the downward strokes below the baseline (y, g, f) indicate the need, at least at the level of imagination, to incorporate the "other" within himself; also the left margin diminishes, i.e., moves towards the left, which is an additional confirmation of that trait. In this context, according to Max Pulver, a Swiss philosopher, psychologist, and researcher on the symbolism of handwriting—born on 1889, and considered as a point of reference for the most part of graphologists, the regressive left margin means also a hyper-attachment to the maternal world, which symbolically is an impediment to autonomy. In any case this HW is very clearly of a person profoundly open towards others.

A simple soul

One of the characteristics of Nines is a certain candor of spirit, an inclination towards idealizing the other, and a sense of profound innocence. It is as if Nines start off well disposed towards others and willing to underestimate their dark side.

We can see this in the simplicity of the graphic strokes that have nothing contrived about them. The unfavorable flip side could be over-simplification when approaching essential problems. The need to avoid conflict carries the risk of not facing situations in their full complexity and trying to find solutions that are conventional and lacking in imagination. These traits in a HW are mainly seen if two signs, *Calm* and *Naturally Graceful*, are present.

The sign **Naturally Graceful** is when:

- The carefulness of the graphic movement is not excessive or artificial;
- The rhythm is spontaneous and fluid;
- The graphic context is simple.

In essence, this sign denotes gentleness of spirit. Moretti defines *Naturally Graceful* as "Someone with spontaneity of heart without phoniness. The smile is open and confidence inspiring like that of an innocent girl. Gentleness is already present when a new thought or feeling arises and it is maintained with freshness and innocence." He then adds that it is generally a more feminine sign and when found in males it may show awkwardness.

This is a sign of amiability, of being profoundly human, of gentleness without agenda, and of being naturally disarming. The drawback in this sign is absence of an adequate level of aggressiveness, so that gentleness can become compulsive and used to avoid conflict, or cultivated to create an image of "calm," identifying in this role to the exclusion of other options.

Samples 2, 3, 4, 5 and 6 illustrate this attitude of complacency and simplicity.

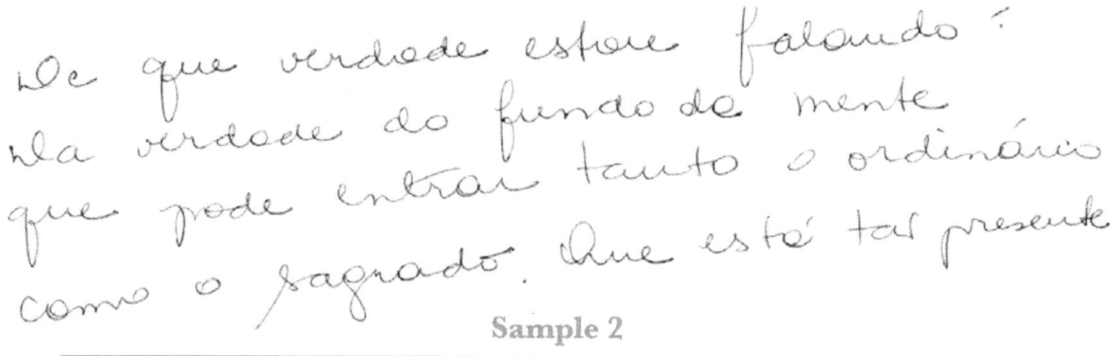

Sample 2 Female – Type Nine, Self-Pres. Hw showing the signs *Naturally Graceful, Calm, Curved, Narrow between Words, Extensions Concave to Right.* The low level of energy is also seen in the "stepping up" rise of the words. If you observe carefully, you can see that while the line as a whole is continually rising vis-à-vis the baseline, each word starts just below where the previous word ended.

molto affetto, quando abitavo da
mia mamma e ne avevo altre tre,
uno maschio e due femmine –

Sample 3

Sample 3 Female age 26 – Type Nine. Hw showing the signs *Naturally Graceful, Calm, Curved, Narrow between Words, Extensions Concave to Right, Loops*.

Quando você já não busca fora esta
enfermidade cura e agora é preciso de
deixar esta medicina. Se você se prende,

Sample 4

Sample 4 Female – Type Nine, Self-Pres. HW somewhat less calm than the previous samples visible in the lack of homogeneity of pressure. The HW as a whole gives the impression of softness.

e la prima leggerezza della pioggia e
cresciuta fino a farsi sentire, nell'aria
è rimasta una quieta che l'aria del
una nuova pace a

Sample 5

Sample 5 Female age 24 – Type Nine, Sexual. HW showing the sign *Calm* (less so than samples 2-3, because the space between words is larger indicating that she is more analytically inclined and restless. The *Leftward Slant* shows a need to control. Here too, as in sample 2, the line is "stepping up.")

shadows. The words I exchange with familiar or unfamiliar faces are phases for which I have no dictionary, though I have an idea of what they mean. They ss speak, they ss

Sample 6

Sample 6 Female age 63 – Type Nine Social. A simple HW, soft, gentle and not fast. Keeping in mind that American writings are generally more angular than the Mediterranean ones, we can label this HW as *Curved* with Extensions *Concave to Right* and with adequate *Space between Letters*. Note the end strokes of words that curl and drop below the baseline (*Strokes of Phlegmatism* explained later).

The sign *Calm* is when:

- The graphic rhythm is continuous and restful;
- There is an absence of strokes of impatience, highly visible strokes, as well as horizontal and vertically exaggerated ones;
- Angularity is low. Actually, angularity is the opposite of *Calm*.

Calm is not compatible with:

- Characteristics that show a strong inclination towards analysis; for example, *Disconnected*, *Meticulous*, or a high degree of *Space between Words*—all typical of the Five.
- Exaggerated reactivity and control seen in the signs *Angular*, *Straight Extensions*, and *Twisted*—common among Ones.
- Impulsiveness of Twos and Sevens expressed with the signs *Flung Out* and *Thrusting*.
- Overcompensation due to insecurity of the Six, the sign *Pompous*, doubt, or the sign *Wavering*.
- Excessive preoccupation with image, or the sign *Careful* as found in Threes.
- Emotionality of Fours which is mainly expressed with the sign *Methodically Irregular*.
- The intensity of Eights shown in strong graphic pressure.

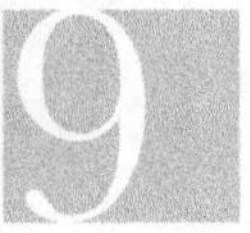

The graphological sign *Calm* is found in a person who loves peace, quiet, and stability; who operates at a low level of emotionality—not fast but steady, not fastidious, but not too loosely sloppy either. These are people with a practical approach to life who do not treasure intensity and are not particularly prone to be perturbed by affections or spiritual ambitions. *Calm* rarely indicates creativity and is more inclined to follow the lessons learned in school; it also does not allow much space for transformation as would be expected with the Jungian intuitive function.

Calm or Lazy?

It is difficult to find people who are genuinely calm. It is easy to confuse calm with laziness or apathy. Nines are typically not into action, unless the action is a comfortable and stress-free puttering from one distraction to another. Even when hyperactive, Nines are usually not fully engaged, with a low output of vitality, tending to remain even keeled, good natured, and avoiding of problems.

These characteristics are not immediately obvious but generally come to the surface after knowing the person better. In the HW they manifest as a concealed indolence, the so-called *Strokes of Phlegmatism* at the end of words. In graphological terminology these are called *fugitive strokes* because they are tacked on at the end of a word and not very obvious. It is as if the writer was heedless, seeming to say, "Whatever I have written so far is not that important," then drawing a final sagging stroke that peters out, giving the impression of deflation.

Strokes of Phlegmatism manifest in the following ways:

- Final strokes that sag below the baseline and then return dragging on tiredly.
- Final strokes that extend a little bit forward and then stop dead in their tracks forming a minute squiggle.
- Final strokes that sag below the baseline and then stop.
- Final stroke of letter "i" which sort of extends itself towards the dot.

This example comes from a graphological manual showing a variety of *Strokes of Phlegmatism.*

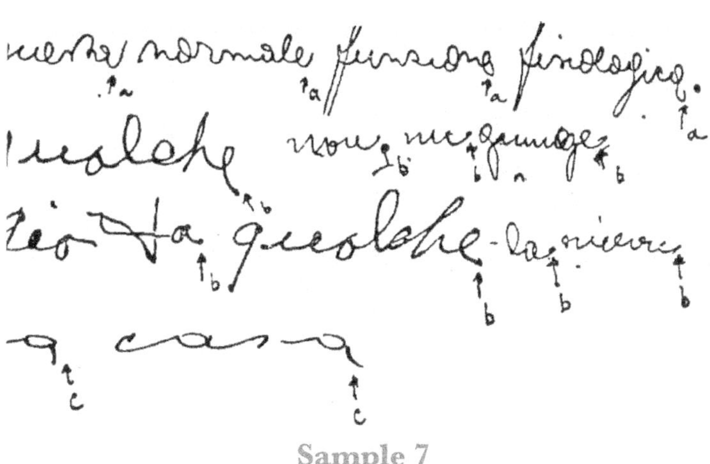

Sample 7

Sample 7 Example of different *Strokes of Phlegmatism*

Ci sono giorni nei quali ogni persona che
incontro e, ancor più, le persone abituali
della mia convivenza obbligata e quotidiana,

Sample 8

Sample 8 Female age 49 – Type Nine Social. Hw showing the signs *Strokes of Phlegmatism* (see arrows), *Curved, Slow, Narrow between Words, Flat.* The Hw is very scholastic.

"The healthy nine can be defined as
deeply receptive, accepting, unselfconscious,
emotionally stable and serene. They are
trusting of self and others, at ease
with self and life, and innocent & simple

Sample 9

Sample 9 Female age 52 -Type 9w1. Hw showing the sign *Strokes of Phlegmatism* (see arrows).

Three score and six years ago I arrived here. "Here" was a small town in northern Minnesota.

Sample 10

Sample 10 Female - Type Three, Social. Hw showing the sign *Strokes of Affectedness.*

Sample 10 was already used in the article about type three. Note the ample final strokes and curviness. To the inexperienced observer this HW may look as if it contained *Strokes of Phlegmatism.* However their energetic nature is very different. They project forward, do not contain any passive or backwards movement, and are generally more decisive compared to the HW of the Nine.

In this context they are not called *Strokes of Phlegmatism* but *Strokes of Affectedness.* The former is typical of the Nine and indicates resignation and renunciation. The latter comes from a need to attract attention.

The behavior of someone who has *Strokes of Phlegmatism* is hard to read. It requires time and intimate exposure to get to know such a person; only then do the attachment to habits and the lack of interest in facing complex problems emerge. There is a general feeling of tiredness and wanting to be left in peace.

Ci sono giorni nei quali ogni persona che incontro e, ancor più, le persone abituali della mia

Sample 11

Sample 11 Female age 40 – Type Nine. Hw showing the sign *Strokes of Phlegmatism* (see arrows). This HW is also slow, with a flat rhythm, keeping to a scholastic style.

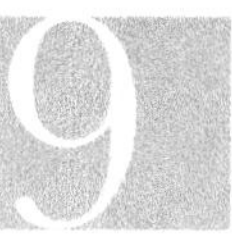

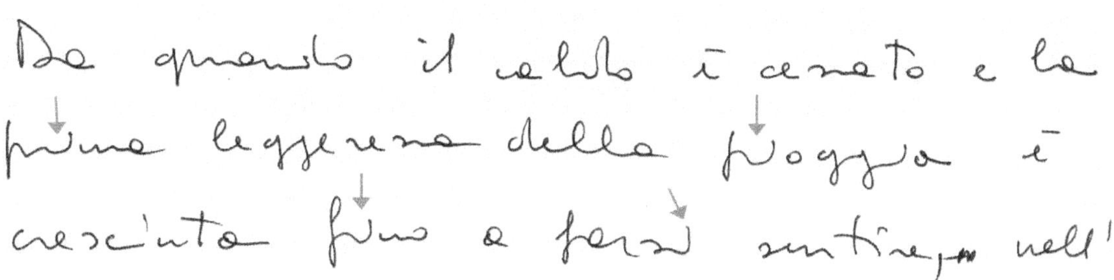

Sample 12

Sample 12 Female age 50 – Type Nine, Sexual. Hw showing the sign *Strokes of Phlegmatism* (see arrows). This Hw is more original then sample 11, but they share the tendency toward phlegm.

Is the struggle worth it?

Relaxation for type Nine is a psychophysical condition, and a characteristic that wreaks havoc on will power. It is mainly a form of excessive surrender. Every type surrenders to something:

- Type One gives in to anger.
- Type Four gives in to excessive emotionality.
- The Six gives in to their doubts.
- The Seven surrenders to impulsiveness.
- The Five analyzes excessively.
- Twos give in too much to what they feel.
- Threes give their all in order to be successful.
- Eights need to dominate at all costs.
- And the Nine surrenders to the idea that "that's how it is and what's the point in struggling to change it?" According to Naranjo there is a stoic element in this approach.

Enneagram students often see this characteristic as resignation or excessive ability to adapt. These traits are so natural to the Nine that they are often unaware of the price in frustration it costs them.

In the HW this attitude is seen in the small dilations in the strokes, with the slight dropping of some letters below the baseline. It is as if a person while walking had stepped into a hole; the rhythm of the writing suffers a bit in its

overall harmony. One can make a comparison to a trumpet player who occasionally runs out of breath and toots a feeble note in an otherwise pleasant performance.

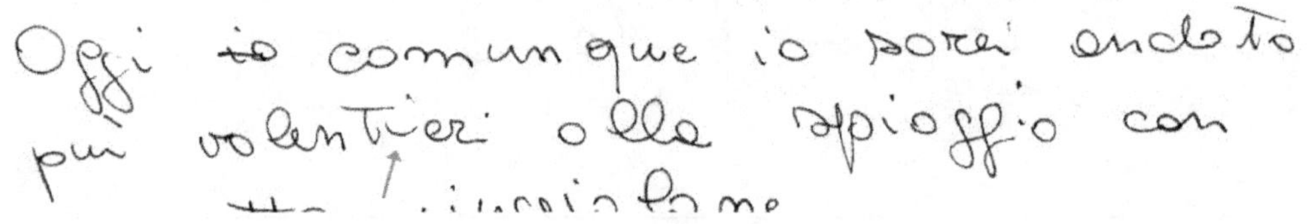

Oggi ~~io~~ comunque io sarei andata
più volentieri alla spiaggia con

Sample 13

Sample 3 Female age 39 – Type Nine. Hw showing some dilatations and relaxations. The context is slow and curved. Difficulty in respecting the baseline.

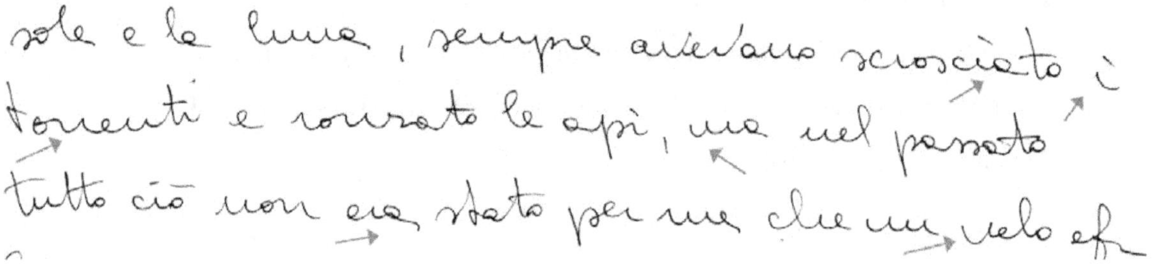

sole e la luna, sempre avevano sciosciato i
tormenti e rovinato le api, ma nel passato
tutto ciò non era stato per me che un velo ef

Sample 14

Sample 14 Female age 48 – Type Nine, Social. Same characteristics as sample 13.

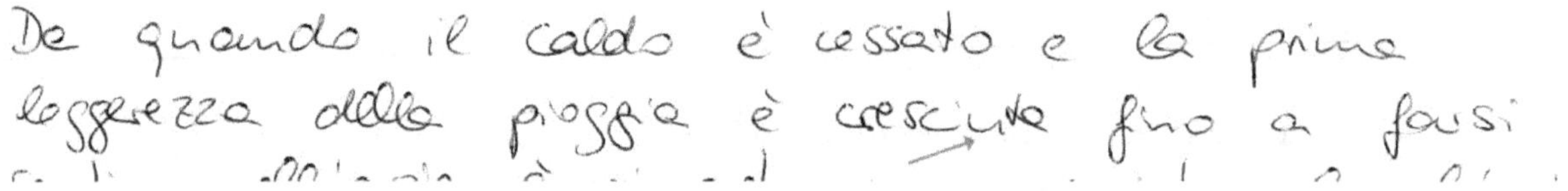

Da quando il caldo è cessato e la prima
leggerezza della pioggia è cresciuta fino a farsi

Sample 15

Sample 15 Female age 35 - Type Nine, Social. Hw presenting some relaxations of movement.

pero están apegados a la formas. No saben que deteniendo su pensamiento conceptual y olvidando

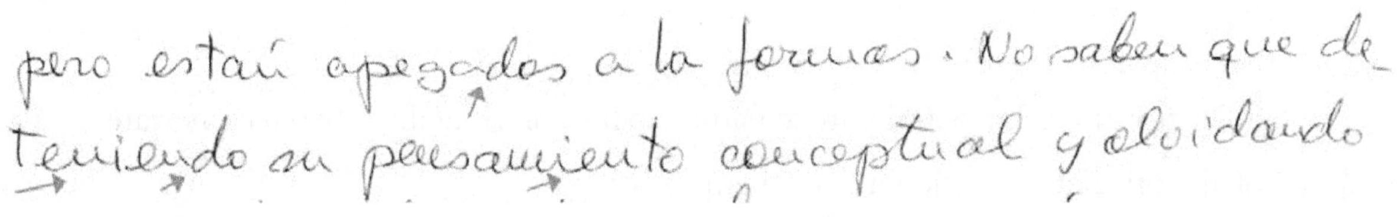

Sample 16

Sample 16 Female – Type Nine, Sexual. Hw presenting some relaxations of movement (see arrows).

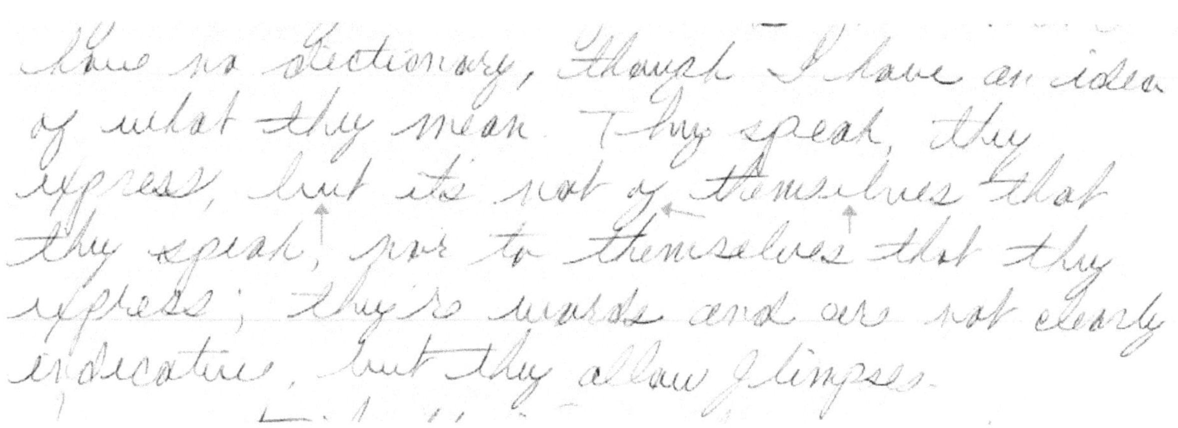

Sample 17

Sample 17 Male age 47 – Type Nine, Sexual. Highlighted are some forms of relaxations of graphic movement, also *Narrow between Words*.

Sample 18

Sample 18 Female – Type Nine, Sexual. Dilations and relaxations of movement.

Please note that for the most part the Nines' samples seem to struggle with maintaining the steadiness of baseline. The jumps on the baseline should not be mischaracterized as *Springing* that we have seen in the type Seven—those are due to an excess of vivacity and impulsivity. The Nines' jumps are caused by drops of energy and motivation.

Apathy—Looks like type Five?

It is a short slide from relaxation to apathy. The classic definition of apathy is lack of energy for both physical and psychological action. In Jungian terminology it would correspond to dominant Introverted Sensing, but as we have seen with all types, these functions can be expressed or directed inwardly or outwardly. This may be the reason why Naranjo generally sees the Nine as Extrovert Sensing and Riso/Hudson as Introvert Sensing.

The handwriting (HW) samples of Nines generally show both qualities; the

HW of the Introverted Sensing Nine is more static while the Extroverted Nine's leans more towards sloppiness and neglect.

The apathetic Introvert is more stable and able to concentrate and pay attention than the distracted Extrovert. In the apathetic person sensitivity and emotionality appear to be dampened even though Nines rarely behave in a detached way. Their HW is mostly curvilinear, a sign of generosity and acceptance, but it is rather monotonously flat and thereby showing limited nuance.

Apathetic Nines can be mistaken for Fives, but there is a fundamental difference. Fives carry a hint of depression that comes from isolation from the environment (see article about type Five where we talk about the Five's large spaces between words). Nines on the other hand remain in touch even when they feel dissatisfied or malcontented—they even seek "fusion" with the environment (seen in the spacing: *Narrow between Words*) which in Jungian terms means suppressed Thinking function, as if critical evaluation of circumstances and people is put on hold in order to avoid conflict.

Such an attitude would obviously protect relationships with others at the expense of assertiveness about your own desires and rights. *Narrow between Words* also hints at innocence and childlike trust that others' motivations are without guile.

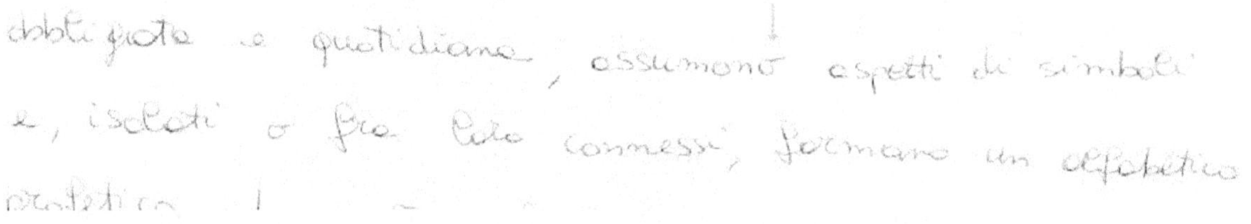

Sample 21

Sample 21 Female age 34 – Type 9w1. HW with a low level of vitality. Note how the final strokes in some words seem withered and without thrust.

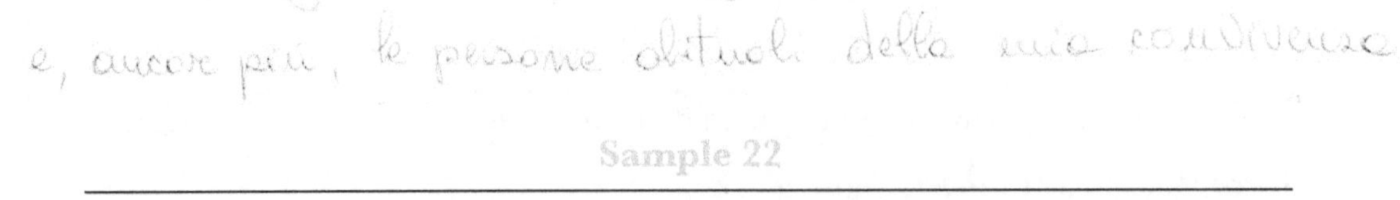

Sample 22

Sample 22 Female age 48 – Type 9w1, Social. *Slow*, static handwriting.

Samples 19, 20, 21, & 22 have the sign *Regular* (or *Flat*), the opposite of *Methodical Irregular* typically found in HW of Fours. **Methodical Irregular** is when small letters (a, e, i, o, u, m, n, etc.) vary in height in a rhythmic way, a sign indicating that the inner life is active, lively and creative. **Flat** or **Regular** is seen when the small letters vary little, giving the impression of a HW that:

1. Is monotonous and impersonal.
2. Shows a flat movement rhythm. The HW emanates a sense of fixedness, showing a few variations.

Such HW belongs to those capable of being precise, patient, able to perform boring and repetitive tasks—in other words, salt-of-the-earth valuable members of society instrumental in upholding schemas and conventions.

When the signs *Slow*, *Curved*, and *Flat* are pronounced it may mean emotional numbness and depersonalization, as if the writer is indifferent to everything that is happening outside of direct sensory perception.

Sloppiness—Nine can be mistaken for type Six

Nines sometimes express apathy; if they are more vivacious, it may actually be a form of subtle negligence that is rather charming, as in a "cool" style of slouching. In the HW this is seen in the lack of care in the graphic forms, which are at times vague and imprecise with little tension in the strokes. Depending on the degree of this tendency, the person may fall into a range between slight laziness to lack of vitality on all levels: mental, emotional, will, and even body posture. The signs are *Neglected* and *Careless* (The sign *Careful*, common to Threes, would be the exact opposite).

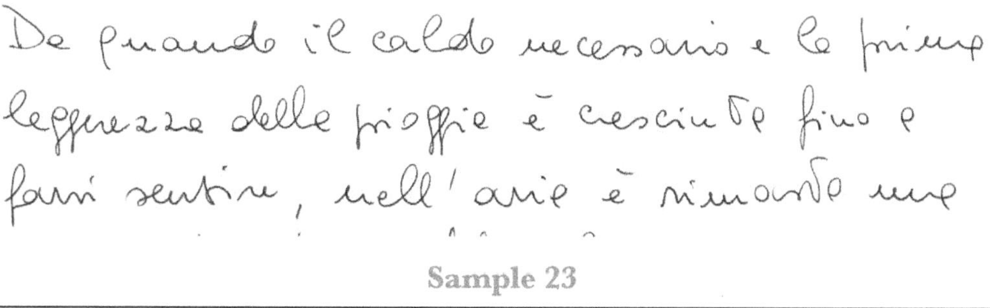

Sample 23 Female age 51 – Type 9w8. HW showing the sign *Neglected*.

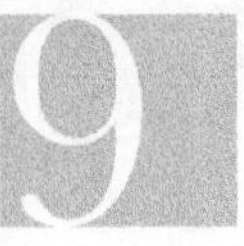

leggerezza della pioggia è cresciuta fino
a farsi sentire, nell'aria è rimasta una
quiete che l'aria del caldo non aveva, una

Sample 24

Sample 24 Male age 48 – Type Nine, Sexual. HW showing the sign *Neglected*.

There are days when everyone I meet appear
as symbols, and individually or together they
form a prophetic or occult writing that describes
life in shadows. The word I exchange with
familiar or unfamiliar faces are phrases for
which I have no dictionary, though I have a
sense of what they mean. They speak, they
express, but it's ...

Sample 25

Sample 25 Male age 44 – Type Nine, Social. This handwriting is predominantly *Curved* and soft in movement. Yet it contains a descending baseline and many relaxations of movement.

Sono fortunato, anche se spesso ho pensato o
temuto di essere sfortunato. La mia fortuna si

Sample 26

Sample 26 Male age 48 - Type Nine, Sexual. HW showing the sign *Careless*.

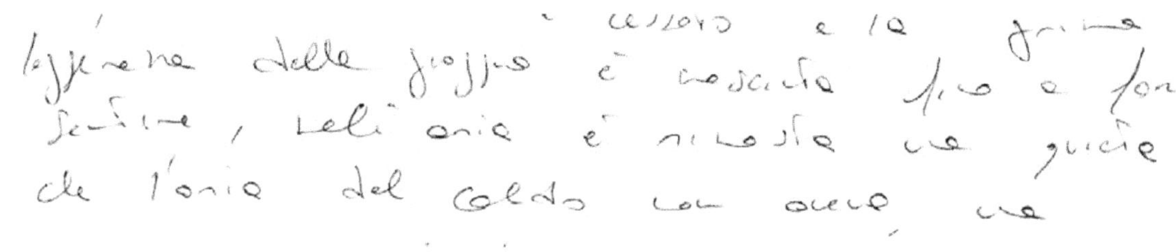

Sample 27

Sample 27 Female age 30 – Type Nine, Sexual. HW showing the sign *Careless*.

Samples 23 – 27 are certainly more vivacious than 19 – 24 and these Nines are more active. What they have in common is general lack of tension in the writing. In contrast to the Three who is preoccupied with image, the Nine downplays the value of their presence. That's the root of the sloppiness and here there are similarities mainly with the phobic Six. It is not by chance that the connecting line of integration for the Nine is to Three; a move in that direction would include improvement of the self-image.

Other styles of Nines

It is rare to find Nines who write small. Such HW is more common among Fours and Fives who often are introverts. Nines' HW is "naturally" medium in size. This indicates a balance between exhibitionistic expansive, and schizoid contractive impulses, and points to a practical adaptation to reality without too many flights of fantasy or too much closing off into isolation. The same principle applies when comparing the internal and the external life. Here too Nines are inclined to strike a balance.

Exceptions exist and some Nines are more focused, thoughtful, deep, and introverted. They can easily be mistaken for a Five. But their HW is generally slower than that of Fives and less cutting.

Insecurities and doubts afflict Nines differently than Sixes. Because Nines wish to avoid conflict, they strive to avoid disagreement itself; the content of the ideas with which they disagree is less important. In samples 28 – 30 we can see how the strokes below the baseline, which in graphology represent our instinctual energy, tend to wither.

Nines with a small HW often also have a *Leftward Slant* (most, not necessarily all letters lean to the left). This points at several common characteristics

among Nines: a defense mechanism against excessive fusion with the other and being overly dependent or influenced; repression of the need for contact; and most of all, an attempt to avoid conflicts at all cost, which are reminders of rejections and emotional pain in early childhood. Thus, it's not laziness or negligence that is at play here but a defense against an excessive neediness for others.

Sample 28

Sample 28 Female – Type Nine, Sexual. HW showing a high degree of *Leftward Slant.*

There are days when everyone I meet appears as symbols, and individually or together they form a prophetic or occult writing that describes my life in shadows. The words I exchange with familiar or unfamiliar faces are phrases for which I have no dictionary, though I have suppositions about what they mean

Sample 29

Sample 29 Male age 50 – Type 9w8. HW predominantly *Curved*, and with some hints of *Leftward Slant.* Note how the strokes below the baseline appear to be atrophied. The influence of the 8 wing is seen in the strong pressure. This Nine seems to repress expressing anger a lot.

Sample 30

Sample 30 Female – Type Nine, Self-Pres. HW showing the signs *Curved*, *Leftward Slant*, and a distinct lack of vitality

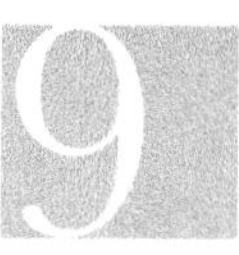

Then there is the more extroverted Nine with larger writing, not that size matters all that much. Samples 31 – 33 are fairly *Slow*, *Curvy*, with little *Space between Words*, slight *Rightward Slant* but with *Extensions* that are almost *Parallel*, probably due to the influence of the wings. There are also indications of controlled aggression seen in the rhythm which appears restrained, and in the monotony of the slant. The HW appears to have an element of containment while still being spread out on paper. The Jungian Sensing function seems to be prevalent from the "pasty" pressure and scarce spacing between words—as if the writers were absorbing and retaining impressions from the environment. The appearance of heaviness comes from the laboriousness they encounter when trying to express what they really feel. Mainly, it is aggression that needs to be suppressed in order not to risk compromising contact with others.

De la verdad del fondo de la mente. Que puede
entrar tanto en lo ordinario como en lo sagrado

Sample 31

Sample 31 Male – Type Nine, Social. Although this HW is mid-sized, we can't say it expresses vigor; rather, it is slow and heavy.

sentito fino a farsi sentire, nell'aria
è rimasta una quieta che l'aria

Sample 32

Sample 32 Female age 56 – Type Nine, Sexual. HW has a slow rhythm. Note that although the writing is fairly large, the end strokes of the letter "a" look withered and without energy.

There are days when everyone I meet
appear as symbols, and individually
or together, they form a prophetic
or occult writing that describes my
life in shadows. The word I
exchange with familiar or unfamiliar
faces are phrases for which I have
no dictionary, though I have a
sense of what they mean. They speak

Sample 33

Sample 33 Female age 53 – Type 9w1, Self-Pres. At first, this HW resembles that of an Eight or a One. To detect the subtle differences takes something of a trained eye. Even the pressure is pretty good, and size is medium (both indicators of a decent level of energy), the rhythm is restrained and contained. Eights and Ones tend to "fire into the paper" with more vitality and less restraint. This HW also has a mix of slack and relaxed forms; there is *Narrow between Words* and all loops of the extensions are slanting leftward as if there was a fear to openly own up to having needs and to show pith. If the extensions were to slant to the right, it would imply a need for contact with others.

Similarities with the Two

Twos and Nines can have similarities and their writing often shares such signs as: *Curved*, *Narrow between Words*, good *Space between Letters*, *Loops* and *mid-sized letters*. Yet the Nines' HW tends to hold the baseline less firmly, is usually descending, and has an aura of calm or monotony about it. Twos' HW is more lively and exuberant.

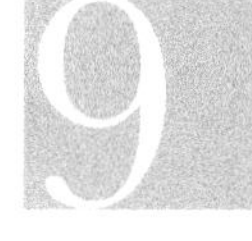

ordinario como en lo sagrado. Está tan
presente en lo pequeño como en lo inmenso.

Sample 34

Sample 34 Female – Type Nine, Social. HW with many *Loops*, that in this instance signify a loving and open nature. It is *curved*, slow, with a *descending baseline*, and somewhat *careless*. She is very attentive to the needs of others and a Two look-alike. Yet the HW has the flavor of resignation, visible in the lack of tension, as if she had given up on herself.

Thank You

We are ending this series of graphological exploration and enneagram types in the sweet and peaceful space of Nines.

I would like to thank the readers who assisted in the research by sending in samples of their handwriting and suggestions. Their contribution was essential and without it this research would not have been possible.

Most of all I thank Jack Labanauskas, the editor of the Enneagram Monthly, who had faith and was supportive of this project, patient with the translation, and contributed many useful suggestions.

The research is ongoing and continues to deepen the understanding of the connection between graphology and enneagram. I would appreciate more samples. Workshops in recent months on this subject triggered much interest and new ones are being planned by graphological associations in several countries. To people familiar with both systems it is immediately obvious how powerful combining the two can be.

Thank you for having been fellow travelers in this journey.

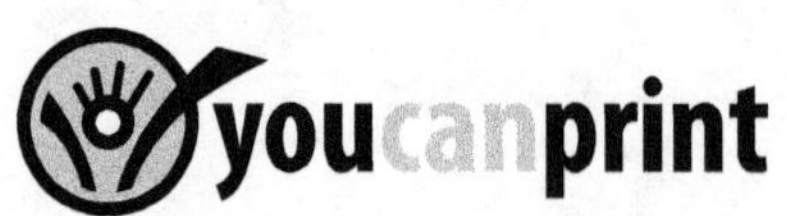

Printed in March 2018
by Youcanprint *Self-Publishing*

www.ingramcontent.com/pod-product-compliance
Lightning Source LLC
Chambersburg PA
CBHW080830170726
48000CB00022B/2762

* 9 7 8 8 8 2 7 8 1 6 7 2 1 *